Praise for *The Dance of We*

This is one of the most accessible books on the power of organizational systems and the visceral impact they have on those who work in and lead organizations. A **must read** for leaders of complex (not necessarily large) private and public sector organizations who know they have to go beyond the personal and interpersonal dynamics to understand and bring about transformation.

– ROGER H EVANS, founder of CLC, a leadership consulting company and author of *5DL - Five Dimensions of Leadership* (2014) and *The Creative Manager* (1999)

Horowitz skillfully explains often-overlooked dynamics of power and love so central to complex human systems, and does so with remarkable clarity — and with much heart. The Dance of We is, clearly, an invaluable resource to anyone truly serious about engaging the transformations of our family lives, of our institutions—and of our very culture—transformations demanded by these challenging times.

– RAÚL QUIÑONES ROSADO Ph.D., author of *Consciousness-in-Action: Toward an Integral Psychology of Liberation & Transformation*

Bravo! In this fresh and very timely book, Mark Horowitz gives us a new pair of "human systems glasses" that helps us see why things go wrong in our relationships, our organizations, and the political and economic systems that govern our lives. More importantly, he provides us with a set of proven principles and practices that can help us join with others to create dynamic human systems that foster mutual respect and common purpose.

– BILL JOINER, co-author of *Leadership Agility* and President of ChangeWise, a leadership and organizational consulting firm

In this clear and comprehensive work, Mark Horowitz applies systems thinking to the challenge of understanding the interactions between individuals and the groups to which they belong — whether it be family, organization or business — showing how a fuller appreciation of these dynamics can help repair dysfunctional attitudes and foster more life-affirming behaviors. A most valuable book for anyone wanting to improve human relationships within a group.

– PETER RUSSELL, author of *The Global Brain* and *From Science to God*

As a state legislator in a political system that often becomes stuck in dysfunction, this book offers me ideas and thoughts about how to overcome these obstacles. We legislators strive to serve our district, yet often don't see beyond our own ideologies. This book offers a perspective on how to get beyond ourselves and achieve our shared goal of improving the lives of the people of our state.

– REPRESENTATIVE JOAN WELSH, Maine House of Representatives

Mark Horowitz does a remarkable job in this insightful and practical book, helping us to see and understand the system dynamics and dysfunctions of our families and organizations. With humor, personal stories, and real world examples, he demonstrates how we can transform our human systems into Life-affirming ones.

– **MOLLY YOUNG BROWN**, author of *Growing Whole: Self-realization for the Great Turning*, and co-author with Joanna Macy of *Coming Back to Life: The Updated Guide to the Work That Reconnects*

For the fifteen years that Mark Horowitz has been coming to teach Systems to our students, they have asked him where they can read the remarkable material he teaches. We are happy that his wisdom and humor will now be available in writing.

I am sure this book will help to kindle the spirit of love in its readers and support them in owning their power in systems. This is the kind of book that encourages us to transform our ways of seeing as well as our ways of being.

– **ALEXANDER BADKHEN, MD**, Co-founder of the HARMONY Institute, Director of the International School for Psychotherapy Counseling and Group Leadership. (St.Petersburg, Russia)

Mark Horowitz was one of my closest (and wisest) friends growing up. I read this product of his life's work with great interest. My three terms as a Denver city councilwoman grew out of the values that Mark and I have shared for a lifetime - a firm belief in community. But when that community breaks down in disagreement, we often blame ourselves or we blame the other people. *The Dance of We* moves us past blame with both wise and practical approaches.

– **JEANNE ROBB**, Denver City Councilwoman

This is a book that every helping professional should read,because if we delude ourselves into thinking that any client has a problem that is theirs alone, we are not doing our job. Every client, every diagnosis, every move towards health is embedded in systems. As we turn our eyes to the bigger picture, we can help our clients, and ourselves, to take a just and rightful place in the world.

– **DR. DOROTHY FIRMAN**, professor of psychology and the author of a number of books including *Engaging Life: Living Well with Chronic Illness*

Mark Horowitz's *The Dance of We* is a creative, thoughtful, and literate vision of an emergent Jewish psycho-spirituality. Horowitz blends psychology, theology, humor and life experience into a fine read.

– **RABBI LAWRENCE KUSHNER**, Emanu-El Scholar in residence at Congregation Emanu-El of San Francisco and author of a score of books on Jewish mysticism and spirituality

THE DANCE *of* WE

For Abby, Rachel and Eli
my very own Life-affirming system

THE DANCE *of* WE

THE MINDFUL USE OF **LOVE** AND **POWER** IN HUMAN SYSTEMS

FOUR PRINCIPLES for strengthening the family, humanizing the workplace, and transcending the politics of separation

MARK HOROWITZ

SYNTHESIS CENTER
PRESS

Published 2014 by Synthesis Center Press
Amherst, Massachusetts
www.synthesiscenter.org

ISBN: 978-0-9678570-8-4

Printed in the United States of America

Designer: Isobel Gillan
Cover: Oxidized silver bracelet by Selda Okutan: www.seldaokutan.com, used with permission
Diagrams: Emma Levitt

PERMISSIONS:
Pages 14, 171, 280: MR. BOFFO © cartoons reprinted through the generosity of Joe Martin
    and Neatly Chiseled Features
Pages 282, 293: HAGAR © cartoons reprinted by permission King Features Syndicate, Inc.
    World rights reserved.
Page 103: DILBERT © 1993 Scott Adams. Used By permission of UNIVERSAL UCLICK.
    All rights reserved.
Page 112: CALVIN AND HOBBES © 1992 Watterson. Reprinted with permission of
    UNIVERSAL UCLICK. All rights reserved.
Page 37: WUERKER © 2011 Politico. Dist. By UNIVERSAL UCLICK. Reprinted
    with permission. All rights reserved.
Pages 173, 174: Woodcarving images are reprinted from *The Art of Gaman:
    Arts and Crafts from the Japanese American Internment Camps, 1942-1946*
    by permission of the author Delphine Hirasuna (Ten Speed Press, c.2005).
    Photographs by Terry Heffernan.

Copies of this book may be purchased through author's
website: www.newcontextcoaching.com, www.amazon.com,
www.ingramcontent.com or by pleading with your local bookseller

For digital editions, visit www.newcontextcoaching.com

CONTENTS

It is well to remember that the entire population of the universe,
with one trifling exception, is composed of others.

JOHN ANDREWS HOLMES

AUTHOR'S NOTE

Human systems can be either affirmingly positive or oppressively negative. I know, because I lived through the whole range in one organization. In 1974, when I was 27 years old, I joined a group of remarkable men and women dedicated to bringing existential, humanistic, and spiritual principles into psychology. The institute, which I will refer to here as the Psychotherapy Institute (PSI), was founded a few years earlier by a husband and wife team trained in the school of psychology that we practiced. The group was made up of psychologists, social workers, family therapists, doctors, nurses, college professors, and other educators. We were all in our 20's, 30's and early 40's. Almost all of us had advanced degrees and most of us were already doing creative work in our fields. We were committed to functioning as a group and not just as a loose association of professionals working under the same roof.

Working as a group, those of us who comprised PSI published a biannual psychological journal, created and ran a successful psychotherapy training program and counseling center, and offered personal growth programs for the general public. People came from all over the world to study with us. Building on our success, we also designed and opened a graduate school with a cutting-edge integrated curriculum that offered advanced degrees in psychology and counseling. But, by 1981, the group had unraveled and PSI was defunct. Most of us would come to refer to those years as some of the most wonderful and simultaneously the most painful of our lives. What happened?

We were an intelligent, well-meaning group of people committed to helping others. We believed that by helping people discover and express their essential selves, we were contributing to the world becoming a better and more loving place. For us, this was not just a job or career, but a mission, a kind of spiritual work that we were undertaking together, as a team. We were committed to working extremely hard in service of this mission.

At first, like any start-up, we told ourselves that our hard work was a temporary necessity, even though this meant less time with our families and friends, and less time for having fun or taking care of our health. We worked long hours designing new programs and expanding proven ones in order to bring in more income to support the growing number of people who were attracted to our work and who wanted to join PSI. But over time, the numbers of people who wanted to participate in our programs and the success of our mission began to go to our heads. As a group we became arrogant and justified our continuing long hours and our isolation from others by telling ourselves that our work was extremely important and the kind of psychology we were doing was unique and much better than anything else around at that time. Slowly, we became more competitive and more black-and-white in our views of other types of psychology and other psychology institutes and training programs. We began to believe that other forms of psychology were either good or bad depending on whether or not they thought the way we did. But, on the other hand, if they were too similar to us, we suspected them of stealing our ideas without crediting us and we accused them of such.

Of course this didn't create many good feelings toward us from our colleagues in the field. We fell into seeing other institutes and other forms of psychology as threats and competitors, rather than simply as other ways of helping people to heal. This stance produced increasingly more negative feelings toward PSI. We started believing that the amount of resistance and negative feelings we were encountering was a measure of others' jealousy, and that reinforced the importance of our mission. Our mantra became, "We must be doing something very important if so many people are trying to copy us or shoot us down!" If colleagues outside of the group, who cared about us, tried to give us feedback about our arrogance and behavior, they were seen as one of those critical "others" who were trying to discredit us, and we had nothing more to do with them.

Over time, we became more focused on perceived enemies and spent more time on attacking others and defending ourselves than on serving our clients and students.

If this was so extreme and problematic, why didn't we catch it at the time? Partly, I think we were dealing with the "boiled frog syndrome," the meme often reported as fact: If you drop a frog into boiling water, it will hop right out, but if you put it into a pot of water and bring it to a boil slowly, the frog will keep trying to adjust its internal temperature until it eventually boils to death.

Our behaviors evolved slowly over a long period of time and we took them to be normal or natural outcomes of the work. I think we were also experiencing a kind of group delusion of grandeur, not unlike a family system that feels it is better than other families just because it is wealthy, or because it has several generations of people who all attended Ivy League universities.

Had the problem been simply with our arrogance or our "competitors" and our obsession with them, we might have been able to survive or even thrive. However, our obsession with "others" outside of the group also affected the relationships within the group. Over time, we, began to treat each other in ways that seemed consistent with the beliefs that a) our form of psychology was the best, and therefore, the only form worth practicing, and b) that others were out to either copy us or denounce us and our work. The directors of PSI, of which I was one, created rules to ensure loyalty, for example, not allowing group members to teach at "unapproved" psychology programs or speak at conferences of groups that had said negative things about us. Group members, who objected to this, even if they were directors, had their allegiance questioned. The job of teaching students was taken away from them and they were given more menial office tasks. Imperceptibly, over time, we became collectively more and more paranoid, withdrawn, and isolated from outside friends and colleagues, and more controlling of members' behaviors and more disconnected from one another within the group. We sacrificed our feelings, and our friendships and ourselves for the good of the group, as well as for the "important" mission of spreading our school of psychology.

This may sound like a form of collective insanity and, even though I left the group in 1980, I am still somewhat ashamed to be writing about it. It is hard to fathom how I could have given up so much of myself, so many of my deepest values, to participate in such a group. In the beginning of the group's life, we created an amazing institution that was reaching out to and helping hundreds of people. By the end, we were closed off, mean and divisive. At the time, I had no idea of what had happened to my colleagues, our shared mission, or me.

Leaving a Dysfunctional System

When I left PSI, I was one of eight directors of the institute and the vice-president and one of the lead professors of the graduate school we had founded. I could no longer tolerate the internal group conflict and endless directors' meetings to deal with it. The meetings only seemed to make things worse. Rather than solve anything, they increased the finger-pointing and blame and separated us even more. The graduate school was the fulfillment of an exciting personal and group vision and was doing quite well. It was challenging and thrilling for me to work with such talented students, but at the same time I was extremely unhappy. I was spending so much time in the contentious directors' meetings that I did not have time to prepare adequately for my teaching or mentoring of students.

When I resigned the school and left the group, I did not immediately feel relieved. I was lost, lonely, and felt like a failure because I thought that I didn't have the strength or courage to do what was required to fulfill my purpose in life. I was afraid to have contact with colleagues outside of the group because I still saw them as "those others" whom we had attacked because they were critical of PSI. The people who were still in the group did not want anything to do with me because, as they saw it, I had betrayed them and our ideals by leaving. I was very depressed and the powerful beliefs, feelings, and attitudes from the group continued to haunt me.

After a time, I finally reached out to a woman who had left PSI before me. She and her family welcomed me with so much love and understanding that I could not imagine how I had once felt that she was bad for having betrayed the group, and me, by leaving. My guilt and depression vanished almost immediately – simply from their acts of loving kindness – and my energy returned, as did my humor and my love of life. It happened so quickly and so completely that it seemed like a miracle. It was as if I had awakened from a trance. Suddenly I was seeing the beauty of people and the world again.

However, at the same time, I was shocked to realize how distorted my perceptions had been while in the group at PSI and immediately after.

Suddenly, most of what I had thought was wrong was right and everything that I had so fervently believed in was terribly distorted. It was as if my whole worldview had shifted 180 degrees in a few short hours. How could an intelligent, caring psychotherapist and teacher like me, who wanted to do good in the world, go so far astray? How did I – we – get so caught up in such a twisted worldview that I behaved toward others, both inside the group and outside, in ways that were uncaring, controlling and psychologically abusive? How did I come to unintentionally act against my highest values? I was appalled by my transformation while in the group and immediately set out to try to make sense of what had happened.

Systems Theory

This quest for understanding about the dysfunctional behavior of groups and organizations eventually led me to the field of General Systems Theory and, more specifically, to human systems theory.[1] It is a way of thinking about groups, organizations and systems of people as entities in their own right, and not just the sum total of the behaviors, both competent and incompetent, of the people who make up the system. Human systems theory is a way of seeing "wholes" – larger units of identity – which operate as if they are autonomous entities, with their own history, and if you will, personalities with conscious and unconscious behaviors, values, and purpose. My study of human systems theory helped to shed light on much of what happened at PSI, as well as on much of what is going on in the world today. This journey ultimately led me to writing *The Dance of We*.

In my consulting, in my studies, and in my life after PSI, I have also witnessed and participated in what I would call healthy, Life*-affirming systems. These are families, businesses, and schools that nurture their people and whose people take care of the wellbeing of the system. These are systems where there is a free flow of information and where members are treated as human beings rather than objects so that they can make informed choices for themselves and for the system as a whole.

---

* *Life is capitalized throughout the book because, a) I am using this term to indicate the largest whole that contains everything else and, b) because I believe that this whole is mysterious and sacred. I do not see Life simply as a container for everything, but as a source and a force, constantly pushing outward, encompassing and creating diversity and complexity as it does so.*

In this book, I will present what I have learned about seeing more systemically, understanding how human systems work, and how to help make them more Life-affirming. I also want to share the dilemmas and questions I still have, in the hope that others in the field will supply or continue to search with me for answers. Most of the examples in the book come from my experience as a family therapist, management consultant and professor in undergraduate and graduate programs. I also draw heavily from my personal family history and my experience at PSI, as well as from the political and cultural arenas.

I hope that what I have lived through and what I have learned about systems will shed some light on some of those everyday experiences that may baffle or frustrate you about your family, workplace or other organizations in which you participate. I also hope that what I have written will help you to see differently and understand better those complex problems we all face together as members of one human family.

INTRODUCTION

THE PROBLEM WITH OUR CURRENT WAY OF SEEING

Have you ever wondered, "Is what's going on in this family / organization / country crazy, or is it just me?" Yes, things are crazy *and* you are involved as part of the problem and part of the solution, but not for the reasons you might think. You, and everyone on this planet, live, work and play together in human systems in ways, that over time, *unintentionally* (and sometimes intentionally) create the perfect conditions for either craziness or well-being.

Human systems are collections of people that are so interconnected and interdependent that a change in one person affects the whole and a change in the whole affects each individual. *The Dance of We* will help you learn to see beyond simple "you and me" relationships in order to understand what happens, for better or for worse, when you and I (and others) become "We."

We've all been in or around families, groups, or organizations that are lively, fun, and productive and bring out the best in us. We've also experienced other groups that are always fighting, blaming, or stuck in dysfunctional decision-making or power dynamics and that make us feel unseen, abused or angry. What makes the difference?

Most of us would point to various individuals in the group as making the essential positive or negative difference. However, in *The Dance of We,* you will begin to understand that each group or organization is an entity, a whole unto itself, that is, a system. This system emerges out of the multitude of relationships of the people within it and takes on a life of its own which, in turn, affects the people within it. Much like an individual, this entity has its own identity or personality, its own behavior, and its own conscious and unconscious rules of operation. To the people in the group, the system's behavior and rules can either be Life-affirming, like a supportive and energizing corporate culture, or Life-deadening, as in a sports team with low morale and a lot of in-fighting.

The Importance of Seeing Systemically

We spend most of our lives as members of collections of people – families, corporations, churches, civic groups, gangs, book clubs, sports teams, ethnic groups, economic systems, cities, nation states–to name just a few. Unfortunately, we have very little understanding of how these groups or systems work. We tend to see groups or organizations as simply the collection of people that make them up. We also interpret events that happen in groups in very personal, one-to-one, linear, cause-and-effect ways: X caused Y that caused Z. For example, "Sybil's constant complaining made everyone tense and people started to leave the party." When something goes wrong in a family or group or company, and this is our only way of seeing and interpreting events, then some person must be at fault, as in, "The director of manufacturing can't manage his people so product quality has deteriorated."

This way of seeing often leads to finger pointing, blame and polarization among the very people who need to be working together to solve the systemic problem. It also leads to paralysis and gridlock as we wait for those "other" people who are causing our problems, to change. Yet they rarely do. So we change wives, or the director of manufacturing, or the president of the United States, but nothing really changes. Here you will understand why real change is so difficult and what to do about it.

Once you are able to see an organization or system as a whole, an entity that takes on an identity and life of its own which then affects all of its members, you will begin to better understand some of the baffling dynamics of everyday life, such as:

- Why fights with your spouse or boyfriend/girlfriend often feel like you are having the same argument over and over whether the content is politics, how messy the house is, or whose turn it is to walk the dog.
- How in some groups you come alive and are creative and respected, while in other groups you can't seem to do anything right.
- As a parent, you are trying so hard for the family to eat meals all together but most often there is someone missing from the table and sometimes it is you.
- How so much time, money and energy can be spent fighting drug addiction, crime, or poverty and yet they still exist or are getting worse.
- How a baseball team with the highest paid superstars does not make it into the World Series, while a team of merely competent players, working together, does.
- How everyone in a group can agree to start meetings on time, but somehow they never do, even when the chairman demands it.
- Why your children seem to need attention just when things are most tense (or most intimate) with your spouse.
- Why it might be that the company mission statement says, "We put our employees first by encouraging a healthy work/Life balance," but there is always *just one more meeting* before you can go home or *just one more weekend* you need to be out of town with an important client.
- Why long-standing international tensions such as those between the Israelis and Palestinians have not been solved.

Seeing systemically means observing the whole gestalt of a group or organization and looking at the behavior and rules of the entity as a whole. For example, "What is it about how we all live our family life that makes it seem so tense and leads to so much fighting?" or "What are all the factors and pressures throughout our company and externally that are effecting quality right now?"

All of the dynamics in the list above involve *relationships* within couples, families, or other institutions. However, when we try to fix these issues, we usually try to change the behavior of one of the individuals or one of the units involved. Of course, it's mostly "them," not "us" who we attempt to change. We look at our spouse, our boss, the pitching staff or the Israelis, because they are easily visible, but we rarely look at ourselves.

But all relationships happen within larger contexts or systems that we often don't see or understand. Nonetheless, they exert significant pressure on our relationships and us. Most of us have had the experience of blowing up at a spouse or child and then feeling ashamed a short time later when we realize that our anger or frustration really had nothing to do with them. It was really about other outside pressures – the family budget not balancing, sick parents, feeling underappreciated at work, etc. – that we were dealing with. In the moment, though, it truly looked like the spouse or the child was the problem. We don't see the larger systems that are affecting our relationships with each other and instead make it personal between or among us.

Similarly, if we could step back far enough to get a sense of the entire Israeli/Palestinian conflict, we would see that there are myriad internal and external pressures on both. These include fundamentalists both within and outside their countries, the shortage of water, Iran's nuclear threat, the upheaval in Egypt, the global economic situation, the need for other countries to identify an enemy in order to unify their people – the list goes on. Each party is forced to deal with all of these pressures while simultaneously surviving with the other. So of course these larger systemic issues are also affecting how they look at, and behave toward, each other. But when we look at the situation from the outside, usually all we see is Israelis versus Palestinians, and depending on which "side" we are on, one or the other is to blame for being the bad guys.

Human systems

Organizational systems are comprised of many different kinds of relationships and processes including decision-making, financial relationships, production systems and technology systems. The emphasis in *The Dance of We* is on the human component of systems and the things we can do when the socio-cultural human systems we create to serve us become dysfunctional, destroying our aliveness and our sense of self.

The primary focus of this book is the functioning of the system in relation to its people and whether or not the system is Life-affirming or Life-deadening.

I believe that an organizational system can function adequately in relation to its basic purpose, but still be dysfunctional in relation to its people. Throughout the book the term dysfunctional will be used interchangeably with Life-deadening, as it applies to the people within a system. I will also be using the terms group, organization, and system interchangeably to connote the various collections of people of which we are a part, defined by a boundary, such as ethnicity or paid membership or common purpose.

We create human systems to make our lives better, but unless we understand how they work, they can take on lives of their own and end up dictating the conditions of our lives. One only has to look at the unpredictability of the global economic system, or the 2010 – 2012 gridlock of the American political system and its unresponsiveness to its constituency, to get a sense of what I mean. Who or what is in control in these systems?

Understanding systems requires new ways of seeing the relationships among us and seeing the wholes we are a part of. Changing our experience in systems to be more Life-affirming requires new, more powerful and more caring ways of being in those systems. *The Dance of We* will introduce you to these new ways of seeing and being.

Learning from Aberrant and Abhorrent Group Behavior

One might simply write off my experience at PSI (see Author's Note) as an aberration of the tumultuous culture of the 1960's and '70's with its upheavals in the areas of civil rights, free speech, religion and spirituality, sexuality, and community. In those days, ours was not the only organization experimenting with working as a group of peers to try and make the world a better place. It would be easy to label PSI as a cult and to dismiss our behavior as an extreme example of the zealous group fads of the time.

Today, there are still groups that are referred to or that behave as, cults. These include groups with powerful, charismatic, controlling leaders, zealous missions, bizarre rituals or behaviors, strong ideas about what is good and bad, as well as rigid rules about who is in or out of the group.

While these extreme groups may be cults and on the fringe of society, simply dismissing them as irrelevant prevents us from seeing that they can serve as valuable learning opportunities about the behavior of human systems. I believe that many of the system dynamics of cults, or the dynamics that we experienced in our PSI group-gone-bad, are being demonstrated every day, with various levels of intensity, by families, religious groups, and other political, social, and economic institutions.

I believe some of the extremely dysfunctional system dynamics of cults, such as secrecy, isolation, paranoia, control of members, and sense of righteousness, were demonstrated strongly, for example, in:

- The Bush administration's deception about weapons of mass destruction that led us into the war in Iraq.
- The behaviors of the companies involved in the mortgage derivatives scandal both before and after the 2008 collapse of the U.S. financial system.
- The gridlock between Democrats and Republicans in the U.S. Senate and House of Representatives throughout the Obama administration.
- The Catholic Church's handling of the child abuse scandals.
- And also less extremely in:
- Families with parents who feel the need to micro-manage their children's lives and futures.
- Corporate cultures with significant amounts of conflict, blame and finger pointing.
- Non-profit service organizations with high levels of burnout, where employees are often overwhelmed by their caseloads and work long hours but never seem to get on top of things or have time to plan or enjoy their successes.
- Schools or school systems where there is an authoritarian administration, unhappy teachers, parents who don't feel heard, and students who seem unmotivated about their own education.

As you read, you will come to understand what happened to us at PSI and be able to identify the clues when your families, groups and organizations are becoming dysfunctional. You will also learn some useful ways of seeing and interpreting group dynamics, and some more effective ways of behaving in all types of systems. These include:

- Several key principles to improve your interactions in one-to-one and group relationships in family, organizational and business settings.
- A visceral awareness of how groups disempower individuals and how to step back from these disempowering system pressures in order to have more freedom and more power as a member of a family, group, or organization.
- How to see the behavior of other people as the result of their attempts to cope with these same disempowering group pressures rather than as an indication of who they are as individuals. This gives you more understanding of what life is like in their system and more possibility of creating win-win solutions to mutual problems.
- How to see past the surface behaviors and the mindsets you have about another to the part of them that is worthy of respect simply because he or she is a unique expression of Life. Knowing that when another person feels seen and respected, they are more likely to try to see, understand and respect you and others.
- Understanding that blame in relationships is irrelevant and a sign of dysfunction in groups. The path to a workable solution is being able to look at any family, group or work situation and ask, "If no one is to blame here, but WE are all responsible, who needs to be at the table to discuss what path of action we need to take together?"
- An understanding that the antidote to the dysfunctional forces within systems is the effective, balanced use of both love and power, including:

  How to own your true power in relationships by developing the courage to express who you are, what you have to offer, and what you need from others.

  How not to give away your power while empowering others and how to use "feeling like a victim" as a wake-up call to reclaim your power and choice in any situation or relationship.

How to express love and caring in groups in practical (non-romantic) ways in order to bring people closer together.

How to extend empathy and compassion for another person or group's situation without giving up your own needs or the group's needs or goals.

How to listen carefully to others because they are expressing information that both you and the system need to learn and to grow.

The Power of Systems Over People

Part One deals with the power that systems have over the people that comprise them. I will define what I mean by a human system and describe some of the properties of systems that will help us understand how they behave and how they affect us as members by either deadening our spirit or enhancing it.

Systems, of course, are usually not totally dysfunctional or perfectly functional. They operate somewhere on a continuum between Life-deadening and Life-affirming depending on the combination and strength of certain conditions.

As a family therapist and an organizational development consultant, I have seen what systems can do, both positively and negatively, and know that it requires a great deal of power, as well as humility, to change them. There is much good work being done about how to create positive, Life-affirming systems and how to develop the leaders to run them.[1] However, I also think that it is beneficial to pay attention to how dysfunctional, Life-deadening systems operate, hence the strong emphasis on them in Part One. Without this understanding of the dynamics of dysfunctional systems, the work on Life-affirming systems can be undermined by these dynamics because they operate outside of members' awareness.

When the people in the system, whether it be a family or corporation, can become "viscerally" aware of how the system affects them, this "felt sense" of system pressure gives individuals the possibility of being mindful of the symptoms of dysfunction *in the moment.* Members can then make choices in relation to those systemic pressures rather than being controlled by them. Part Two focuses on how to do this.

The Power of People Within Systems

In Part Two, you will discover the power that people possess within systems and how they can re-humanize dysfunctional systems by learning to step back, or disidentify, from the pressures of the system and reclaim their agency, one of the hallmarks of a human being. Once people regain their autonomy, they become capable of changing the primary mode of operation of the system from domination and control to empowerment. The result is strong people standing in relationship to each other to change their own experience within organizations and to make their systems more Life-affirming. This is a shift from power *over* to power *with*.

In Part Two we will also explore more fully what I mean by "Life" in the phrases "Life-affirming" and "Life-deadening'" by referring directly to your personal experience of being alive. Until that meaning is more fully explored in Part Two, note that I am using the term *Life* as being synonymous with Spirit, Source, Being, God or whatever term you use to describe the Largest Whole of which we are a part.

I believe that all human systems, whether families, communities, the military, or businesses, have as a part of their purpose to further the growth, development and expression of their individual members. I also believe, that, in addition to its specific concrete goals, the system itself has a larger purpose. That purpose is to express and enhance Life as fully as possible. I believe that when systems are truly doing this, they will accomplish their basic purpose more effectively, and their members will have a more fulfilling experience in doing so.

At the end of Part Two there are four principles that arise naturally from Life as I understand it. We will look at how the practice of these principles serves as an antidote to the dysfunctional characteristics of systems. They can help guide you in the practical, balanced expression of power and love and the creation of more Life-affirming families, groups, and organizational systems. There is nothing new about these principles. These principles have been expressed in various spiritual, religious, and wisdom traditions for millennia. *The Dance of We* is simply a reminder that their practice is absolutely essential in the human systems we create and inhabit. Very briefly, they are:

1 The Principle of Honoring Life
2 The Principle of Interconnectedness
3 The Principle of Respect and Inherent Value
4 The Double Golden Rule

I emphasize these principles because tools and techniques for growth and change are often taught without reference to the Life-affirming principles behind them. This can limit their effectiveness. Sometimes the techniques work in making things better and sometimes they don't. When they don't work, they get cast aside and we tend to grasp at the next tool (or fad) that comes along. However, if you understand the principles behind the tools and techniques, then when a technique doesn't work the first time you attempt it, you can reconnect with the principles behind the technique and try again, perhaps in a slightly different or more creative way. In Appendices A and B, I show how the skills and techniques in two crucial relational and organizational areas flow from the above principles – how you communicate and how you work with mindsets. It is the principles you are trying to practice, not the techniques.

And practice is key. If you want to overcome the dysfunctional and disempowering forces of the systems we have created and make them more responsive to human concerns, it is necessary to learn to see the world in new ways and to practice treating yourself and others differently.

Systems are powerful. They maintain their control over your behavior because they limit or distort how you see yourself and others and how you understand life. Seeing things differently and behaving differently will begin to change your personal and collective experience within a system, even if you are not immediately able to change the system as a whole. By practicing these new ways of seeing and ways of being, individually and in consort with others, you will bring more love, power, and Life into the system. This is the purpose of *The Dance of We*: to help nurture more Life-affirming families, businesses and other organizations. May you find it useful and may it fulfill its purpose.

PART ONE

HUMAN SYSTEMS AND THEIR DYSFUNCTIONS

COMPUTERS HOLDING ARMS DATA MISSING

(Washington, DC) The office in charge of protecting American technical secrets about nuclear weapons from foreign spies is missing 20 desktop computers, at least 14 of which have been used for classified information, the Energy Department inspector general reported last week. This is the thirteenth time in a little over four years that an audit has found the department has lost control over computers used in working on the bombs.

(New York Times news service in Boston Globe 2008)

CHAPTER ONE

WHAT IS A SYSTEM?

Some firms, university departments or neighborhoods seem to have a warming esprit de corps, offering a much greater likelihood that someone will laugh at your jokes, regard your effort as valuable and tell you so, or be interested in what you have to say. In other settings you feel less witty, somehow everyone else seems to be doing something more important than you are, and things that come to mind to say seem boring. Often those immersed in one or the other of these situations are not even aware of its properties until they move to another and experience the difference, often a difference not only in how one is treated but in how one finds oneself treating others.[1]

PAUL WACHTEL, *The Poverty of Affluence*

You probably have some sense of what a system is. Perhaps you've said, "You can't fight City Hall," or "I'm going to stick it to 'the man'" or that you feel like "the system is working against me." When thinking of systems, you might consider large organizations that are either working for you or against you. These organizational systems have people at the "top" who are running them. These leaders are usually viewed as either competent or incompetent, depending on whether the system is helping or hurting you. It usually looks like the system is "out there" and its impact seemingly beyond your control.

Sometimes it is confusing and frustrating because, in certain systems, such as our democratic political system, where you are supposed to be in control, you feel powerless. Sometimes the political system does something good like send a stimulus check but then turns around and uses taxpayer money to bail out bankers who are making tens of millions of dollars. Unless you are a banker, this seems like an outrage and makes you feel more powerless and out of control. In response, you get angry and elect new representatives. But nothing really seems to change with these new politicians. "The system is broken," you lament, and blame it for not hearing your concerns and being more responsive.

Or you look at a religious system like the Catholic Church that is committed to saving souls and creating the kingdom of heaven on earth. Therefore you are baffled, sad and angry when the Church, which teaches spiritual values, covers up incidents of child abuse and protects the abusers within its own clergy. You feel in your gut that something is wrong, but your vague understanding of systems and how they operate doesn't help you explain what is wrong or how to fix it. Instead, you point to the leaders and say, "They didn't do their job."

This "gut sense" or visceral feeling about systems can be very useful if interpreted correctly. It can be used as a signal that you are losing your self and your power in the system. You can utilize it as a trigger for appropriate action. But in order to do this effectively, it is important to have a deeper understanding about systems and how they operate. We need to develop what Barry Oshry calls "system sight,"[2] the ability to see *the whole system as an organism* in its own right and to see how it is affecting the people who are parts of that system. This is very difficult because, as an individual, you are one of the members who make up the whole system, but you are imbedded in it, so it is difficult to see. It is hard to step back far enough in your mind, as well as in reality, to get a view or sense of the whole. As the saying goes, "You can't see the forest for the trees."

Visualizing a System

So what does it mean "to see the whole and not just the parts?" To get an idea, try this simple visualization exercise: Imagine that you are a tuba player in a marching band at halftime in a football game. (I'll bet no one has asked you to do that before!) As you march, you concentrate on staying in step, playing the music, swiveling your tuba, not getting out of breath, etc. You may not be able to see the drum major but you know she is there and you trust that she is performing her role. When the band shifts formation, you do the steps you have practiced and trust that the resulting configuration looks like it is supposed to, but you don't really know because you can't see the whole band.

Now imagine that you are one of the fans at field level. You can see that there are a large number of people marching around with different instruments. You are looking for the tuba player, but he only comes into view occasionally. From the sidelines you can't get a view of what is happening on the whole field.

Now imagine that you are one of the fans looking down from higher in the stands. You are back far enough and high enough to get the sense of the marching band as one whole entity, moving and changing shapes. It is your distance from the field that allows you this perspective of the whole.

Again imagine that you are the tuba player and you are looking at the video re-play of the band's performance. You might be impressed to see that what from your perspective seemed like a bunch of individual people playing music and trying to stay in step, actually looks like an "entity." There is one moving, seemingly living thing flowing over the field. You now have two perspectives and two sources of information about the same event: your view as a part and your view of the whole. It is this "helicopter view" of the marching band *as an entity* that I am pointing to when I talk about "seeing wholes." What can you see and learn from this perspective that you are not able to understand from closer in, where you see only individual parts?

Seeing "wholes" is not our usual or natural way of perceiving the world. This way of seeing and understanding is not taught in schools. What is taught is how to understand things by analyzing their parts – the atoms that make up a molecule, the characters involved in a historical event, the parts and sub-systems of the human body, etc. While this "dissecting" type of learning can be useful, it also misses much of the deeper understanding that comes from looking at *the interactions among the parts* and *the "whole" that emerges out of those interactions*. Consider a dance producer. He cannot create a remarkable performance just by hiring the best choreographer and the best dancers. Something emerges out of their relationships that determines what kind of ensemble or group they will be together. And, in turn, how they are together as a group will influence their individual performance.

Looking at the whole and not just its component parts it gives rise to many difficult questions like, "What is causing what?" or "Who's running the show?" or "Who do I blame if things aren't going the way I want them to?" and "How can I change things around here?"

System Definitions

A system is a whole that is defined by its function in one or more larger systems of which it is a part. It cannot be divided into independent parts; its behavior and properties depend on how its parts interact, not on how they act taken separately.[3]

RUSSELL ACKOFF, Systems Theorist

An organized whole – a complex, mutual influence relationship of parts following a design or order. For example, the difference between the piles of materials and a house.[4]

MARCO DEVRIES, M.D., Ph.D., Medical Pathologist

While there are many ways of looking at systems,[*] I find that these definitions cover a lot of areas. They apply to all systems, non-living (like an automobile or a computer), and living (like an ecosystem, a human being, or an organization of human beings). My focus here is on human systems or the human elements of systems.

There are four key principles in these system definitions:

- Wholeness
- Mutual influence relationships
- Design, order, and rules
- Emergence

---

[*] There are many different frameworks or schools for understanding systems, such as general systems theory, organizational dynamics, family systems theory, system dynamics, systems modeling, deep ecology, to name a few and many of these theories have different schools or theories within them. In other words, there are many ways of looking at systems. The purpose of this book is not to be an exhaustive overview or a detailed understanding of systems, but rather to encourage experimenting with this way of 'seeing.'

In the following chapters in Part One, we will look at these four principles and other aspects of systems, as well as how all of these aspects affect the behavior of systems and contribute to their dysfunction.

Wholeness

Again, systems are a united, organized whole or entity that maintains its existence and cannot be divided into independent parts (without losing its essential properties). As systems educator, Fred Kaufman, jokes, "When you cut a cow in half, you don't get two cows."[5] Some examples of human systems include: a football team, a family, a girl scout troop, the U.S. Senate, the board of directors of a country club, a book group, the government of Egypt. All are easily recognized as functional wholes, single entities, often with names, for example: the New England Patriots, Troop 61, or the Mother Bears Reading & Knitting Circle.

These "organized wholes" are distinguishable in purpose, structure, and behavior from other entities, even those in the same category or field, doing the same things. Even without knowing their names or seeing their uniforms, but by watching their behavior over time – the types of plays they run and the level of teamwork, for instance – some would say the New England Patriots are clearly distinguishable from the Pittsburgh Steelers. The Mother Bears Reading & Knitting Circle definitely does not look or act the same as the Witches and Warlocks Book Coven.

The system as a 'living' whole. One way to begin to try to understand what a system is and how it behaves is to imagine it as a living organism, an entity, or a kind of "being" with a life of its own over time.

Think about Girl Scout troop #61. It is comprised of individual girls and their leaders, each of whom has her own unique identity, purpose, goals or personality. The troop was formed in 1955 and has continued over the years even as individual girls and leaders have entered and moved on. Over the years, the troop as a whole developed its own unique identity, purpose, goals and personality (or culture). It is these aspects that make it distinguishable from other troops. Troop 61 became known in its district as the "outdoors" troop, the troop that trains its girls in camping, canoeing, and wilderness survival skills. Girls who join this troop know, because they have heard stories, that it has strong rules and discipline and that they will not be babied. And even though they do all the other things that a Girl Scout troop does, this has become the "identity" of the group, in contrast, for instance, to Troop 33 which is known as the "social service" troop, or Troop 19 – the "fashion and paint your fingernails" troop. So the troop seems to live over time with its own identity and personality, even though the members are constantly changing.

The life-blood of a human system is information. When information is flowing freely into the system, out of the system, and among its people, the system receives feedback – from within and without – that it needs to regulate itself, know itself, and grow and develop over time.

When the leaders and girls attend council meetings, parent meetings and troop meetings where information is shared, the Troop develops a collective sense of how they are doing in relationship to other troops at any given time in such things as enrollment, cookie sales, parental support, and the girls' levels of satisfaction with the troop.

This sense of itself as a whole is referred to in a living being as "self-consciousness." It can be aware of itself, its existence over time, and its own behaviors.

The Troop has a sense of pride when it wins the cookie sales contest and a sense of disappointment when it loses the inter-troop field days. Troop 61 keeps scrapbooks of its history, its awards, and has developed myths about itself and as well as rituals, both of which are passed on through stories.

Like most living beings, a system will feel resistant to changes and threatened by death: one challenges its self-identity, while the other, its very existence.

At one point, Troop 61 was asked by the district to merge with another troop because its membership had declined significantly. Rather than face the prospect of the troop's demise, and the need to take on or create a new identity, culture and history, the girls conducted an energetic recruitment campaign to bring the troop back to life.

At the same time, like most living beings, systems have within them a drive and ability to learn, to grow in complexity and maturity at their own pace, and to adapt to changes in their environment as needed. As we said above, information and feedback is crucial to this ability.

Through feedback from the girls and parents and from council trainings, the troop learned over time how to better involve and educate the girls, as well as how to adapt over the decades to such things as the evolving needs and interests of its members, or the changing environments in which they were camping.

But is a human system really a living being? It is not living in the bio-organic sense that a person or an orchid is living, nor is it a being in the sense that an ant, or elephant, or human is a being. But a system is an integral, unified whole, an entity with boundaries that delineate its existence. In this sense it is analogous to a being. And because it can learn, grow, adapt and change over time, be self-aware, and cease to exist, in this sense it is "as if" it were living.

Exercises and Reflections

The next time you are watching a family drama or sitcom on television, see if you can look at the whole family and get a sense of its nature. How would you describe the personality of the family? Who or what controls what happens to the family? Has the family "grown" or developed or matured over time? If so, how? The exercise here is to try to practice seeing the family as one whole entity with a personality and behaviors that distinguish it from other families. You can still focus on individual family members, but you might also want to look at how these individuals are affecting the whole family, and how the whole family is affecting the individual.

Mutual Influence Relationships

All parts of the system are interconnected and all are influencing each other. It is not just the leader of a group that is influencing the followers, but the followers are simultaneously influencing the leader and each other. This property of interconnectedness and interdependence of relationships means that in a system, a change in one part affects all other parts and quite often, therefore, the system as a whole. This fact of interconnectedness and interdependence is a central principle in the largest whole – the *Web of Life* – and we will return to it often in later chapters.

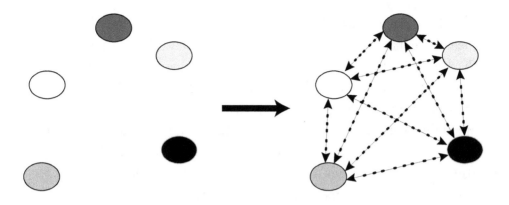

Parts mutually influencing each other

In the preceding diagram, each circle represents a person and the arrows signify the strength or intensity of a given person's connections to the other members of the group. You can see that the myriad interconnections make it look like a single entity with everyone linked and pushing and pulling on everyone else. Virginia Satir, a pioneer in the field of family systems therapy, used to demonstrate this by having family members hold lengths of rope that represented their relationships to other family members. Short ropes equaled close ties to others, long ropes equaled distance in the relationship, and medium ropes equaled somewhere in the middle.

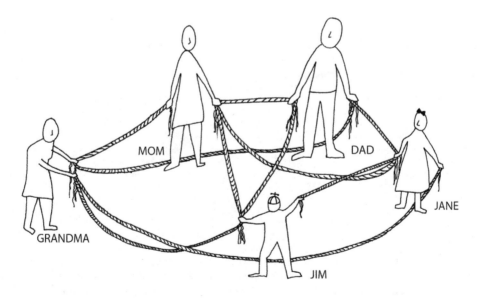

Virginia Satir's demonstration of mutual influence relationships in a family.

If one person moves in any given direction, it will pull the other group members either closer to or further from other individuals depending on the length of their ropes. Satir used this to demonstrate, among other things, the principle that a change in one part affects every other part and the shape of the whole. For example, when the children in a family system are old enough to be in school all day this would affect a stay-at-home mother who suddenly has more time on her hands. If mom decides to take part time work, then this, in turn, affects the kids and her husband who may need to take on some of her former responsibilities.

The system as a whole, however, is also participating in these mutual influence relationships. The people in the system are influencing each other *and* the system as a whole, while at the same time being influenced *by* the system as a whole. In the family example, the particular combination of lengths of rope in this family determines the degree of movement for any one member. It is not just that the mother is responsible for the changes in the family because she wants or needs to work; the family and all the dynamics of its members (such as kids and husband being gone all day) are also affecting the mother who may want to do something interesting and/ or contribute to the family income.

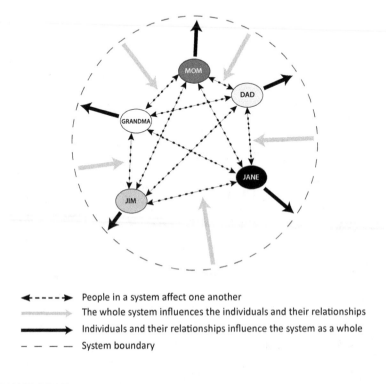

- ◄----► People in a system affect one another
- The whole system influences the individuals and their relationships
- Individuals and their relationships influence the system as a whole
- - - - - System boundary

Cause and effect. As you begin to view systems as the result of mutually influential relationships, you immediately discover that the whole notion of cause and effect, and therefore blame, is called into question. In the family (diagramed below) roped together by what family therapists refer to as 'the ties that bind,' when Bruce moves around, all the other members are forced to move also. Even if Gracie has a long rope connected to Bruce and therefore isn't pulled by him, Gracie might still be required to move because she has a short rope connected to Alison and Alison has a short connection to Bruce. So when Bruce moves Alison, then Alison moves Gracie.

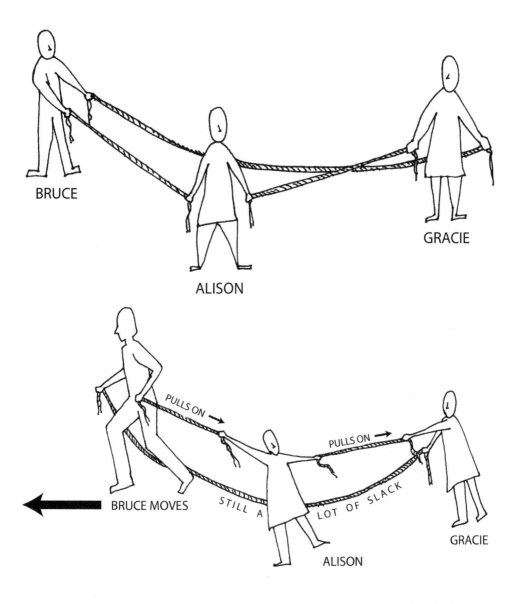

BRUCE

GRACIE

ALISON

PULLS ON

PULLS ON

BRUCE MOVES

STILL A LOT OF SLACK

GRACIE

ALISON

So who causes Gracie to move? Is it Bruce or Alison? Or was it the interconnected relationships that they built up over time? If they were not bound together as a family, Bruce's movement would not affect anyone.

Delays and Unintended Consequences. Let's look at a real-life example of the family above that will also demonstrate two other system dynamics, namely *delays* and *unintended consequences*. In this family, Bruce is the father who loves his wife Alison but wants to feel even closer. He worries that she is paying too much attention to, and cares more about, their daughter, Gracie. Gracie distances herself from her father because she is scared of his moods and on some level senses that she is in competition with her father for her mother's attention. Bruce speaks with Alison about his concerns and since she loves him and wants to be closer to him too, she starts paying more attention to him, cuddling more, etc. Over time, Gracie feels that something is changing in the family and that mother is pulling away and not paying quite as much attention to her. One day, Gracie says she doesn't feel well but has no temperature or other symptoms. She needs her mother to take care of her and to stay in her room with her because she is so miserable. This goes on for several evenings and Bruce begins to suspect that there is really nothing wrong. He gets mad at Alison for not seeing this. His anger just confirms Gracie's fears about her father's moods and she gets even more upset, needing more comfort from mother.

Because it took a while for Gracie to feel her mother's lessening attention, there was a *delay* between Bruce's talk with Alison and Gracie's not feeling well. Because of the delay in time no one involved sees them as connected events within the dynamics of the system. This is not to say that Bruce's talk with Alison caused Gracie to get sick, or that Gracie is to blame for pulling her mother away from her father. A more accurate description of the dynamics might be that the mutual influence relationships (the length of their ropes) are such that when Bruce and Alison move closer together, it has the *unintended consequence* of making Gracie feel more distant. Seeing the more complex, inter-related dynamics of the system opens up the possibility for more creative, Life-affirming solutions, than does blaming Bruce, Alison, or Gracie or any of their separate relationships.

UNINTENTIONAL CONSEQUENCE OR MORE TIME TO PONDER THEIR CRIMES?

Inmates outliving people on outside (Washington, DC)

State prison inmates are living longer on average than people on the outside, according to a Justice Department study released yesterday. State inmates are dying at a yearly rate of 250 per 100,000. By comparison, the overall population of people between ages 15 and 64 is dying at a rate of 308 per 100,000 a year. For black inmates, the rate was 57 percent lower than for the overall black population — 206 versus 484. (AP)[6]

Blame. In most systems, because of the intense complexity and multiplicity of relationships, and because of delays and unintended consequences, it is usually very difficult to determine what is causing what. Therefore seeking and blaming the cause of a problem becomes less useful in identifying a strategy for changing the behavior of a system.

For example, who is to blame for the problem of gun violence in this country? Is it the gun manufacturers, the NRA, the gun laws, the people that pull the triggers, the people that have not stood up to the gun lobby, the climate of fear in this country, the economic disparity between rich and poor, or the full moon?[7] So instead of wasting time blaming and trying to find the 'cause' of gun violence, let's look at the *relationships,* the interconnections between these various aspects, for leverage points where a change in the relationships might bring about a change in the whole.

> *There is real opportunity for action in learning to view every system as the cause of its own behavior. First of all, if the entire concept of blame is removed, you can stop arguing about who is at fault and get on with solving the problem.*[8]
>
> DONELLA MEADOWS, systems theorist

Even in simple systems made up of only two parts, like a couple, the mutual influence relationships make it very hard to determine cause and effect.

Example:

A husband is sitting on the couch watching television. His wife, feeling out of touch with him says, "Let's go for a walk."

Husband: "Not right now, maybe later."

Wife: waiting fifteen minutes – her "later" – comes back into the room and says, "Come on, it's nice out tonight, let's go for a walk."

Husband: who would in fact like to walk later, is just getting to the suspenseful part of his show and doesn't want to be interrupted, says, "Not yet. Just wait a minute."

Wife: now feels that the husband likes television more than her and feels even more distant. She comes and sits on the couch, curls up next to him and says, "What's happening to our relationship honey?"

Husband: who just wants to see if Jack Bauer can defuse the bomb before it blows up half of New York City, and wondering what this could possibly have to do with their relationship, puts his arm around her but doesn't respond.

Wife: feeling totally ignored and worthless, is the one who blows up and goes storming out of the room just as Jack cuts the red wire and the time bomb stops ticking down.

Husband: gets up, ready to go for a walk, and finds his wife sulking in the kitchen. He says he's ready to walk.

Wife: is angry and withdrawn, and says she doesn't want to walk anymore. "I want to talk about our relationship and why we are so distant."

Husband: frightened by what this means and of her feelings (and his own), withdraws into his shell and wonders why this is coming up now when he thought they were going for a walk.

You've just read about one incident in this marriage, and depending on whether you are a husband or a wife, a man or a woman, or like TV or taking walks, you probably have your clear favorite for who's to "blame" for the problem in the relationship. What you don't see is this "mutual influence relationship" playing out *over time,* an approach-avoidance dynamic occurring over and over again with differing content. The problem is not about the content, that is, the TV watching or walking. Rather, it is about *the patterns of interaction*. Whose fault is it, the approacher or the avoider? Once the vicious circle is rolling, trying to determine the cause is often time-consuming and futile. Assigning blame often just escalates the viciousness of the circle.

Blame and Responsibility. A large amount of blame is one of the indicators that a system is dysfunctional. Blame separates people, creates distance and breaks the bonds among the parts of the larger whole. It also keeps us from looking at the system as the source of the problems we blame each other for. It is in our human nature to attribute cause and to blame as a way of avoiding responsibility. Even blaming the system means whatever is wrong is not my responsibility. However, as you will see in Part Two, removing blame in a system does not remove responsibility. The system may be causing its own behavior, but we make up that system and therefore we are the ones who are responsible for changing that behavior if we don't like it. No one is to blame, but all of us are responsible.

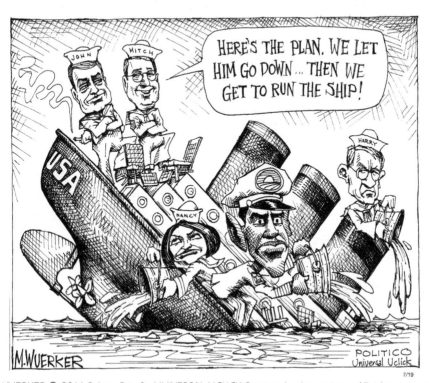

Exercises and Reflections

1 Think of a situation between two of your friends or in someone else's family where, from the outside, you can clearly see how each of the members is contributing to the problem. Try to describe the situation as a series of events: "When he does this, then she does that and when she does that, he responds by doing this and when he does this, she then does that, etc." See if you can describe it without taking sides or seeing one or another as causing the other's response. Try to imagine it as a series of 'dance moves' where it doesn't matter where you start the dance, the dance always stays the same. What is it like to see the situation this way?

2 Think of a situation where you are blaming someone for making your life difficult. Think about the actual behaviors that are causing problems for you, e.g. phone calls not being returned. (Don't attribute a motivation for this behavior, e.g. "He doesn't like me" or "He just wants power.") How do you respond to these behaviors? What do you do when he/she behaves in this way? What is the other person's response to your behavior, etc. See if you can describe it as a series of dance moves with no causal relationship between the steps, e.g. "When she steps here, I step there, and then she steps . . ." Now ask yourself two questions about this dance: a) "In what ways am I contributing to the continuation of this dance?" and b) "Does seeing this as a dance open up any new possibilities for steps that I might make that would change the nature of the dance?"

So how does a system as a whole cause you to behave in certain ways toward one other in your mutual influence relationships? For the answer to this, we will look at the third component of the definition of systems: ". . .a *complex, mutual influence relationship of parts **following a design or order**.*"

Design, Order and Rules

A heap of building materials, or a bunch of men milling around, are not a system. They only become a system when they start interacting with each other in a regular way over time. How the materials or men interact is determined by the design or order or rules of the system to which they belong. If you have a pile of building materials, it will be made into totally different structures depending on the blueprints that are used. Members of a baseball team and members of a hockey team interact differently among themselves and with their opponents because of the rules of the game they are playing (the system they are in).

If you want to begin to understand and attempt to change a system, you need to understand the order, the structure and rules of that system:

- How are the members of the system interconnected: by contract, by family bonds, by common interests, by common employer, by random assignment, etc.?
- How is the system structured? Most systems are hierarchical by nature, but what kind of hierarchy? Does this system have many levels with a rigid command and control structure, or is it a "flatter" hierarchy with leadership being determined by competency at tasks as they arise? Or is it a circle structure with no leader or rotating leadership?
- How are decisions made: by majority rule, leadership fiat, through consensus, etc.?

In essence you are looking for the rules that determine how the members of the system behave with each other and as a whole.

Espoused Rules vs. Behavior in Action. Unfortunately, as you start to look for the rules or order of the system you run into a big problem. It soon becomes clear that the written, espoused, contracted, and agreed upon rules do not adequately explain the behavior of most systems. It turns out that a system, like an individual, has unconscious, unspoken, not-agreed-upon and habitual rules. And because they are unconscious, and therefore unspoken, they are very hard to uncover. It is these rules that are usually at the source of most recurring problems that seem to defy attempted fixes. If you observe the behavior of the members of a system, it is as if they are subliminally aware of these rules and, on some level, feel a pressure to follow them. (There is more about these pressures in Chapter 3.)

Most of us have experience with these unconscious rules in our families. In some families, it is just not okay to speak about sex. In others, the rule is about money, while in others the ban is on religion or politics.

No one ever said that these topics were out of bounds; but as a child, for instance, you just know that they are. You might not even realize that they are forbidden subjects until you go to a friend's house and hear them spoken about openly. Your first response might be embarrassment or discomfort to be in the presence of someone talking openly – with their parents – about sex. Or you might judge these people as impolite, uncouth, or uneducated, not realizing that they only appear this way because they are violating your family's unspoken rules.

In larger, more complex systems, there are always multiple unconscious rules, and they are often even harder to uncover because of the myriad behaviors of the system. And to complicate matters further, the conscious and unconscious rules are often in conflict with each other. I have consulted with several companies and non-profits where the workers were stressed, exhausted, and overloaded with work, and where the morale in the company was dropping. And yet the number of banked, unused vacation days was astronomical. The number was so big that in one company the human resources department was actually encouraging the employees to take time off so that they wouldn't lose their vacation days. But the vacation days still did not get used to their full extent. This was not the CEO's fault. He was being just as influenced by the system dynamics as everyone else. The CEO recognized the burnout potential among his immediate staff and practically ordered them to take their vacations. But because he could never seem to find the time to use all of his vacation days, they didn't want to let him down by not carrying their full weight. As a consequence, the stress kept building.

In these companies, it is as if everyone is following an unspoken rule that "we don't take vacations here" or "short-term company goals are more important than my well-being." The individual (including the boss) always has a good reason why he or she cannot take his or her vacation. There is a project deadline, fear of not looking committed, concern about the piles of work that will be waiting when he or she returns, etc. But when one steps back and looks at the system as a whole, one sees that it is not an individual problem. Rather, it is a *systemic* problem caused by the unconscious rules or design of the system.

Exercise and Reflections

1 Think about the spoken and unspoken rules in your family of origin. Were the spoken rules always followed? If not, what were the consequences? Did your parents ever say, "Do as I say, not as I do"? What did this communicate to you? What rules were unspoken in your family? What was okay to speak about, what not? Who could you touch, who not?

2 Now ask yourself the same questions about your current nuclear family.

3 At work, what unspoken pressures do you feel? What do you intuitively know you are supposed to do or not do? Do other people feel this too? How do you know? Is it discussed? Where do you and others imagine these pressures are coming from? What might you and others be doing that contributes to these unspoken pressures?

It is crucial to understand both the conscious, espoused rules of the system and the unconscious, unspoken rules because all of these rules together over time create a recognizable pattern of interactions among the people in the system. Out of this pattern of interactions over time, the personality or culture of a human system emerges, often with new, unpredictable, and sometimes unintentional characteristics.

Emergence

You think because you understand "1" that you also understand "2," because 1 and 1 equals 2. But you must also understand "and".[10]

SUFI SAYING

In a given system there is a coming together, a synergy, of all the behaviors of the individual parts, the relationships among the parts, and the rules, structure and order that guide those relationships, to form *a whole which is greater than and different from the sum of its parts.*

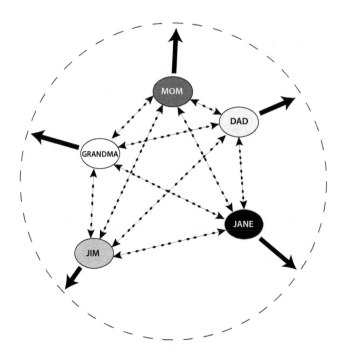

The "personality" or culture of the whole emerges out of the interactions of the parts

This whole or entity, is 'greater than' its parts because it is able to perform functions beyond what the collection of individual members can do, the same way a hospital is more than the sum total of all the functions contained within it. The system is "different than" because characteristics *emerge* out of this synergy that are not chosen or exhibited by any of the component parts. An example: My institute's (PSI) obsession with loyalty and betrayal that were not concerns for any of the members when our group began.

Even if you walked into a biology lab and saw a table full of organs and limbs, and recognized them as human and studied them intensively, you would not be able to predict or understand the emergence of a unique personality, let alone the existence of consciousness. Out of this conglomeration of flesh, bone, blood and brain there arises: 1) individual personality and identity 2) consciousness of your surroundings and 3) the ability to be aware that you are aware. Where did those characteristics come from? Were they contained in the spleen, the brain, the heart, the little finger? And yet somehow they emerge.

And once they do emerge, they become a part of the mutual influence relationships:

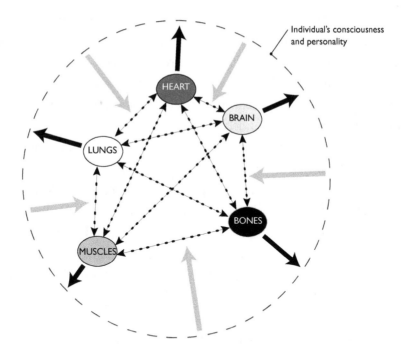

The consciousness and personality of the whole person affects the body and all of its parts through what we choose to eat, how much we sleep, etc. while at the same time the health of our body and its parts affect our personality and consciousness.

The Emergence of a Cult. In my case, with PSI, I asked myself: How could a group of loving, well-educated, helping-professionals become so psychologically abusive amongst themselves and to others? How did a group of people whose school of psychology was based on seeing and drawing out the highest and best in people become so paranoid and obsessed about "us = good" and "them = bad"? How did a group that was committed to helping make the world a better place become so isolated and cut off from that world? We had come together because we liked and respected each other and what we were individually trying accomplish in our lives. We saw the potential of doing more, of doing it better, of learning and having fun along the way if we could do it together.

And all of these things did happen. We had fun together. We learned together. We became life-long friends. We started a graduate school that no one of us could have started alone. And yet, other negative characteristics also emerged and ended up consuming the organization we had created.

Many theories could be put forth to try to explain why our group turned into what I now see as a cult: unresolved parental issues, collective shadow, peer group pressure or "group think," brainwashing, or an authoritarian leader. But the *why* is not as important as *the fact* that a whole emerged out of the mutual influence relationships of the members that none us consciously intended.

One might argue that a cult is a rather extreme, rare, and therefore irrelevant example of the emergence of characteristics in a system that are different from, and not chosen by, the component parts. However, I think that when we use this human systems perspective and the property of emergence to look at debacles such as the Enron and Worldcom scandals, the Abu Ghraib prison atrocities, or the 2008 financial derivatives crisis, we can understand better how they might have happened and how they involved so many individuals who, on their own, probably would not have undertaken these actions or intended the devastating results. It was only when the individuals all came together and began influencing each other within given systems, like free market economics or the Iraq war, that these horrendous behaviors and characteristics emerged.

Responsibility and "Positive" Emergence. Emergence, sometimes called synergy, is a property of human systems. From a systems perspective it is not necessary to arrive at a definitive cause, or to attribute blame (or praise) for what emerges. Trying to assign cause or blame is a distraction and often a way of avoiding accountability. It is, however, crucial as individuals and as a group to take responsibility for our behaviors and to learn from our mistakes, to fix the problems we have created, to apologize and make reparations where possible, and to foster behaviors that will prevent these events in the future.

As members of human systems we can learn, individually and collectively, to be aware of the characteristics that are emerging in our systems, and to step back and ask, "Is this how we are *choosing* to behave? Is this what we want to be valuing in this moment and therefore to reinforce, or are we being pressured by the forces of the system as a whole to behave in ways that go against our highest nature?"

However, not all emergent qualities are negative. The sports team made up of rather ordinary players that rises to the occasion and succeeds against all odds is an example of the emergence of positive qualities. Both positive and negative qualities can emerge in the same group and, in fact, most human systems will have both. In our group there was also an emerging quality of communal creativity that was very exciting to participate in. It was like being part of a group creative mind. All of the "100 Best Companies to Work For" lists attest to the fact that there are human systems that are getting it right. And we've all seen families, clubs, or organizations that seem energetic, lively, creative and fun, even if we have not ourselves been members.

Exercises and Reflections

Think about the various groups of people of which you are a part, eg, your family, a team at work, your workplace as a whole, your church, maybe a sports team. Are there characteristics or behaviors, either positive or negative, which have emerged in any of these groups that you and others were unable to predict when the group was formed? What do these emergent characteristics look like in action?

Systems within Systems

As you begin thinking about human systems and your role in them, you begin to see just how many systems you are involved with and, therefore, influence and are influenced by. You are a member of a family and maybe a church, temple or synagogue. You probably work, either taking care of a family or for a corporation, for a non-profit or for yourself in your chosen field. You may belong to various clubs, service organizations, or sports teams. All of these are examples of systems. You are a whole being, a system unto yourself, participating in other whole systems. These systems are in turn participating in even larger systems thereby influencing these larger systems as well as being influenced by them. Your synagogue, for instance, might participate in a particular form of Judaism such as reform, reconstructionist, conservative or orthodox. Your local church, along with others, inhabits a particular diocese that in turn is a part of the Catholic Church as a whole. Your family is a member of a community that is a part of

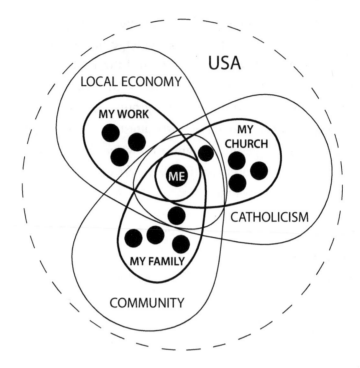

a city, state, country, continent and world. Your work is part of an industry among other industries. It also participates in your local economy that is in turn part of a regional economy, a national economy, and a global economy.

As a member of each of these human systems you possess an opportunity to influence their behaviors over time. However, the larger the system is, or the more levels of hierarchy it has, the harder it is for one person to exert influence. On the other hand, as part of all of these human systems, you are also constantly being influenced by them in various ways and to differing degrees of strength and consequence. Sometimes, the systems in which you participate may even be in conflict with each other and therefore trying to pull you in different directions.

For instance, when the diocese wants to close your local church because of budget issues you may become torn between your support for the diocese's ministry to the poor in your city as a whole and your love for the community at your specific place of worship. When your boss needs you to make an important business trip on the weekend of your daughter's championship soccer game, the pressure on you to act in the way that each system needs can be excruciating.

The Relationship between the system and its people

In a healthy, Life-affirming system, the people in the system look out for the wellbeing of one another and of the system as a whole. In addition, the whole system strives for its own wellbeing as well as promoting the growth, development and health of its parts. There is a process of mutual care-taking and nurturance between the parts and the whole. Each realizes that because of their interconnectedness and interdependence, the health of one is dependent on the health and wellbeing of the other.

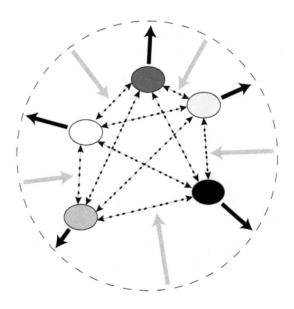

Parts taking care of the whole
and
Whole taking care of the parts

When the company thrives, it is more likely that the people within the company will thrive. When the individuals within the company are happy, secure and growing, the company is more likely to do well and grow.

The parts not taking care of the whole. In contrast, a system becomes unhealthy and Life-deadening when the whole and the parts do not support each other. When the people in a company try to get as much as they can for themselves, without caring about each other or the company as a whole, the result is a dysfunctional company such as Enron, WorldCom or AIG. The hubris and selfishness of the top echelons contributed to the death of the first two companies. AIG had to be put on life support by the federal government because its demise would have had a disastrous effect on the larger economic system of which it was a part. In these cases, the parts of a system did not take care of the whole system(s) to which they belonged. (Systemically, a case could be made that the AIG bailout was a larger whole, namely the U.S. government, taking care of the American and global economic system and protecting the other parts that comprise it, as well as itself.)

The whole not taking care of its parts. It can be equally damaging when the whole doesn't support the parts that comprise it. For example: a system such as a non-profit, might focus so strongly on its important mission and the people it is serving, that it loses sight of its own staff's well-being. The non-profit might be doing good work and attracting grants and funds for its survival, but its staff are over-stressed and there is high turnover. The non-profit keeps replacing burned-out staff like one might replace worn-out parts in a machine.

Benign systems. There are also, of course, benign systems, systems that are neither Life-affirming nor Life-deadening but somewhere in-between. Benign organizations are probably the majority of all systems. They are companies, non-profits, families, etc. that take care of their members, and whose members take care of each other and the whole just enough so that every person and the whole can survive, but not enough so that the people and the whole can really *thrive*.

Exercises and Reflections

Review the list of systems in which you participate (from the last exercise) and identify which are healthy, benign, or dysfunctional in terms of whether the whole nurtures the people within it and the people nurture the whole.

Who's Running the Show?

So what makes a system either Life-affirming or Life-deadening? Why do some systems take care of their people and vice versa? Who decides this? In the next chapter, you'll learn about the principle of wholeness and how it leads to a system developing a personality and taking on a life of its own. Once the system takes on a life of its own, there are major implications for the individuals who comprise it, the most important being the answer to the question, "Who's running the show here, us or the system?"

CHAPTER TWO

WHO'S RUNNING THE SHOW?: SYSTEMS HAVE A LIFE OF THEIR OWN

No one wants or works to generate hunger, poverty, pollution, or the elimination of species. Very few people favor arms races or terrorism or alcoholism or inflation. Yet those results are consistently produced by the system-as-a-whole, despite many policies and much effort directed against them.[1]

DONELLA MEADOWS, author of *Thinking in Systems*

In my classes and workshops I often do a simple experiential exercise that I call the ballgame. It is adapted from a more complex systems exercise created by systems educator and consultant, Michael Goodman.[2] In this exercise, I ask for volunteers to form two circles of about 12 people each. I tell them that they are a manufacturing group that makes widgets. Each person has a part to contribute to the widget, represented by a ball that is passed or thrown around the circle. The group makes one widget once everyone has touched the ball. There are only four rules:

- Everyone must touch the ball once and only once for each widget made
- You cannot simply pass or throw the ball to the person who is currently standing next to you
- Once you establish a manufacturing order you must keep to it
- If a ball is dropped it must be picked up and put back in play

I remind them that this is just a game and the purpose is to learn about systems and not to win the game. I give them time to establish their manufacturing sequence: they throw it around and across the circle until everyone has touched it and it comes back to the person who started the process. Once they have established their sequence I tell them that they have one minute to see how many widgets they can make. Once they start, I feed more balls of different shapes into each group so that more than one ball is going around at a time. Invariably, chaos ensues.

The groups always go as fast as they can and there are balls flying everywhere. It is often the case that when Bob drops a ball and goes to get it, Sue, the person throwing to him, has to stop because there is no one to throw to. But the balls keep coming to her. She can't catch them and hold them all and more balls end up on the floor. At the end of a minute I call "stop!" and ask each group how many widgets they made.

Two things usually happen: 1) it is hard to get people to stop when I say to – they always seem to want to make one last widget; and 2) the group that made the most widgets cheers and the other group moans. They usually think the game is over because one of the teams has won. But then I tell them that the local newspaper just reported that the manufacturing company down the street has just set a new world record of X number of widgets in a minute (with X being a number somewhat greater than either group had made).

I then suggest they try it again for one minute. Most of the time the groups are excited to try to beat the world record. I remind them, again, that this is just a game and the purpose is to learn what they can about systems. They start right up trying to go faster and faster, with even more balls dropping. At this point people start yelling suggestions into their circle for how they might do it differently. Sometimes the group will follow a suggestion, but most of the time people just yell over each other and the balls keep flying.

Sometimes I add complexity by taking Mary out of the circle for what I shout is "an offsite meeting" thus assuring that they can't simply maintain the same order. But usually they do. They are going so fast and there is so much shouting that some people don't even notice that I have removed a member and the balls keep going to where she used to be standing. Once the person that was throwing to Mary notices her absence, he usually tries to slow things down by shouting, "wait" or "who was she throwing to so

I can throw to him?" But, because of the chaos, usually no one hears or responds, the balls keep flying, and he has to keep throwing to where she was or to someone – anyone – else or he will end up holding (and dropping) too many balls. The game turns into an out-of-control madhouse.

At the end of the second round, the groups have usually improved a little, but sometimes they actually produce fewer widgets because of all the shouting and speeding up as they try to do even better. Again the group with the most widgets cheers and the losing group moans and looks dejected. I tell them that while they were improving, the company down the street had also improved and broken their own world record by producing X widgets. After the third round I tell them that the company down the street had doubled their production producing Y widgets, a seemingly impossible number.

Usually the groups take this as a challenge, and realize that they have to make some changes in how they are doing things because they can't go any faster with the current process and structure. They start talking among themselves with some talking louder and more forcefully and others sitting back and listening or looking bored. They often ask me if they can do A, B or C and I just repeat the above four rules to them. At this point, groups usually start coming up with creative possibilities such as changing where they are standing in the circle or getting one person to carry four balls around and everyone touches it. But sometimes they cannot come to an agreement before the next round starts because Jane came up with a better idea or Robert thinks they are breaking the rules or they aren't listening to each other. The groups that do listen to each other and end up changing the process usually make quantum jumps in numbers of widgets produced and always beat the "world record" easily.

We play the ballgame for about half an hour and could spend hours processing the various insights group members have about systems. I start by asking about participants' personal experience of the exercise. I hear things like "I was incredibly stressed," "I was excited," "No one listened to me, so I just didn't care," "It was total chaos. I couldn't stand it," and so on. When I remind them that it was only a game, they all laugh. Clearly they had invested a lot in it, even though it was 'just' a game.

When I ask why they were so invested, I hear comments such as "it was a challenge to us," "I wanted our team to win," "I knew our team could do better," etc. I point out how quickly they became a team. They went from being 12 volunteers out of the larger class to being a group almost instantaneously. As soon as the 12 had a task (a purpose), rules of the game, and a manufacturing order, they immediately became a 'team' with an identity and a boundary that set them apart. They individually became parts of a larger whole.

The first thing the class sees about systems is how quickly and unconsciously an entity can form with a boundary that determines who is, and who is not, a part of that entity. They also see that the entity develops an identity – an "us-ness" that sets "us" apart from "them." This becomes startlingly clear when I ask the class who the "them" was that they were trying to beat. Some say that it was the other circle; a few say it was the company down the street, and some say both were the "other."

> Me: "So what made you think that this other circle was another team?"
> A few class members speak up: "Well, there were two circles" "They were trying to beat us" "*You said* there were two teams".
> Me: "*I said* there were two circles. And I also said that both circles were part of the same manufacturing company."
> Class: silence
> Me: "Did anyone realize that, together, both circles always produced more widgets than the company down the street?"
> Class: All shake their heads side to side.

There are a lot of implications for communication and collaboration between teams, within families, vertically-structured (stove-pipe) organizations, in-groups and out-groups, and much more.

The class begins to see how a system almost immediately takes on an identity and life of its own. This gets even more clear when I ask them what happened when balls were dropped or when I took someone out of the circle.

> Class: "You took someone out of the circle? I was too busy throwing and catching; I didn't even notice!"
> "Everything was chaotic, but we kept going."
> "I didn't know who to throw it to so I just threw it to anyone."

Me: "How many of you knew that something was wrong with the process, that it was getting out of order or breaking down?"

Class: Almost all of the hands go up.

Me: "How many of you said anything or tried to stop the process?"

Class: One or two hands out of the whole group are raised.

Me: "Those of you who knew something was wrong but didn't speak up, why not?"

Class members: "There was too much momentum."

"I didn't want to slow us down. We had to win."

"I couldn't see how to fix it."

"I don't know why. I just couldn't."

Me: "For the few of you who did speak up, what happened?"

Class: "Nobody listened."

"I didn't hear anyone speak up."

"Everybody else just kept going even when I started to hold on to the balls to get them to stop."

Me: "So it was hard to find your voice and be heard in the midst of the chaos? It was hard to get information or feedback into the system?"

Class: No one speaks, as the implications of this sink in.

Me: "Let me ask one more question: As you were in the middle of this fast-paced game, what were you focusing on?"

Class: "Who I was getting the balls from and who I was throwing them to."

"Everything was going so fast I could just focus on the task at hand, which was moving the ball from one person to another."

Me: "What was that experience like? How did it make you feel?"

Class: "Like cogs in a machine."

"Like a robot just doing a repetitive task."

"Like an object that was just moving another object (the balls) around another object (the circle)."

Me: "Were you aware of how many widgets were getting made, or what was going on in the whole group?"

Class members: "No way! We were too focused on the balls coming at us and the need to keep them moving."

"We were parts in the system. We couldn't see the whole system."

Me: "So it really was like the group took on a life of its own and had to keep going no matter what. You, as members of the system, did not consciously design it to be that way plus you were unable to control it. Would you say it was like the system was controlling you?"

Class member: "Yes. It was like that scene from 'I Love Lucy' where Lucy and Ethel were working in the chocolate factory and the conveyor belt started speeding up. They were forced go faster and faster. They started eating chocolates to keep them from falling on the floor. Then they heard the supervisor coming and started stuffing the chocolates into their dresses, their hats, their mouths. It was hilarious. When the supervisor came in and saw the conveyor belt empty, she complimented them on their job, and yelled to the machine operators, 'Okay, boys speed 'er up!' It was like whatever Lucy and Ethel did, the factory was going to keep going in its own way. It felt just like that!"

This is what it looks like, whether it is in a ballgame or an "I Love Lucy" episode, when a system takes on an identity and life of its own, often beyond the control of the individual parts.

Exercises and Reflections

Think about any groups, organizations (systems) that you are a part of. Do any of them feel chaotic or out of control? How much ability do you have to make a difference in any of these systems? How easy or difficult is it to get feedback into these systems? How creative is the group or organization in changing its processes or structure to improve its performance? Who is the 'us' in these systems and who is the 'them?'

Homeostasis: The system 'ego' and its resistance to change

One of the major implications of a system taking on a life of its own is that, over time, it develops a 'personality' much like an individual. As with an individual, the system has a drive to grow and develop, or in systems terms, to self-organize, like the teams in the ball game wanting to improve their manufacturing times. At the same time, it also has the drive toward preservation of 'selfness' or identity, or in systems terms, homeostasis, as when the teams kept going in the same process over and over even when they saw it wasn't working. As with an individual person, these two drives in a system are often in a healthy tension, because growth that is too much or too fast can overwhelm an individual or a system, but rigid clinging to the status quo and fear of change are also not healthy.

It is as if the system or organization develops an identity much like an individual 'ego' that it consciously and unconsciously strives to hold on to and protect. (I am using the term ego here not in a strict psychological sense but in the more colloquial sense of a perceived self-boundary that becomes threatened and defensive when others try to point out faults or try to change a person.)

You can sense this systemic identity when two companies try to merge. Which company name will prevail? Whose culture will survive? Which company will lose the most employees in this merger? You can also sense this self-boundary in the fear that arises, for example, when a non-profit organization's main funder goes bankrupt, threatening the very survival of the organization. It is not just that the individual members are worried about what will happen to them; there is a collective fear of the whole system dying. This sense of "who we are" is also present in families and can be felt most strongly during significant family changes such as deaths or marriages. But the identity of the family might also be felt or challenged at other times, for example when a gay or lesbian member comes out to the family, or when two people from very different ethnic or religious backgrounds intermarry. In each of these cases the questions of "who have we been and who are we now?" are felt very strongly by the system as a whole.

This sense of systemic ego or self-boundary helps to explain a system's resistance to change and the unconscious collusion among the parts to preserve the identity of the whole. This need to maintain the system as it is, or to return to a state of familiarity or balance, is called the drive toward homeostasis. One of the key ways that a system maintains its homeostasis is by controlling the amount or type of information or feedback that is allowed into the system. This can be seen clearly in dictatorships or fundamentalist religious groups, but it was also apparent in the description of the ball game where it was difficult to be heard in a system driven by its rule to produce as many widgets as possible.

Homeostasis in My Family

The first in my Kansas, second-generation-immigrant family to go to college, I was excited to leave home in 1965, to get out of the boredom of the mid-west and out from under parental control. I was accepted into two mid-western universities and one on the east coast. I chose Brandeis University in Boston, even though I had never visited it, because it was the farthest from home. And even though it was a Jewish-affiliated university, which meant a lot to my parents, they wanted me to stay close to home and go either to Northwestern in Illinois or Purdue in Indiana, where we could see each other more easily and therefore, more often.

Somehow I convinced them, over several long phone calls, to let me stay until the end of the first semester and we would discuss it when I returned home for the holidays. When I got home, we spent the whole time fighting about the Vietnam war and whether I would be able to go back to Brandeis. In the mid-60's, many families were fighting over differing views of the war and since my father had served in the Army in World War II and was politically very conservative, none of this was very surprising. What was surprising was the strength of my parents' feelings and their willingness to pull me out of a first-class university. To me, the consequences seemed way out of proportion to the fact that we had differing political views.

It wasn't until many years later, when I began to study family systems theory, that I understood what had been going on in my own family during that first year of college. Jay Haley, a prominent family therapist, wrote a book called *Leaving Home*,[3] about how certain families encounter problems when a child goes away to college. For some families, removing a member from the home can (unconsciously) be very threatening to the balance of relationships within the family and therefore, to its identity. Haley describes different scenarios by which these families try to preserve the homeostasis: a parent gets sick and the child has to come home to take care of him or her; the child can't handle the stress or the workload and has to drop out; or, the student over-indulges in the newfound freedom and ends up being sent home. In all cases, the end result is the same: the child returns home and the family preserves its life as it had known it. No family member consciously chose to get sick or act out. Often the reaction is, "it just happened that way." The life of the system goes on in its familiar safe way even if it has to sacrifice the growth of one of its members to do so.

That is what I think was going on in my family at the beginning of my college years. My being the first person to leave a very close-knit family was threatening to the identity of the family as a whole on two counts: 1) by removing one member from the makeup of the family, my father, mother, and brother would have to come into new mutual influence relationships with the fear of not knowing what that might be like; and 2) I was bringing new and sometimes very different ideas and beliefs (information) into the family, which challenged how it saw itself and the world. We had many fights and became very polarized as no "commie propaganda" or "right-wing diatribe" would change either my father's or my mind. The system as a whole would not let new information in. No wonder the feelings seemed out of proportion to the circumstances.[4]

Fortunately, in my family's case, the systemic drive to grow and develop was stronger than the systemic forces that were resisting change. My parents agreed to continue paying for college and I was able to graduate from Brandeis. Others are not so fortunate when the preservation of the identity of the system prevails and has more drastic consequences for the individual members of that system. One only needs to look at how long it is taking to undo racism in America, or apartheid in South Africa, to see the oppressive effects on the members of a system that is unwilling to change its way of being in the world.

Exercises and Reflections

As you read or listen to the news in the next few days, listen for examples of systems resisting change or trying to maintain their identity. There are always good reasons why the system is acting the way it is, but the end result is that the system preserves its homeostasis or identity. Some examples might be: certain states in America insisting on English only education, or France prohibiting Muslim women from wearing veils. What do you see or hear in the news?

Who's Running the Show?

When I first read Donella Meadow's quote at the beginning of this chapter, it seemed to sum up everything I was wrestling with when I left PSI. None of us were choosing to hurt each other. None of us wanted to cut ourselves off from our families or our friends outside of the group. Everyone complained about the late hours and lack of sleep. And yet, somehow this was what we were creating. When one or more of us, including the leader, would realize a symptom of our dysfunction and try to change it, there was always a good reason or a perceived crisis that would come up that would send us back to the familiar ways of doing things.

As a small example, we would try to end our meetings by 10:00 pm so that we could get some sleep and be in good shape to teach the next day, but somehow, the agenda was always too long or too important and we would keep going late into the night. Even when someone would say that she had to leave because she was teaching first thing in the morning, there would be one more item that the group needed her for. This seems crazy when I write about it now from the outside, but then, from the inside, it was just the unfortunate way things were. Who was making this happen? Was it the leader? No, it would go on even when he wasn't at the meetings and even when he explicitly said that he was concerned about our health and that people needed to get more sleep. But then some emergency would arise that we were needed for and that couldn't wait until morning and we would continue with the same dysfunctional patterns. Who was running the show?

As the reader, you might be tempted to write this off as an extreme case; it was a cult after all! But look at the organizations that you are a part of and see if there aren't less extreme (or maybe even more extreme) examples of the group or organization behaving in ways that no member is really choosing, and yet no members have been able to change. Think about your city's sports team that has internal tensions everyone realizes are hurting the team's performance, but no one is able to do anything about. Or think about the non-profit-that is losing people to burn out despite its efforts to take care of its members. Or consider a family where everyone, consciously or unconsciously, feels that they are growing further apart and spending less and less time together. Individual members might try instituting new rules such as always eating dinner together, or family movie night. These might work for a while, but then end up petering out because something more important always comes up. these are examples of what I mean when I say that *the system takes on a life of its own*. And this is what Meadows means when she says that a system-as-a-whole, consistently produces the same results in spite of efforts to change it.

To answer the question of "who is running the show?" let's look at the family growing apart. Initially, it might look like mom is running the show because she is the one who feels the family separation most strongly. She comes up with the idea of at least eating dinner together. She also is the one who uses her power and makes it happen, at least for a few weeks. Then, her daughter Irene's soccer team schedules an evening practice to get ready for regionals, so the family eats dinner that night without Irene. Then dad is required to be out of town for three nights on a business trip, so mom makes sure that they still eat dinner together without him. However, on one of those nights Daniel, the son, stays at school to help with an emergency on the stage crew, so it is just mom and Irene at the dinner table. That doesn't go so well because mom, in an effort to connect, asks too many questions about how Irene is doing in school and about her friends. Irene ends up leaving the table as quickly as possible. Dad comes back in town and they all go out to eat as a way of celebrating being together. But then, on another night at the last minute, mom is forced to stay late at work and it becomes 'every-person-for-himself' for dinner.

It seems obvious, in this case at least, that it is life that is running the show. These are the demands of life today, of the busyness of our 24/7 culture. But this culture is a human system in which we participate. Many cultures today do not have the same difficulty establishing family time. There have been many books written about the power of our frenetic culture and what to do about it, including *Finding the Deep River Within: A Woman's Guide to Recovering Balance and Meaning in Everyday Life* by my wife, Abby Seixas, in which she refers to the "disease of a-thousand-things-to-do" and the "tyranny of the to-do list."[5] But the power of our culture to keep us stressed and out of balance often seems to persist in spite of our attempts to right the imbalance. Thus far, individual choice and our collective will do not seem to be strong enough to change a speed-obsessed culture that has taken on a life of its own.

In 2008, Barack Obama was elected president of the United States on a platform of hope and change. He campaigned against the gridlock in Washington and pledged to reach out to Republicans and seek bi-partisan collaboration on the crucial issues facing our country. He was elected by a significant percentage, with 60 Democratic senators and enough members of Congress to over-ride the threat of a filibuster and make change happen. We had replaced the leaders of the country who had created two wars and one of the worst economic crises since the Great Depression. The potential for change was in the air.

And then what happened? Even *stronger* gridlock! The Republicans fought Obama's health care bill and battled the financial reform bill, while accusing him and the Democrats of reneging on their pledge of bipartisanship. Anger and hate speech took over, black Senators were spat on, and members of Congress, overcome by the heat of the moment, yelled slurs at each other and at the President during the State of the Union address – behaviors that had not been seen in Congress for decades. All of this was ostensibly caused by Obama trying to provide health care for 30 million people who didn't have it and by his attempts to rein in the power and costs of the health care industry, which were severely adding to the deficit. But what was it *really* about?[6]

In the middle of all of this rancor, Ted Kennedy died, and Massachusetts, arguably one of the most liberal states in the country and one that had had Democratic senators for many years, elected Scott Brown, a Republican senator, to take his place. This took away the Democrats' super-majority and assured even more gridlock – the very thing that we the people had resoundingly voted against. So who is running the show here? We the people? The Democrats? The Republicans? The healthcare industry? The voters in Massachusetts? None of the above?

If we disengage from the anger, blame, and one-line sound-bites and step back far enough to look at our country as a living entity, what we see is "same old, same old," only more of it. We see that the resistance to change by the system as a whole is tremendous. We have replaced the leaders of the system and still nothing has changed.

Of course this is not just true in America. We see this playing out in political systems all over the world. A new leader is appointed or elected or takes power in a coup and enters office with many ideas and much energy to change things but soon gets mired in the day-to-day pressures of the system, or the corruption of the system, and nothing really changes. We tend to blame the leader for not delivering on his promises and wait until we can elect a better one. We keep looking for a leader that can make the system more effective. We rarely look at how the system-as-a-whole 'lives its life' and ask, "what do we need to change about the system to allow the leaders to be more effective?"

Disidentification: Stepping Back to See the Whole Picture

In order to demonstrate how systems take on a life of their own, I encourage you to step back, to disidentify from your point of view within the system and try to see that no one individual or group of individuals is producing these results *"despite many policies and much effort directed against them."* This disidentification is an attempt to achieve the perspective of the people in the upper tiers of the football stadium who are far enough away to see the patterns that the marching band is making. (see p. 26) These are the patterns that the tuba player on the field is unable to see. Don't worry about how to change the system *yet*. The first move is to learn to step back from individual and group blame, and to soberly acknowledge that the system, which we created for our own benefit – be it a government, family, business, or social service – has taken on a life of its own and is largely out of our control. And, in fact, the system seems to be controlling us.

Several years ago, my partners and I were hired as consultants to a large chemical company that was under financial pressure because of quality problems. They hired a new vice-president of manufacturing who had experience with quality improvement methodologies. He began right away to implement his ideas for improvement. But because of a company financial crisis, all budgets needed to be cut, including manufacturing. This meant that he couldn't purchase all of the quality control equipment he needed and he had to lay off staff, forcing the remaining staff to do more with fewer resources. Not only did quality not improve; it got worse. A lot of blame was focused on the new VP. When he tried to defend himself by pointing to the economic pressures he was dealing with, he was perceived as weak and defensive. There was talk about replacing him before things got even worse. Here was a strong, competent, collaborative individual who had been successful in his last position (as was the VP of manufacturing before him, by the way). He came into this system and was unable to make a difference. The company began to doubt him, and he began to doubt himself while at the same time blaming others for his problems. This just reinforced the other executives' desire to replace him.

Things in this company began to change when my partners and I were able to get the executive team to look at the quality situation systemically rather than just as a manufacturing problem. We encouraged them to step back as a team and imagine the organization as having a life of its own. We asked them, "What is it about how this organization lives its life that results in it turning out a lower-than-desired-quality product?" and "What is it about how this organization lives its life that takes strong, competent, creative vice-presidents of manufacturing and turns them into incompetent, weak, and ineffective people?" These questions gave them enough distance to begin to see how the "the life of the system" was pressuring each of them, and the system as a whole, to behave in certain ways. They were known as the high-quality, reasonable-cost, and superior-customer-service company in their industry. The attempt to maintain this identity in the face of rapidly changing market conditions was putting significant pressure on every department. This caused each of them to make decisions which, in order to preserve the reputation of the company and the success of their own department, ended up making unrealistic demands on the manufacturing group, leading to more mistakes and lower quality. Seeing this, they could begin to ask, "What can we as a group do to change the way the system as a whole lives its life so that it would better support excellent quality?"

From this more disidentified perspective, the management team was able to see several actions they could take, company-wide, to ease the pressure on the whole system and therefore on manufacturing, such as:

- Changing the reward system for salesmen who were promising anything to the customer just to close the deal.
- Agreeing to re-allocate the budget in order to purchase some of the quality control equipment needed to measure their progress.
- Training customer service personnel to better resolve problems from the customers' perspectives (some customers were angrier about how their problems were handled than about the original quality problem. This made their concern with the quality of the product seem bigger than it actually was).

- Most importantly: establishing a cross-functional team of managers to do whatever was needed company-wide to get the quality back to the customers' desired standards. The new vice-president of manufacturing was the head of this team and went on to a successful career with the company.

Exercises and Reflections

It is not easy to disidentify from the family, group, or organization that you are a part of. It takes practice. The main idea is to change your perspective in order to see the system more from the "outside looking in" or from a more detached or dispassionate point of view. This allows you to see the system as more of a whole entity and encourages you to come up with more creative, system-wide solutions to problems. It also helps to take the blame out of the process and to describe clearly what you see from this different vantage point.

Sometimes it helps to imagine the system as something else or yourself as someone else who is observing. Try these exercises:

1 Imagine that your family or organization is an animal. What kind of animal? How does this animal behave? What are its strengths and weaknesses?

2 Imagine that you are a customer approaching your company for the first time. What are the first things you notice? How does this company feel to you as you make contact with it? What really attracts you? What pushes you away?

System Forces

A system can take on a life of its own, developing an identity or ego in the process. In doing so, it exerts subtle but powerful pressure on its parts – its people – to behave in ways that maintain that identity. This was apparent in the ballgame when the players felt pressure to just keep going so they could beat the other team even though balls were dropping all over the floor.

These system pressures often influence or have power over the members of the system in ways they are not conscious of. This played out when my leaving for college set off behavior which tried to pull me back home and preserve the family's sense of itself.

Until we become aware of these unconscious system forces, they will continue to control us. With the chemical company, our consulting company was required to get the whole executive team to step back together and become aware of how the system pressures on each of them (not just on the VP of manufacturing) were producing the problems with quality. After doing so, rather than working in the way that the system was determining, they could then stand together to change the system to work in the way they wanted.

In the next chapter we will explore in more detail these subtle but powerful system forces and learn how to recognize, in the moment, their effect on us as individuals and on the system as a whole.

CHAPTER THREE

SYSTEM FORCES – WHAT THEY ARE AND WHAT THEY DO

Human systems—organizations, families, nations—in addition to their amazing accomplishments, persist in living out self–limiting and often destructive stories . . . Members do not wake in the morning and say, "Hey gang, I've got a good idea, why don't we just re-create the same old destructive story?" Instead, they simply rise, go about their business, do what they do—and then the familiar story happens.[7]

BARRY OSHRY

The Reality of System Forces

How can an invisible system, which is really a concept, put pressure on us? Surely the pressure is coming from the people within the system pressuring each other? Yes, it is. But some of these pressures and behaviors are identical and predictable in completely different systems and even though the people may come and go in those systems over time. You may think that has to do with how the system is structured and how the rules are set up. That is true. But why, then, do we keep structuring our systems and making rules that keep producing the same negative behaviors and results over and over?

First, let's look at this notion of "system forces," the pressure on people within systems to behave in certain ways. If they are invisible how do we know they are there and that they are real? The answer is that when we become more aware and more mindful in the moment, we can learn to sense them and feel them. They are palpable. How we act in relation to these system forces is our choice, *but only if we are aware of them.*

When we are not aware of system forces, they cause us to behave in certain ways, thinking that we are doing so of our own volition. Our economic system, for instance, is based on growth and has therefore created mechanisms of advertising to subtly (and not so subtly) influence, or pressure us to consume in order to keep the system alive.

Also, when you are not aware of system forces, you are likely to point to, and blame, other people for making you act a certain way, when in fact you are all responding to the pressures from the system. ("She made me take the fundraising chair position at the kids' school. She wouldn't take no for an answer.") The system exerts pressure and, typically, you respond in unconscious and reflexive ways. These responses seem so familiar that it doesn't even occur to you to question them. I see this process of being influenced by system forces as similar to how our individual unconscious may guide our actions without our awareness.

But are these pressures real or are we just making them up? I say they are real. We are all familiar with terms such as market forces, the pressure to perform, or peer group pressure. Many of us have experienced these forces as very tangible. Are they being created by the system or by your own thoughts or feelings? I would argue that they are a result of both.

Consider peer group pressure. Most of the time you are not aware of it and don't feel it. You just happen to like the same clothes or drive the same car or live in the same-sized house as your friends. You just happen to dislike, or make fun of, the same people as your friends. But when you try to do something differently, suddenly you feel uncomfortable, out of place, guilty or afraid. You feel a pressure to go back to the old way of behaving. While that pressure might be coming from your own fears of being excluded or humiliated, it is probably also coming from friends who are talking behind your back, regarding you strangely, or not returning your calls. The pressures are coming from inside and from outside. For me, the more intriguing point is to notice that, somehow, we all get the idea that driving a BMW is in and that Aruba is the hot vacation spot, but that driving a family van or vacationing at Disneyland is not. Sometimes one person is dictating the style or coolness but more often it is through the mutual influence relationships of friends with each other and with the environment in which we live. The point is not about how it happens, but that it happens and that we can feel these pressures.

Families are smaller systems that provide good examples of how strong system pressures can be. Here's an example: As I was growing up, each member of my family sat in the same seat every night around the dinner table. These seats were not assigned, didn't have our names on them, and the arrangement was never discussed. I came home from college once and happened to sit in my father's chair at the dinner table. When the others came to the table they just stood there. No one knew where to sit because I had unintentionally broken one of the dinner table rules. We all laughed because everyone was so uncomfortable. It felt as if there was an actual force keeping the others from sitting down while at the same time pushing me to get up. It was only after I had moved to "my seat" that everyone else was able to sit down.

Many people become aware of the system pressures of their country of origin, for instance, when they go to other, very different cultures. A friend working in a third-world country described how free and unburdened she felt and how easy life was when there were few choices of what to buy and very little advertising promoting products. She felt the absence of the pressure of the western economic system pushing people consciously and unconsciously to consume. She felt lighter and to her it was freeing.

The Emperor's New Clothes[8]

One of my favorite stories describing the dynamics of system pressures is Hans Christian Andersen's "The Emperor's New Clothes." Most of us know the story, and particularly, the exciting ending when the young child breaks the spell by announcing, "But he hasn't got any clothes on!" You may not remember how the Emperor came to be walking down the street naked or what this has to do with system pressures, so let me remind you.

The Emperor was very fond of clothes and spent lots of money buying them. Two swindlers heard about the Emperor's passion and came to town claiming to be weavers who could make very elegant cloth with special powers. They claimed that their magnificent cloth was "invisible to everyone who was stupid or not fit for his post." This was the real magic – planting the seed of a kingdom-wide belief in how things work – a 'rule' in our language.

The Emperor sent his advisors to check on the progress of the weavers. Each advisor was dismayed not to see anything on the looms, especially when the swindlers were pointing to the non-existent material, exclaiming at how beautiful it was turning out, and asking the advisor if he didn't agree. Each man, in order to try to hide his imagined stupidity or unfitness, would return to the court raving about the beauty and magnificence of the cloth. Of course, this made every succeeding advisor believe even more strongly that he was the only one who could not see the material. Information that the system needed was not being circulated and the belief stayed in place.

Eventually the Emperor could not stand the suspense any longer and went to see the cloth himself. He took a group of ministers with him and was shocked to see nothing on the looms. Did this mean that he was unfit to be the Emperor? His worry was only exacerbated when all the ministers, in order to hide their own fears, exclaimed over the beauty of the cloth and suggested he have clothes made out of it for the next day's procession. Assuming they could all see it even though he couldn't, and that therefore he would be elegantly dressed in front of his people, he had to agree.

By this time the story of the amazing cloth and its special powers had spread across the kingdom, so as the Emperor paraded through the streets everyone cheered and cried out about how splendid the Emperor's new clothes were. Of course they did. No one dared to admit they couldn't see anything because who would want to appear stupid or unfit for their job?

The belief only began to crumble when the little boy made his exclamation about the Emperor's nudity and the other people began to talk among themselves about what they were *not* seeing. This, then, circulated the more accurate information that the system needed to break the spell of the rule they were all following. The story also demonstrates how leaders in the system can be caught by the system rules as much as, if not more, than everyone else. The story ends, "The Emperor himself had the uncomfortable feeling that what they were whispering was only too true. 'But I will have to go through with the procession,' he said to himself.

So he drew himself up and walked boldly on, holding his head higher than before, and the courtiers held on to the train that wasn't there at all."

This children's story is an excellent example of the power of system forces and of the unspoken rules, beliefs, and myths that hypnotize or enthrall a group of people, including the leader of the system. These forces cause people to behave in ways that none of them would have if the system were not in place. And while the leader may be contributing to the creation of the system forces, he or she is being influenced by them as well. Many of us would like to be able to point to the leaders of the various systems to which we belong and blame them for the faults of the system, thus absolving ourselves from any responsibility for our behavior. One of the recurring themes of this book is that *no one of us is to blame, but each of us is responsible* for the systems in which we participate.

To be effectively responsible for the systems of which you are a part, you first must become aware of these forces, then step back from their pressures, and make choices about how you want to respond.

Exercises and Reflections

Think about some of the systems that you inhabit. Where do you feel these system pressures in your life? Are there unspoken family rules that you are aware of? What does it feel like (in your body, mind or feelings) when you are tempted to or inadvertently violate one of these rules?

Are there systems where you feel compelled to behave in certain ways that you normally wouldn't? How are you expected to behave in these systems?

Are there places, situations or systems where you have wanted to speak up, give feedback, or tell your truth but haven't been able to? What was keeping you from doing so? (There might be internal fear, but also try to notice any system resistance to new or divergent information.)

A Real-Life (and scary) Example

In 2007, Bill Moyers ran an exceptional journalistic piece on television about Iraq. In the documentary, called *Buying the War: How Big Media Failed Us,*[9] he and producer Kathleen Hughes ask, "How did the mainstream press get it so wrong? How did the evidence disputing the existence of weapons of mass destruction and the (lack of a) link between Saddam Hussein and 9/11 continue to go largely unreported?"[10] To me, it is a graphic and frightening example of the power of system forces and how destructive they can be in a dysfunctional system. In this case, destructive to the Iraqi people who died there, as well as to our own sons and daughters who died, to our country's worldwide reputation, and to our economy.

"Buying the War" focuses on the reporting of John Walcott, Jonathan Landay, and Warren Strobel, reporters for Knight Ridder news. Their reporting raised serious questions about the Bush administration's continuous barrage of claims that Saddham Hussein was connected to the 9/11 World Trade Center disaster and that Iraq had weapons of mass destruction. "Many of the things that were said about Iraq didn't make sense," says Walcott, "and that really prompts you to ask, 'Wait a minute. Is this true? Does everyone agree that this is true? Does anyone think this is not true?'" However, as the documentary shows, few newspapers or other media were willing to report the Knight Ridder investigative pieces, and few reporters within the Washington, D.C. beltway were asking those questions on their own. Not only were they not asking the questions; they jumped on the bandwagon and were extensively promoting the administration's assertions, most of which turned out to be completely false.

"From August 2002 until the war was launched in March of 2003 there were about 140 front page pieces in *The Washington Post* making the administration's case for war," says Howard Kurtz, the *Post's* media critic. "But there was only a handful of stories that ran on the front page that made the opposite case. Or, if not making the opposite case, raised questions."

Moyers asks how the mainstream media got so caught up in the pre-war fervor that it lost any semblance of objectivity. Some of the reporters and analysts cite a fear that they felt or sensed (the following italics are my own emphasis):

- "There was a patriotic fervor and the Administration used it so that if you challenged anything *you were made to feel* that there was something wrong with that."
- "Everybody on staff just sort of *knew* not to push too hard to do stories critical of the Bush Administration."
- "Especially right after 9/11. Especially when the war in Afghanistan is going on. There was a *real sense* that you don't get that critical of a government that's leading us in war time."

Comments like "you just sort of knew. . ." or "there was a real sense that you don't get that critical. . ." point to system pressures. There is a vague sense or understanding that controls behavior. Sometimes one is conscious of it and sometimes not.

Often, you feel the pressures most strongly when you violate or are about to violate the conscious or unconscious rules or norms of the system. In the case of the run-up to the Iraq war, the right-wing media used the system forces and inflated them to their own ends, becoming the enforcers of the system rules.

Even prominent and respected newsman Dan Rather succumbed to the pressure. He says, "And every journalist knew it. They [the right-wing media] had and they have a very effective slam machine. The way it works is you either report the news the way we want it reported or we're going to hang a sign around your neck." As in "The Emperor's New Clothes," if a reporter questioned or spoke his truth he would be seen as stupid, un-American, and unfit for his job.

In the documentary, Strobel and Landy talk about the system forces being so great that even with the mounds of data that they were uncovering about there being no links between Hussein and 9/11 and no weapons of mass destruction, they, themselves, started questioning what they were doing. Landy explains, "But there was a period when we were sittin' out there and I had a lot of late night gut checks where I was just like, 'Are we totally off on some loop here?'"

"Buying the War" points to the potentially disastrous effects of system pressures and what Moyers (and others) call groupthink. Not only were the system pressures limiting the choices about what could be published; they also were strongly prohibiting feedback and information from entering the system in a way that might challenge and, therefore, change the homeostasis or identity of the system. As Michael Massing identified, "The media have become sort of like the whipping boy, because they [those in power] know that the press can provide information that runs counter to what the government is claiming, to what the Bush Administration is claiming." The first step in having some choice in relation to system forces is to become aware of them. Yet in the heat of the moment, or over a long period of influence, it is often difficult to see how these forces are affecting us.

Barry Oshry: Power and Systems

I am indebted to Barry Oshry for his lifetime of work to make system forces understandable and viscerally tangible to people in organizations. It was through Oshry's work that I first was able to make sense of the pressures I had been feeling in every group or organization in which I participated, including PSI as it devolved into a cult. I had felt these system pressures in my gut, my neck and shoulders, or in my feelings of anger or blame. I would assume that I was somehow inadequate to handle the demands of the situation, or I would blame others for causing me to have these feelings, thoughts, or body tensions. In other words, I had always taken these system forces personally or made them personal to others.

Oshry, in his Organization Workshop[11] and his books *Seeing Systems*[12] and *Leading Systems,*[13] makes it clear that it is not me, not you, not them, but the system that influences our behavior, and until we become aware of this fact we will continue to blame each other and nothing will change in the system as a whole. He demonstrates, through his elegant simulation exercise, the power of system forces and how they affect us at all levels of the hierarchical systems that we generally inhabit.

Throughout this book I will be referring to other system theories, but I find Oshry's to be one of the easiest to grasp experientially and therefore, one of the best examples to draw from in making my key points about system pressures. Here is a brief overview of his theory:

Since most of the organizational systems we participate in are hierarchical (obviously corporations and the military, but also most non-profits, families, clubs, teams, etc.), Oshry focuses particularly on the system forces that affect the people at the top, middle and bottom of the hierarchy.[14] He clearly describes and demonstrates the nature of the system forces that come with each of these "worlds," as he calls them. He points out that these forces are a given in each world, and that depending on the world we step into, the pressures on us are different and, therefore we behave differently. "Not always, but enough of the time to make it predictable," he says. And because we are unaware of these forces or take them personally, they cause us to behave in predictable ways that only exacerbate the pressures of that world. Oshry also makes it clear that on any given day we operate in several, if not all, of these worlds. I might leave the house feeling like the responsible head of my family (a Top in Oshry's vernacular), and go to work where I am just one of the thousands of workers with little authority, being told what to do (a Bottom). Then I go home and find my wife and my mother arguing about something that the kids did, and suddenly I feel torn between defending my wife and not hurting my mother (a Middle).

As you continue reading, think of places where you are living in one of these worlds and see if you can recall what the system pressures are like for you. When you are in this world, how do you think or feel about things? How does it affect your body and your behavior? By asking yourself these questions, you will be able to identify mental, emotional, or situational clues that will alert you to be mindful of the system pressures so that you have some choice in how you react to them.

The Life of Tops

Tops are those people who are viewed as, and who experience themselves as, responsible for the system, for a project, or for a particular domain or area in an organization. If you are an executive director of a non-profit, a parent, a project leader in a company, or the chairwoman of the garden club's fundraiser, for example, you know what it is like to experience the conditions that come with being a Top. You handle a lot of responsibility and accountability to others; there are probably many important and urgent things on your list, and more than you can possibly do. All the problems that you juggle are complex and involve multiple people.

Given these very real conditions of your world, it feels like you are under pressure to deliver results and to do so you need to be in control and not let things get out of hand. The system pressures at the top might feel something like: "I am accountable for all of this so I have to make sure everything is being done perfectly;" or "Life is so chaotic; I'm afraid that if I don't stay in control, everything will fall apart;" or "I need to keep my finger on everything I am responsible for so I know what is going on or I might look bad."

Some examples of how Tops behave if they are not aware of these system forces might be: the CEO who micromanages or makes all the decisions himself; the mother who doesn't want her son to fail, so she does the homework research for him because he's procrastinating and it's due tomorrow; the fundraising chair who does things herself because it is easier than explaining to others exactly what she wants and trying to get them to do it right.

The problem, as Oshry points out, is that all of these predictable, normal responses to the system pressures result in drawing even more responsibility to the Top. Those in a leadership role then feel even *more* burdened by having even more to do and even less time.

The Life of Middles

Middles are those people in positions where they are required to meet the needs or demands of multiple constituencies simultaneously. If you are a parent trying to navigate multiple medical systems for your sick child, a mid-level manager in a corporation, or a non-profit executive caught between your board's demands and your staff's needs, you know what it is like to experience the conditions that come with being a Middle. When you are a Middle, you are being pushed and pulled from all directions as you try to meet multiple and often conflicting needs and demands.

Given these very real conditions of your world, it feels like you are under pressure to keep or make people happy and you need to work very hard to meet everyone's needs. The system pressures in the middle might feel something like: "It is urgent that I run around finding out what people need and taking care of them" or "I'm frustrated having to constantly answer for one party's behaviors or defend them to a third party" or "I am constantly fighting fires and fixing things between or among other people or groups" or "What about me? Doesn't anyone care about me in all of this?"

Some examples of how Middles behave if they are not aware of these system forces might be:

- The person who spends time phoning back and forth trying to mediate between two friends who are fighting;
- The manager who is "just carrying out orders" for the Tops and feels obliged to defend them to the workers even if she doesn't agree or doesn't know what she thinks about the situation;
- The soccer mom who is running everywhere trying to take care of her kids, her husband, her home and her community responsibilities.

The problem is that all of these predictable, normal responses to the system pressures result in the Middle being pulled even more in multiple directions and he/she ends up feeling *more* torn apart by others' demands.

The Life of Bottoms

Bottoms are those people who are seen as, and experience themselves as the ones who have the least power and authority within a hierarchical system. Their behavior usually involves following other people's directives. They often have little autonomy or decision-making ability within the system. If you are a worker in a large corporation, a child, an elderly person in assisted care, or a minority or immigrant in America, for example, you know what it is like to experience the conditions that come with being a Bottom. Other people make the rules for you and can change them whenever they choose; you may be willing to work hard, yet you have very little power, authority, or access to the resources needed to succeed. The distance (economic, social, and spatial) between you and others seems vast. You are vulnerable to a world you have very little control over and get very little recognition from.

Given these very real conditions of your world, it feels like the system is pressuring you to do what you are told, to be the good soldier and wait for orders, to be invisible and not rock the boat. The system pressures at the bottom might feel something like: "I'm discouraged because I am doing what I'm supposed to do but I don't get rewarded or acknowledged," or "I'm afraid that if I get creative, I'll attract too much negative attention," or, "I'm lost. I'm being told to do this but I have no idea why," or, "I feel like an unappreciated cog in the machine."

Some examples of how Bottoms behave if they are not aware of these system forces might be:

- The worker who sits around and waits to be told what to do;
- The adolescent who acts out in order to be seen or recognized;
- The non-profit receptionist who sees that things could be better, but doesn't say anything because she thinks, "I'm not responsible. That's their problem;"
- The individual who feels like such a victim of circumstances that he can't even imagine that there are areas where he could take initiative or be creative on his own behalf.

The Results of System Pressures

There are several points that Oshry makes about these dynamics. First, it should be obvious that if you reflexively behave in the way the system is pushing you, you only make the conditions of your life worse. If I am a Top who micromanages and makes all the decisions, I only add to the things on my plate and my life becomes even busier and more complex. If I am a Middle who keeps running around fighting fires and trying to make everyone happy, I feel even more torn and lose myself further in the needs of others. And if I am a Bottom who sits back and waits to be told what to do, or gives all the responsibility for my condition to others, I end up feeling even more vulnerable, more helpless and more like a victim.

Second, the conditions of your life come with the territory. For instance, if you are a Middle, people will always be making demands on you to meet their needs. That is a given. However, you do have a choice and the ability to do something about your situation by recognizing how the system is pushing you to behave and asking yourself, "What do I want to do here?" Just because your kids each want to do a different activity on a given afternoon doesn't mean you must jump into the middle and make a choice for them, making some happy and others sad. Instead you might tell them to hold a siblings' meeting and come up with a solution that they can all live with. If they can't, no one gets what they want. By becoming mindful of these forces, stepping back and asking, "What other choices do I have here?" you begin to empower yourself and master your world.

Third, because these conditions of the Top, Middle and Bottom worlds are a given, *different people* placed in these worlds will experience the same pressures and behave in remarkably similar ways. It is also true that *the same person* placed in a different world will behave differently according to the pressures of that world. Some individuals may be better trained or their personalities are better suited for the pressures of certain worlds. But usually much of the person's behavior is being determined by the pressures of their world *and not by who they are*.

This is demonstrated quite graphically in one of Oshry's simulations. In the first round of the simulation, people are randomly assigned positions as Tops, Middles or Bottoms. In the second round, everyone is required to change roles. Even before the second round starts up, their behavior changes! The Tops, who have been carrying all the burdens and responsibility of the organization and blaming the Bottoms and Middles for being inept, audibly sigh in relief when they become Bottoms. Suddenly they feel lighter because they are no longer responsible and can sit back and wait to be told what to do. Or the Bottoms, the same people who just minutes ago had been laughing, joking, or threatening to go out on strike, suddenly become serious and worried about the organization. They barely hear the instructions for round two of the exercise because they are already planning how they might run things differently since *now that they are called Tops,* they are responsible.

In changing roles and inhabiting a different world, the individuals almost instantly feel the pressure to behave exactly like their predecessors about whom they had recently been complaining. Oshry implores the participants not to make what happens in systems personal. He makes it clear that it is not the person, it is the pressures of the world they are inhabiting.

Oshry points to several other effects of automatically and unconsciously following the system pressures of one's world. You know what your life feels like, but you have little information about another's world and its pressures, or of the behavior of the system as a whole. Everyone in the system ends up being a victim to other parts of the system: "If only they would change, then my life, and the system, would be better." This victimhood leads to blame, anger, or even revenge. For some, it can lead to not caring and ultimately, to giving up. It also keeps you from seeing your responsibility for your own situation. It keeps you from realizing that by going along reflexively with the system forces, you contribute to your own unhappiness and difficulties. This, in turn, kills your ability to be inventive in your life. If everything is being caused by others, and you want to improve things, then your only option is to try to get them to change or to leave the system. It may not even occur to you that you could be more imaginative about how *you* respond to the system forces of your own life.

Exercises and reflections

Think of situations in your life where you are a Top, a Middle, and a Bottom. Choose one of those situations that is most prominent or most problematic for you right now to work on for this exercise.

- What is this world like for you? What is your life like while in this world?
- How do you feel? What are you thinking?
- What is the effect of this world on your body?
- What are the pressures of this world telling you that you should be doing?
- What physical, emotional or mental symptom in this world would be the best wake up call or 'alert' to remind you that you are under the influence of this world's pressures?

  Try to imagine that the alert works and wakes you up to the fact that the forces of this world are controlling you. At that moment, what other choices or possibilities open up for you?

Choice and Power

When you are not aware of the pressures of a particular world, you succumb to them and act reflexively. You lose your creativity and the ability to choose, that is, you lose your power to act effectively. When you believe you have no choice, you feel powerless.

For instance, when I am a Bottom in a system, the real condition that comes with that world is one of vulnerability to those higher up the ladder. *They* give me my assignments to carry out. *They* are the ones I approach to ask if I want to take a break or vacation. *They* are the ones who determine my pay and my survival in the organization. This condition of vulnerability might be true, but when I buy into it as the whole truth, I lose my self, and behave as if *they* control all aspects of my life in the system.

When we succumb to the system pressures in this way, we fail to realize that we have unconsciously given our power and creativity away. When we hold others responsible for our situation, we fail to ask important questions that would put us back in control of our own destiny. Those are questions like:

- How have I contributed to the situation I am complaining about?
- If I didn't wait for *them* to change, what could *I* do, right now, to make my condition better?
- What *do* I have control of or influence over in this situation?
- If I were inventive right now, how many choices could I come up with other than changing *them* or leaving?

- Are there more imaginative solutions that would make the system work better for me and for others?

These are the kinds of questions with the potential to counteract the pressures of a Life-deadening system and help you to regain your power or volition, your creativity, and the feeling of aliveness.

Synopsis: System Pressures and You

When you are not aware of, and therefore automatically succumb to, the system pressure to hold others responsible for the conditions of your life, you do several things at once. You:

1. *Give away agency for your own life.* You make yourself a victim by ignoring any role that you play in creating your own circumstances. And you give away your power to others because you are waiting for them to change in order for your situation to be better. You don't realize that you have the power to *not* make certain choices.[15]
2. *Lose yourself in the system.* Because you are not aware of the system forces, you are easily overcome by them and lose sight of your own goals, values, and even your own needs. You begin to feel like a cog in the machine fulfilling the needs of the system.
3. *Lose your vitality and creativity.* When you lose yourself and your volition, it is difficult to see any options for behaving differently. You usually feel stuck, resigned, discouraged and enervated. There appears to be no creative alternative to life as it is in the system.

In the next two chapters you'll read one more very important thing that happens when you unconsciously succumb to the pressures of the system: *you lose your humanity.* When you feel as though you are being controlled by outside people or forces and that there are no options, it can be very difficult to have empathy or compassion for *them* – those who have robbed you of your choices. This empathy, this ability to put yourself in another's shoes, and imagine what life is like for them, is one of the attributes that makes us most human. When you are not aware of system forces, you don't consider that others are also dealing with the pressures of their own lives that are causing them to behave in certain ways. Instead, you make it personal to them. You interpret their behavior as a character flaw or as if this is who they are: "Sarah is a bad mother. She's a total control freak." It never occurs to us that Sarah is juggling so many responsibilities as a single mother that she is afraid if she doesn't keep things under control, she might drop something that would hurt her family.

Another example of this seeming lack of understanding and compassion for people in other parts of the system came from Mitt Romney during the 2012 presidential elections. Rather than acknowledging the extreme wealth disparity in America and its effect on those at the bottom of the hierarchy, he attributed their behavior to personal failings: *"There are 47 percent of the people who will vote for [Obama] no matter what ... who are dependent upon government, who believe that they are victims. ... These are people who pay no income tax. ... and so my job is not to worry about those people. I'll never convince them that they should take personal responsibility and care for their lives."*[16]

Like Romney, it is easy to stop seeing others as human beings and to begin seeing them as defective people who are intentionally behaving in ways that are hurting us, others or themselves. When we do so, we not only strip them of their humanity; we lose ours as well.

CHAPTER FOUR

THE POWER OF SYSTEMS
OVER PEOPLE

The problem is that we ourselves have internalized power-over, and too often we reproduce it in the groups we form. We may join a group that promises political or spiritual liberation, only to find that it has simply changed the trappings of oppression, that our own sisters/comrades/ compañeros/ fellow spiritual seekers can still hurt us, disregard us, disrespect us. How do we live a different reality when the ways we perceive, feel, and react have been shaped by this one?[1]

STARHAWK, author of, *Truth or Dare: Encounters with Power, Authority, and Mystery*

Systemic pressures are present in all systems, even ones that are benign or Life-affirming. The latter develop structures, rules and processes that generate enough countervailing positive forces to keep their people from losing themselves and their agency within the system. Rewarding their people for taking initiative and responsibility, they affirm the humanity of the members and acknowledge the unique contribution each makes to the system. Healthy systems encourage creativity and vitality and demand that their members treat themselves and each other as human beings, not as resources to be used. But when the types of system pressures described in the previous chapter go unnoticed and are responded to reflexively by all parts of the system, the result is often dehumanizing, Life-denying, and dysfunctional.

So if there are always system forces at work, the questions remain: Why are there so many dysfunctional, Life-deadening systems? How do these systems have and maintain so much power over us?

Hierarchy

Natural systems are organized in a hierarchical structure where each level contains all of the parts of the lower level, as well as developing characteristics and properties that are greater than and different from those parts. Quarks make up protons, protons make up atoms, atoms make up molecules that, in turn, make up cells that make up organisms. This could be diagramed in the traditional hierarchical way where each level includes all the previous levels:

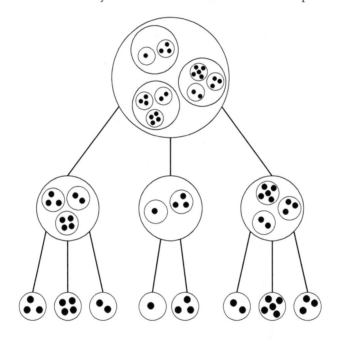

Almost all of our human systems are structured in the same hierarchical way with each higher group containing all of the people in its member groups. Yet these systems take on an identity, abilities and functions that are greater than and different from the people making up that larger system. A human hierarchy as it affects the individual might look like the following diagram. The individual person is at the center to indicate that she is a unique human being, while simultaneously she is a part of all these various systems that are parts of even larger systems.

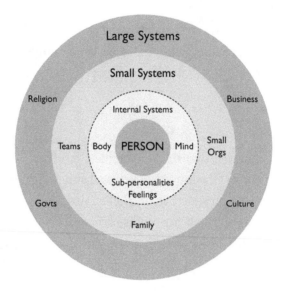

A system is comprised of mutual influence relationships where all the parts influence each other and the whole, while simultaneously being influenced by the whole. In a natural hierarchical system, or in a healthy human system, people realize this interconnection and interdependence with each other and the whole and the whole also realizes its interdependence with its parts. The whole will nourish the life and growth of its people, while the people will nourish the life and growth of the whole.

Another way of saying this is that in a healthy human system there is influence (power) and caring (love) flowing among the parts as well as up and down the hierarchy between the whole and the parts.

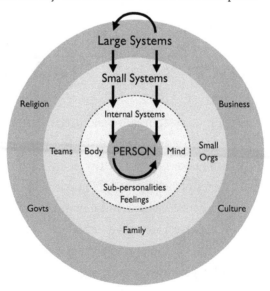

Here are some examples of this mutual influence and caring process in healthy systems:

- Lincoln Filene, co-founder of the department store that bore his family's name, said, "If we were to create contentment in front of the counter, we had first to create contentment behind it."[2] In order to take care of his employees in the early 1900's, he and his brother Edward allowed employee representation in decisions and allowed arbitration of disputes. "The company also provided a clinic, a library, a credit union, profit-sharing, pensions and more." These things allowed them to attract what Edward called a 'better class of workers.'"[3] In return, the workers provided a high degree of productivity and loyalty to the well-being of the company. They were financially connected to the reality that the healthier the company, the better they thrived as individuals.
- The extended family structure where the larger family takes care of all of its members by providing food, shelter and sense of belonging, while the members contribute whatever they can to help the family thrive – income, cooking, cleaning, child and elder care, chores, planning, etc.
- The church, mosque or synagogue that provides spiritual sustenance for its members as well as a community to help individuals during difficult times and a group with which to celebrate special occasions. In response, the members support the religious institution through donations, dues, volunteering on committees, contributing their special expertise, etc.

Here are some examples of this mutual caring and power relationship breaking down:

- The "tragedy of the commons,"[4] where people share resources like water, grazing lands, fishing areas and city parks but only take care of their own interests. In these cases, the shared resources get depleted or destroyed in pursuit of individual short-term gains. An example is the over-fishing almost to extinction of sardine and cod in the early 1900's, or current global warming caused by continued fossil fuel use.
- Military commanders or politicians who are too far from the individual troops. They see the larger system, but lose touch with how their decisions are influencing the lives of the individual soldiers who are doing the actual fighting. They give orders that are not consistent with the

reality on the ground and which the soldiers are forced to carry out even though they know that achieving the desired result is futile. When this is felt strongly by the soldiers, morale drops and they lose touch with, or start caring less about, the system of which they are a part.

Another military example would be the government and the military not taking care of veterans when they return home. The veterans feel abandoned, used, unseen, and unappreciated by the system they served. This was felt strongly by Vietnam War veterans upon their return. And now, veterans from the wars in Iraq and Afghanistan are complaining about the extremely long processing times for disability benefits.[5]

- The abusive or narcissistic family where the parents demand love and respect but don't return it. With narcissistic parents, the children are seen as extensions of the parent and are expected to do what the parent wills them to do and to know this without having to be told. With abusive parents, who were often wounded by their parents, the child is mistreated in order to satisfy the parents' sexual or power needs.

When the mutual caring and influence relationships between the parts and the whole break down, two possible outcomes are: a) the parts stop caring about the whole and the whole dies. For example, when individual fishermen didn't have sufficient understanding of or caring for the ecosystem they were in, they over-fished cod and damaged the ecosystem responsible for their livelihood; or b) the whole stops caring about the parts and the power and influence only flows one way. These systems use their power over their members to fulfill the needs of the whole at whatever cost to the parts, as in the military examples above.

All human systems exert influence over their people and all human systems have *power over* their members when the members are not aware of the nature of this influence. But the most de-humanization, pain and dysfunction arises when this hierarchical *power over* becomes institutionalized.

Power Over

In human systems, the hierarchical structure is particularly good for command and control situations where decisions need to be made and carried out with minimum delay. In these structures, power and influence flows primarily in one direction, from the higher levels to the lower. The people at the lower levels are expected or required to have enough caring for the system and loyalty to the whole to carry out the decisions made by the people at the top of the hierarchy, even if they doubt those decisions. Clearly there can be healthy command and control hierarchies such as fire and police departments that serve their purpose while taking care of their members.

The problem is that not all situations demand or need fast decisions and rapid follow-through, but the command and control structure continues to be our primary organizational model. Often, this type of structure becomes dysfunctional once the people in control try to dictate *all* of the human interactions in the system. The mutual caring and influence relationships break down and the people at the top of the hierarchy use their power to control those at each successive lower level.

Since the people with the power control the structure of the system and make the rules, that structure and those rules almost always end up preserving the power and benefits of those at the top of the hierarchy.[6]

The financial meltdown and bailout of 2008 in the U.S. brought to light the issue of outrageous compensation for people at the top of financial institutions such as banks, hedge funds, and insurance companies. Executives gave excessive bonuses to themselves and others at the top of their companies, while they took risks that would further benefit themselves but ultimately run their companies into the ground. These poor, and sometimes immoral or illegal, decisions resulted in the collapse of the whole financial system and the layoffs of millions of people in other industries and organizations. Still, executives of insurance company AIG took extravagant pay raises and vacations while simultaneously holding out their hands for government bailouts.

To those trained to see systemically, there was something even more shocking that took place in the year following the financial collapse. When the larger system – the U.S. government – in order to preserve the economy and life of the whole country, moved in to bailout the institutions that were "too big to fail," these same CEOs eagerly lined up for the bailout money. Nonetheless, they still defended, and refused to give back, any of their disproportionate salary or perks. That was not surprising. They asked for hundreds of billions of dollars, saying that their companies would go under and threaten the life of the whole if they didn't get it. But because the issue of excessive compensation so outraged a public suffering from the misuse of power by these executives, the government put limits on the compensation executives could take in companies that were receiving bailouts. The executives objected and claimed that no one would want to run such complex organizations without these generous financial packages. That also was not surprising.

But since they had already pleaded corporate financial ruin, they were forced to go through with the bailout loans they had requested even with the compensation restrictions. What was shocking was how quickly many of the banks and other financial institutions (who, just months before, claimed to be on the verge of going under) were able to pay back their loans, so that these executives could return to receiving their former compensation. How did they do it? They slashed staff and expenses, driving millions more into unemployment lines and thereby prolonging the whole economic recovery. The corporate leaders used their power over others to restructure in such a way that they got out from under the power and oversight of the government and were able to return to the rules that re-instated their own benefits and power over others.

The Legacy of Power Over

Historically, these hierarchical, power-over systems, what Raúl Quiñones Rosado refers to as "the culture of imposition,"[7] have been run by men who wield power by virtue of physical strength, wealth (such as livestock or land) or education. "Institutions are created, organized, and directed by people who are simultaneously members of multiple dominant groups within their society. In the United States, for example, virtually all major economic, political, cultural, and social institutions created during its founding years (and since) were established by, and for the benefit of white, owning class, heterosexual, Christian, pro-American men of European descent."[8] And because those in power make and enforce the structure and rules of the system, these rules almost always maintain the status quo of the ruling class and relegate women, children, and ethnic minorities to positions of lesser or no power. These top-down, power-over systems are the source of every major "ism" in the world today – racism, sexism, classism, heterosexism, imperialism, etc. – where the people at the top try to preserve the power and benefits that derive from their being the dominant culture.

And because the structures and the conscious (and unconscious) rules were designed by a certain class of men to preserve their own power, it takes great effort to change those structures and rules to provide more equality for others. Look at how hard it was to abolish slavery or how long it took for women to get the vote in the United States. And even when the rules and structures do change, the belief systems and mental models that produced them still remain and the system pressures of the dominant culture can still be felt. Even though the rules of the system finally changed to give women and blacks equal opportunity and the right to vote, they are still under-represented relative to their percentage of the population, in all government elected offices, corporate executive suites and boardrooms, courtrooms, and other positions of authority.[9] In 2010, even though we have our first African-American president, no woman has become president. Even more telling, women are still only paid, on average, 80¢ for every dollar men earn.[10]

The Perpetuation of Power Over

So even though white, privileged men established the structure and rules to perpetuate their power and benefits, it is interesting to note that when women and minorities do attain admission to the top positions in these hierarchical power-over systems, they often behave just like the men that preceded them.[11] As we saw in the last chapter, all systems put pressure on the people at the top to draw even more responsibility, authority and power up to themselves, no matter who they are as individuals. By doing so, Tops who are unaware of these system dynamics unintentionally perpetuate the power-over nature of the system.

I once led Barry Oshry's organizational simulation for a group of humanistic and spiritually-oriented psychologists. As they drew their roles in the organization out of a hat, it happened that all of the Tops were women. It was clear from the beginning that they intended to be different types of leaders. They immediately called the whole organization into a circle, a promising sign of a lessening of hierarchy, but the leaders then proceeded to give everyone directions about what they should do and sent them off to do their tasks. Under the time and complexity pressures of the simulation, the Tops soon found themselves under great stress to do what they thought was required of them while trying to manage the chaos of the organization. They called another circle meeting to share their problems as well as to hear about what was going on in the rest of the organization. When the women at the top were asked questions about how things should be done in the organization, they answered authoritatively. They never asked how the Middles or Workers thought those problems should be tackled. They also stated clearly what they saw was wrong and gave people suggestions on how they should fix it. And, as is often the case, the Tops were blamed for everything that was wrong in the organization. Not surprisingly, they became defensive and angry and ended the meeting by saying, "We will think about what you've said and get back to you." Sound familiar?

With the exception of creating the circles, all of these were predictable behaviors for Tops in systems under stress. Even with the best intentions, these women leaders succumbed to system pressures by giving orders and suggestions, drawing all authority and responsibility to themselves, and retaining all the decision-making powers. Because they became victims of the system pressures, they perpetuated the power-over structure and rules even though they were trying not to do so.

The Bottom of the Hierarchy

Probably the least acknowledged and most damaging result of the power-over dominant culture is the effect it has on children, both in the United States and globally. In healthy, Life-affirming systems, one would expect the caring relationships to extend to those who will be the future of the system. One would think that power would be used to assure that the needs and the well-being of the young were a high priority for many reasons:

- Because they are loved as kin
- Because they assure the survival of the family and the economic survival of the community
- Because they represent future progress toward a better life for everyone
- Because they will be providing and caring for the elderly at some future time

And yet, these hierarchical systems, no matter what their espoused values, consistently produce intolerable conditions for children. Out of the world's 2.2 billion children, 1 billion live in poverty.[12] In the United States, 21% of children live below the poverty level and 44% live in low-income families.[13] "An estimated 8.8 million children worldwide die before their fifth birthday, with most deaths caused by preventable diseases."[14]

Our traditional systems and our dominant cultures are just that – dominant. People in power-over systems require others over whom to exert their power. The people at the top of the system are distant and estranged from those at the bottom. They treat the Bottoms – women, children, and minorities – not as human beings but as objects, tools or resources to be used to facilitate the system's purpose. This population consistently falls to the bottom rungs of the hierarchical order, thus assuring the continuation of the power-over system dynamics.

Objectification

Once this objectifying worldview gets institutionalized into the structures, rules and cultures of our human systems, the systems then perpetuate this view of the world to justify their behavior. When human systems objectify the people within them, and cause us to objectify one another, it reinforces our experience of being unappreciated cogs in a larger machine that is controlling our behavior.

Because the people at the top are the ones who make the rules that generate the system pressures or the oppression, simply being aware of these forces is not enough. Awareness is only the first step. In order to change these dysfunctional systems and systems of oppression, we must also reclaim our power and our caring. In other words, we must reclaim our humanity. One of the ways that we do this is by refusing to treat others or ourselves as objects. This is the topic of the next chapter.

CHAPTER FIVE

OBJECTIFICATION AND SELF-OBJECTIFICATION

Owing to its inherently competitive nature, [modern capitalism] not only pits humans against each other, it also pits the mass of humanity against the natural world. Just as men are converted into commodities, so every aspect of nature is converted into a commodity, a resource to be manufactured and merchandised wantonly . . . The plundering of the human spirit by the market place is paralleled by the plundering of the earth by capital.[1]

MURRAY BOOKCHIN, author of *The Ecology of Freedom: The Emergence and Dissolution of Hierarchy* (1982), and pioneer of the ecology movement.

When I wrote this chapter, America was in the midst of an extremely nasty presidential race between Barack Obama and Mitt Romney. I couldn't watch much of the Republican convention because every time I'd tune in, someone would be painting a very detailed and very ugly picture of Obama as an aloof, tax-raising liar who made promises he didn't keep. The person speaking kept repeating that Obama was a failed leader who was unable to turn the economy around and create jobs. The speaker would focus only on Obama's perceived shortcomings, blowing them out of proportion, and citing "facts" which were distorted (or made up, for example: 'Obamacare will create death panels to decide when your grandmother should die') to validate his or her point of view.

To me, these partial and/or false descriptions of the president were frustrating and sickening. How could the Republicans blatantly lie and so disparage this good man who was our president? How must Obama feel to hear these ugly qualities and malevolent intentions attributed to him?

The next day, even after the media fact-checkers refuted many of their claims, the Republican speakers would espouse these same "facts" again and again. Their strategy seemed to be to present a very specific picture, or mindset, about Obama: repeat it over and over, and even though it might be distorted, people would begin to believe that is who he really was.

It was, of course, much easier for me to watch the Democratic convention because I agreed with the picture that the Democrats were constructing of Romney as a filthy-rich, out-of-touch, uncaring, corporate raider who wanted to be president so he could give tax cuts to billionaires like himself. At the Democratic convention, Bill Clinton gave one of the clearest and most amazing political speeches I had ever heard. But the next day, the media fact-checkers pointed out several significant ways where he had also lied or distorted the truth. Clearly, the Democrats were also trying to gift-wrap Romney in a very specific (unappealing) box so they could then sell that box to the American people. I just liked their box better than the way Republicans portrayed Obama, so I was more likely to believe it.

Of course, this is how the political system works and most of us are aware of it. My question is: If this is how our political system works, why do we let it work this way? Why do we let the system denigrate two human beings by putting them into boxes that are incomplete, inadequate, and even evil caricatures of who they really are?

If you step back and look at the current political system, you might imagine it as a giant chess game between two political parties manipulating their pieces in order to win. (Each political party is, of course, also part of larger systems that are betting on it to win and threatening dire consequences, specifically the withdrawal of money or votes, if it doesn't.) Each party has its King, and the aim of each party is to try to trap and knock out the other's King by using every piece at their disposal. Each King has its surrogates who defend their leader or attack the other side on their King's behalf. (In this election's game, the Queens, Michelle Obama and Ann Romney, were particularly powerful because of the positive boxes they were placed in by their parties and the public). The surrogates also get attacked (made into caricatures of themselves) and often get captured (in their own lies) and taken off the board.

In each game (election), one side uses its pieces more effectively and wins, and the people who bet on that side get rewarded. Interestingly, the moment one game ends, each team immediately begins to set up its side of the board for the next game. The winning party begins to paint the picture of its new King in a favorable light and starts putting any potential Kings of the other side in unfavorable boxes. The system is preserved and continues on the same track. But even more importantly, the two parties, and the larger systems they are surrogates for, have been preserved and live to play another game, against the same team, only with new people in the roles of King, Queen and Pawns, etc.

This is an example of how a dysfunctional system preserves its identity by turning its people into objects. One of the ways the system does this is by putting targeted people into metaphorical boxes, thereby establishing a simple, distorted, or even inhuman image or mindset about that person rather than seeing the full, complex, human being he or she really is.

Mindsets and Not Being Seen

Objectification is one of the ways a system maintains power over its people. Therefore it is one of the ways to tell the degree of a system's dysfunction.

Objectification is about how you see others and therefore how you treat them. Objectification is dehumanizing and humiliating. It makes others different than and less than who they really are. Many people of my generation became familiar with the concept of objectification through the women's movement of the 1960's and 1970's. It gave a name to the process of objectifying women, that is, seeing a woman not in the fullness and complexity of who she is, but as a thing to be fantasized about or used for sexual pleasure. The operative word here, of course, is "object," a thing to be used or manipulated for a purpose that is either good, benign, or bad.

Similarly, objectification also includes the process whereby a picture is painted of an individual that is a partial or a distorted representation of who they really are. When you witness a teenage girl angrily talking back to her parents, you might label her as a difficult person or a problem child. Such labels or mindsets can be either negative or positive. For example, when this teenager's sister wins the local science fair, she might be referred to as the brainiac, which is an equally incomplete but more positive mindset about her.

Most of us have some experience of other people seeing us differently than we see ourselves. Sometimes this can be an overly positive view that makes you uncomfortable because you are being placed on a pedestal where only your strengths are recognized and not your foibles and fears. At another time, you might get furious at being put in a box by a person who sees you in a certain way – say, as arrogant – and then interprets everything you say or do in a way that proves that you really are who they think you are. In all of these cases, you are being seen as other than who you truly are. In fact, you are not really being seen; instead, others are seeing their image of you.

This process of labeling people or putting them into boxes is automatic, unconscious and natural. It helps you navigate the world. It is what my colleagues and I refer to as creating mindsets[2] about people and the world, or what Peter Senge and others refer to as creating mental models.[3]

While mindsets can be useful to help you understand a person, when you mistake a mindset for the whole truth about who that person is, it becomes a significant problem. You fix this image of the person in your mind and begin acting toward him or her accordingly. Of course, this action has repercussions in the pictures they paint of you. They now also put you into a figurative box, and then react to that box, not you.

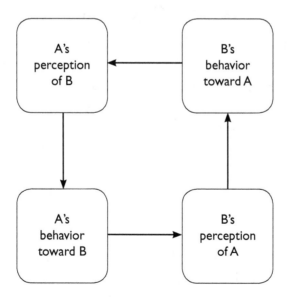

Once there is a fixed image, the person is stuck in that box even when facts show that this image is only partial or not true at all. When you find out that the teenager was angry at her parents for accusing her, once again, of doing something that, in fact, her brainiac sister had done, you might continue to think, "Well she's still a problem because she talks to her parents that way." You don't give any thought to the brainiac and why this golden girl might continually set up her sister to be the fall-girl.

This process of putting someone in a box and holding or fixing them there is part of my definition of objectification. As individuals, we do this in order to make sense of the world, but we also do it so that our view of ourselves and the world will not be called into question. Our views might have to change if we saw this the person not just as our image of them but also as a unique, complex human being who, in most ways, is just like us.

There are three types of objectification:

- When you are objectified by the system and other members of the system;
- When you objectify others; and
- When you objectify yourself.

Objectification, in this case, means not seeing or treating another, or oneself, as a whole, unique, human being, with the corresponding respect that one deserves simply for being a unique living being.

Dysfunctional Systems and Objectification

Dysfunctional systems take this automatic and unconscious process of objectifying others and exacerbate it. Sometimes it is done consciously, as in the example of the Democrats and Republicans. Usually it is done unconsciously in order to preserve the identity of the system, even if it is at the expense of its people.

Ironically, the concept of a human object doesn't make linguistic or rational sense. The two words don't fit together. A human being is not an object, and if something is an object, we don't think of it as being human. But in dysfunctional systems, humans *are* treated as objects. All human systems have a purpose and the members of that system are the *means* by which the purpose is fulfilled. In dysfunctional systems we all become human resources, with the emphasis on 'resource' and not on 'human.'

In the ballgame mentioned in Chapter 2, when I ask the participants about their experience of furiously passing the ball from one person to the next, the usual response is, "I felt like part of a process under stress, like a cog in a machine that had to keep moving." And when I ask how the other people looked to them, the response is often something like, "What people? I was only aware of the 'thrower' and the 'catcher' and myself as the link between the two." The system isn't comprised of people, but of cogs – throwers and catchers.

This might be a familiar situation in your workplace, particularly if you work in a repetitive or boring job. But you might also experience it in other situations as well, such as when your children expect you to make their lunches because you are the mother, or you see a co-worker as subordinate and therefore responsible for more menial tasks. We become each others' means for getting things done. As a result, we see and treat each other as objects, or resources. The more the system is under stress and dysfunctional, the more pressure there is to see and treat each other this way.

Dysfunctional systems are Life-deadening. They focus almost exclusively on the life of the system at the expense of the life of their human resources. A Life-deadening system might function quite adequately, or even superbly, in relation to its purpose and goals, but at the same time be very dysfunctional in how it treats its people. Examples of this dynamic would be a non-profit that is serving its constituency extremely well, but its staff members are burning out and leaving, or a family that provides food and shelter but no stimulation, love, or sense of belonging for the individuals.

Objectification is fairly easy to see and experience in large, impersonal systems like corporations or government bureaucracies where one is treated as a statistic, or as merely another of many customers, or as a social security number, rather than as a human being. But what does it look like or feel like in other settings such as a family or a cultural system like the class structure of a society?

Objectification in Family Systems

Many movies, novels, and autobiographies such as "*The Great Santini*," "*Billy Elliot*," or the animated movie "*Ratatouille*," have a common theme: a parent tries to live or re-live their life through their children. The parent usually does this by pressuring the children to excel in areas where he fell short or to be interested in things she wished she had pursued. This, of course, is understandable. You want the best for your children; you know the mistakes you made and you don't want them to make the same ones.

But it becomes dysfunctional when the parent stops seeing the child for who she is, and perceives her primarily as someone who can provide an opportunity for a do-over in life. There are lots of stereotypes that fit this pattern: the stage mom, the dad who pushes his son or daughter too hard athletically, the professional who pushes his or her child to succeed academically, and so on. In each case, the parent doesn't really see what the child wants or is interested in. Rather, the child is seen as some thing to be shaped into a satisfying result for the parent. This is one form of objectification within the family. There is little recognition that the child is a person in his own right who may have desires, talents, and purposes of his own.

Another version of objectification that many of us are familiar with in our own families happens when children are labeled because of one strong characteristic. The child is then treated as if that one trait or skill or behavior is the whole of their being: "She's the creative one," "he's a schizophrenic," or "our youngest is the shy one." While there is usually some truth in these statements, the problem comes when a mindset about the child is taken as the whole truth, and family members stop seeing her as a unique, multi-faceted being.

In addition, by labeling her in this way, she is not seen as part of a system, the dynamics of which, might be pressuring her to behave in certain ways. She is taken out of context and observed as a completely autonomous individual who fully chooses her behaviors. She can then either be blamed or praised for these behaviors according to how they fit the family's image of her and of itself. Once the system pressures, labels and fixes her in those behaviors or roles, she becomes an object the system can use to preserve its identity.

A Case Study 'The problem child' and 'the brainiac' mentioned earlier were two sisters in a family that came to see me when I was beginning my practice as a family therapist. They entered therapy because the problem child kept getting into trouble both at school and at home. After the first two sessions, where I concentrated solely on her problem behavior, my supervisor asked me, "Are you an individual therapist or a family therapist?" Because I was inexperienced at seeing systemically, I was pulled by the system into focusing all the attention on her as what family therapists call the identified patient. I had lost sight of what was going on in the system as a whole.

As I stepped back, or disidentified, from the system, I could ask myself questions such as, "What is going on in this family that it needs to have a problem child?" As I began to look at its behavior as an entity, not just as a collection of separate individuals, I started to notice certain patterns of behavior that all the members were participating in:

- At each session, one of the two sisters always sat between the parents
- Each session always started by one of the parents or the brainaic reporting on what trouble the problem child had gotten into that week
- Whenever I asked the mother or father a question about themselves rather than the kids, the problem child would make a sarcastic remark or the brainiac would point to something obnoxious that the problem child was doing at the moment.

At one point I commented on how hard the girls were working to keep me from talking to their parents. The next session I seated each girl on either side of me. I asked them not to interrupt and to listen carefully to what their parents had to say to each other. There was dead silence in the room and I could feel the tension rise as if something, or someone, was going to explode. Slowly, the story emerged: the father's workload had increased and he was working long hours and was feeling a lot of pressure to deliver at the office. Mom was feeling neglected personally and unhappy about being forced to deal with all the family problems alone. They had not been intimate in months. They often fought with each other late at night, which the girls overheard. One night the brainiac asked the problem child if she thought their parents were going to get divorced. Problem child was worrying about the same thing. It was shortly after this that the problem child got called into the principal's office for the first time.

I turned to the problem child and said, "I think you are not getting enough credit for holding this family together." She looked baffled, but tears started forming in her eyes.

"What! Her?" exclaimed the brainiac.

"Yes, and you're not getting enough credit for helping her, although she's carrying most of the weight." Problem child was crying now.

"What are you crying about?" the father asked somewhat angrily.

She shook her head and said she didn't know.

"I think she's crying because it has been hard for her to be the recipient of all this anger for getting into trouble. I suspect she's been unconsciously sacrificing herself to take the attention off of your relationship and the fighting between you and your wife. Your daughters are afraid you might get divorced and the family will fall apart." Both girls were nodding yes.

This intervention seemed to open things up for the family. When they came for the next session, the girls sat on either side of me, letting the parents be next to each other. The father started by excitedly reporting that the problem child, Sarah, was so much nicer this week. Also, she was asked to join the soccer team.

"That's wonderful! Good for you, Sarah," I exclaimed, "But now let's talk about how things are going between Mom and Dad, and see what you need individually and as a couple."

If we simply look at Sarah's behavior we begin to form a picture of her and objectify her by putting her into the problem child box. But if we look at her in context as a member of the family system, we get another picture. We begin to see that the system's fear of falling apart required that the attention get refocused away from Mom and Dad. Sarah unconsciously sensed this pressure and started acting out. Brainiac – Samantha – also felt the system pressures and unconsciously helped out by pointing to all of the troublesome things that Sarah did. Mom and Dad were more than happy to shift the focus away from themselves because each of them felt the fear as well. The system preserved itself by objectifying Sarah and quite literally turning her into the problem child.

Objectification of Leaders

In dysfunctional systems, objectification is rampant and extends, to all the people in the system, including the leaders. It is easy to see how those at the bottom of a hierarchy – workers, children, low-ranking soldiers in the military – are only partially seen, put in boxes and made into objects. From their perspective, and often from outside the system, it looks like this is being done to them by those above them in the hierarchy. This is partially true, but they fail to see how they also objectify themselves and each other, and how they objectify the leaders of their system.

The people at the top of the hierarchy are not immune to the system pressures of objectification and self-objectification. Boards of directors replace corporate CEOs all the time for failure to provide a large enough shareholder return. Their performance is taken out of context, as if they were solely responsible for the dynamics of the corporate system or the larger economic system in which the corporation lives. To the board of directors, replacing the CEO is like replacing a part, albeit a critical, very expensive part of a machine to get it to run efficiently again. A CEO might not mind feeling like an object for a while if he or she is an object with a $30 million severance package and no worries about survival. Nevertheless, he is still treated as an object by those who replace him. A vice-president of research at a large pharmaceutical company once complained to me when he was moved sideways into a job of lesser importance and responsibility, "They didn't acknowledge all the sacrifices I've made for the company. They didn't see all the positive things that I've done. They only saw the research projects that didn't come to fruition and blamed me for them."

It is also true that leaders of systems, the Tops, are often seen not as fellow human beings but rather as the role they play, be it mother, general, teacher, boss, etc. I remember the first time I saw one of my teachers outside of the classroom. I was in grade school and she was in the local supermarket with one of her own children. "She doesn't live at school?" I questioned. It disturbed me to realize that we were not her only children. "She has a family? What does that mean about her relationship to me and to the class?" It broke open the box that I placed her in and, as is often the case, was very unsettling to my worldview.

Exercise and Reflection

Try to imagine your mother, father, boss, priest, rabbi, teacher, or president not as their role, but as a human being just like you. Try to imagine them with normal human traits like fears, inadequacies, loves, interests other than their roles, etc. What is it like to see them in this way? How might seeing them in this way open up possibilities in your relationship to them?

Self - objectification

There is also a very common, but more unconscious, experience of feeling pressure from the system to objectify *oneself*. We make ourselves into objects in systems, unintentionally, in many different ways, because we hold an incomplete and fixed view of ourselves within the narrow context of that system. We forget that we possess other qualities that we express outside of that system. This cuts us off from aspects of our creativity that we otherwise might bring to bear on problems within the system. In these cases, we end up feeling controlled by the system, cut off from ourselves and others, less alive and less human. This dynamic is easiest to see when you truly care about the purpose of the system of which you are a part and are therefore willing to make personal sacrifices for that purpose to be fulfilled.

This was the case in the group I belonged to that became a cult. We believed that we were doing "God's work," bringing spirituality into the field of psychology. Because we saw our work as important, we were willing to put in long hours with little sleep and no vacations. We abused our bodies through lack of rest and exercise. We lost touch with ourselves and what we really needed, wanted or thought. Somehow, in the name of spirituality, we lost our humanity. We made ourselves, and each other into 'tools' for doing good or 'vehicles' for spiritual energy to flow through.

I also observed this dynamic in my consulting practice with non-profit organizations. These groups are often staffed by people who are passionate about a cause and who are willing to go the extra mile to help the organization fulfill its mission. These groups are often chronically under-funded, and since the organization as a whole benefits from personal sacrifices like working unpaid overtime or paying for organizational expenses with personal funds, the system unconsciously encourages such behaviors. These kinds of sacrifices for a cause that one cares about is natural and noble when needed, but it is dysfunctional when it becomes the norm (the rule that assures the system's survival) rather than the exception.

Again, there are usually good reasons given by members in such systems for over-extending themselves: "We are understaffed," "My clients/patients/cases have it much worse than I do," and "Who is going to do it if I don't?" But are these well-intentioned employees really making a choice or are they being driven by system pressures to treat themselves as objects? If you are working for such a non-profit and think that you are making a free choice, the question becomes, "Why are you choosing to abuse yourself by working like this?" And in these situations, you often are abusing yourself. You are treating yourself as an object by the way that you are doing the work that you care about.

As a coach in the corporate world, I hear various versions of this same dynamic leading to self-objectification, as well as the objectification of others. It usually sounds something like this:

> *Wow, this is an exciting project I'm working on. Sure, it's hard work with long hours and lots of travel and it's taking a toll on my body. I know I'm pushing people beyond their limits, and they don't like me very much, but this isn't a beauty contest. Besides, it's only temporary and it's for an important project for a key account. I know my wife/husband and kids are complaining about not seeing much of me, and I miss them, too. I'd like to ease up a bit, but I can't. This project is too important. I just have to stick with it a little longer and things will get better when the project is over.*

The problem is that in dysfunctional systems, there is always another project that, because of circumstances, needs to be done in exactly the same way, and the pattern of objectification and self-abuse continues.

Individuals at the top of a given hierarchy are vulnerable to the pressures of self-objectification as well. They are seen by others, and often put themselves in a "leaders should be omnipotent and omniscient"

box. As Barry Oshry describes, Tops inhabit a world of complexity and responsibility that they feel acutely. If they are not aware of, or do not know how to respond to the system pressures on them, they tend to try to micro-manage, control, and draw even more responsibility up to themselves and away from others. They end up feeling burdened by the system, and they objectify and blame others as inadequate, under-performing, or as behavior problems.

What they don't realize is that when they keep trying to control and take on more and more to do, they are actually abusing themselves. They are treating themselves as an object by putting themselves in the box of "a leader should know everything." Therefore they can't ask for help, and they can't be vulnerable as human beings with limitations, needs, and feelings, who have lives outside of that particular role.

Women, especially wives and mothers, are particularly prone to being put in a box by our culture. Abby Seixas says in her talks to women, "We are expected to be all things to all people at all times – while looking beautiful." She says that one of the problems with this box is that women believe it, internalize the system pressures, and try to be perfect wives, mothers, employees, friends, adult daughters, and so on. They objectify themselves. In the process, many women put unrealistic demands on themselves and lose themselves in the stress and anxiety of always trying to live up to the role that they have both been put in and taken on. Abby's work is to help women slow down, step out of the box of perfectionism and unrealistic expectations, and to remember who they are and what is important in life. In other words, to help them become the subjects of their lives again rather than objects.

Exercise and Reflection

Where and how do you objectify yourself: In your family? At work? In relation to an authority figure?

What does it feel like when you are treating yourself as an object? What cues in your body, feelings, or mind can you use as mindfulness triggers to wake yourself up to other choices you might have in the moment?

What rationale do you give when you objectify yourself? What mindset or view of yourself might be more useful to you instead?

The System's Role in Abuse

By far the most damaging forms of objectification are physical, psychological, or sexual abuse. These are also the most glaring examples of the power-over dynamics behind objectification. When individuals see others as outlets or receptacles for their own internal dysfunction, there is no recognition or concern that there is another human being involved. These individuals are disturbed. Others cease to exist when their own needs take complete control and they visit their rage, lust or sickness upon the victim. The terms blind rage or sexual outlet are used to describe these experiences of not seeing another human being in a way that respects their humanity. In these extreme acts of abuse, it is easy to see the individual psychological illness at work.

It might help us to shed light on some of these extreme cases by also looking at the interplay between personal and systemic dysfunction. Without in any way removing responsibility from the individual perpetrator, we also need to ask, "In what way or ways is the system contributing to, magnifying, or justifying the individual's objectification and abuse?" How is it that, systemically, the victims of physical and sexual abuse are primarily women and children? What are the systemic pressures on both men and women that contribute to their physical and psychological abuse of others?

It is easy to see how a man or woman at the bottom of the hierarchical power ladder, who is working in a robotic job, not being seen, and being treated abusively as a cog in a machine, might come home and pass that abuse on to others. On the other hand, not all, or even most, men or women abuse others in such extreme ways. This might lead us to ask, "What is it about the perpetrator's individual psychological dysfunction that might be fed and magnified by the system's dysfunction?" In these cases, it is not either/or, individual or system, but both the individual and the system.

However, it is also true that there are extreme times when the systemic pressures toward objectification of another leads to horrendous acts by otherwise healthy individuals. Examples include the My Lai massacre during the Viet Nam war, the humiliation of Muslim prisoners by US forces at Abu Ghraib during the Iraq war, and the systemic raping of women in the tribal wars in Rwanda. Global occurrences of ethnic cleansing, genocide, and holocaust continue. In these cases a dysfunctional system takes on a life of its own and objectifies an "other," aiming to destroy or humiliate it because it is perceived as a threat to the life of the system.

These extreme cases of objectification of other human beings are easier to see than more subtle cases and, therefore, they help us to understand what is meant by the systemic pressure to make others into objects. But systemic objectification by a dominant culture can also be less explosive and harder to see. While not focused around catastrophic events, embedded cultural objectification is just as powerful because it is chronic, usually invisible to the perpetrators, and works more insidiously over time. This is the description of almost all the major "isms"– racism, sexism, classism, ageism – in the world today. These are systemic problems that, individually, we did not cause, but nonetheless we are individually and collectively responsible for perpetuating. But we cannot act on this responsibility and change our individual and collective behavior until we become aware of the subtle and not so subtle ways that the system causes us to objectify and see categories of human beings as lesser or non-human others.

Objectification Leads to Separation

When you put yourself or others in boxes, or treat yourself or others as objects, the outcome is separation from each other as unique, Life-filled, complex human beings with purpose. You also become disconnected from yourself is a vibrant, creative human being with choices, agency and purpose – the subject of your own life. Finally, you also become distanced from the whole of which you are a part. If you are an object of, or resource to, the system, you no longer experience the healthy, Life-affirming system principle of the whole supporting the parts while the parts simultaneously support the life of the whole.

Recognizing just how much separation is caused by the objectification of self and others in dysfunctional systems is crucial to understanding how the system disempowers the individuals that comprise it, and therefore, what might be done differently. Part Two will explore the inherent power that people possess within the systems they inhabit.

CHAPTER SIX

BLAME: SEPARATION OF THE INTERCONNECTED

Barry Levinson's semi-autobiographical film, *Avalon*, about a tight-knit Jewish immigrant family, contains an episode describing a particularly tense Thanksgiving. The celebration is being held at the home of Jules and Ann, who have moved to the suburbs. Their new home is a long way for their city relatives to travel and Uncle Gabriel and his wife get lost and are late for the meal. The family is gathered, waiting and waiting for them to arrive, but as frustration grows, they finally decide to go ahead and eat without them. When Uncle Gabriel eventually arrives, he is outraged that the family could be so inconsiderate as to carve the turkey without him. He storms out of the house and thus begins a long and intense family feud.

Blame is a major cause of separation in a system. When you don't see systemically, you will view things from a more linear cause-and-effect perspective. You will perceive the person or thing closest to the event in time and space as the cause of that occurrence and therefore deserving of the praise or blame, depending on how you feel about what happened. This linear cause-and-effect perspective produces separation in several ways:

- The very act of focusing only on individual people separates the whole into its components and makes it easy to lose sight of that whole.
- Blaming individuals in the system distances you from your fellow parts in the whole. It pushes them away and allows you to point at them for being the root of the problem.
- Blaming others separates you from any responsibility as part of the whole involved in that event.

If the family is all waiting for Uncle Gabriel to arrive in order to start the Thanksgiving dinner, is he to blame when he is late and everyone is hungry? Or are the hosts to blame for living far from the city and not giving good directions? If the family had waited, would Uncle Gabriel's arrival cause the meal to begin? Or, was the family the cause of the feud for starting the meal without him, or is Uncle Gabriel the cause for storming out and not speaking to them again?

From the system perspective, the cause of the family's behavior is the rules that everyone is following. These are: "Everyone must be here before we start eating, and Uncle Gabriel is the one who carves the turkey." Even though there were no cell phones in the 1950's, had the family, including Uncle Gabriel, been aware of the rules they were following, they might have come up with some creative solutions for the their collective problems of hunger and lateness.

The amount of blame in a system is a good indication of its dysfunction because *blame separates the interdependent and interconnected people in the system into isolated parts.* Blame allows you to abdicate your responsibility for the whole to another, who then becomes the object of punishment or replacement. When you see systemically, you realize that the whole is the cause of its own behavior. You also understand that every member is 100% responsible for doing something about that behavior. You recognize that there are dynamics in the system – the rules, the structure, the belief systems – that are pressuring you to behave in certain ways that produce the results you find unacceptable. Then you, and everyone else, can investigate what rules – perhaps unspoken – are being followed, or what mindsets you might be holding, that result in these undesired outcomes. This coming together to look at the whole is, in fact, a re-uniting of the parts.

Blame in the Dynamics of PSI

At PSI, all of us took part of our identity from being members of an incredible group of people that was doing spiritual work. This meant that the group was good and that each of us individually, by being a member, was good. And since we were good, if something went wrong – a program not filling, a criticism of the group from the outside, or disagreements or questioning from within the group – it was interpreted as something bad, some outside force trying to stop us from doing our good work. By blaming external forces, we were able to unite even more strongly against this powerful enemy. This solidified our identity as God's soldiers (thus objectifying ourselves) and simultaneously separated and isolated us even more from the world outside the group. In doing this, we also avoided looking at what the group as a whole might be doing to create these situations where we were being criticized or where our programs were not filling.

This separation and isolation drove us more and more into cult-like behavior. Since external forces are very hard to fight directly, we needed to find an individual to blame, someone in the group who was, in effect, opening the door and letting in these destructive energies. When that person was identified, he or she was then confronted and helped to see how their behavior was allowing evil in. This person was then "encouraged" to change that behavior in order to close the door to these bad energies.

Of course, this separated us from each other even more. Out of fear, we each kept our reservations about the group's behavior to ourselves, while at the same time searching for which other group members were letting the evil in. The more isolated and righteous we became, the more we were criticized from the outside. Our parents became increasingly concerned and tried to contact or visit us. As we pushed them away, they became even more worried and persisted in their efforts to reach us. According to the group's mindset, this meant that our parents did not respect our wishes and, therefore, must not be on the side of the good. We would then be pressured by the group to sever our relationships with our families. On and on it went in a downward and segregating spiral of separation. And because we were certain that we were doing spiritual work, the strength of the resistance or criticism from the outside just confirmed how important that work was.

We either blamed the outside world or one another. But no matter how difficult things became, we never questioned the assumption that we were doing "God's work". We never looked at the belief system of good vs. evil/light vs. dark, through which we judged everything. By blaming, we cut ourselves off from the world and held it responsible for our situation. Blaming kept us from looking at the system as a whole and how we ourselves might be producing the conditions we were experiencing.

Blame in the World Arena

You might be tempted to dismiss the example of PSI as extreme because it happened in a cult. But this type of blaming behavior, and the separation it causes, happens in dysfunctional systems all the time. Consider the teenager who is either unconsciously or consciously trying to call attention to something wrong in the family or at school. He or she gets blamed for acting out, is separated from others, and is seen as the problem. By assigning blame to an individual, the family or school can shift the blame and avoid looking at the problems in the system as a whole.

When terrorists flew the planes into the World Trade Center buildings in New York, there was a tremendous outpouring of grief and support from the rest of the world. The U.S. no longer saw itself as so removed that we were invulnerable to terrorism. Suddenly we experienced the kind of vulnerability and bloodshed that people all around the world live with on a daily basis, and many of those people empathized with what we were going through. Caring and compassion came to us in the form of offers of aid, rescue technology and workers, military intelligence, and more. There was a coming together of many parts of the world – the whole – around a common rejection of these kinds of horrific, indiscriminate acts of terrorism.

Of course the United States was outraged at the attack and Americans naturally looked for someone to blame. When individuals in this country posed the question, "Is there anything America might have done that could have contributed to people hating us so much that they would be willing to die in order to do us harm?" the questioners were labeled as unpatriotic traitors. They were shouted down and ostracized. Osama Bin Laden and Al Qaeda took responsibility for the atrocity, but somehow, the Bush administration was able to use it as an opportunity to settle old scores and turn the outrage and blame toward Saddam Hussein. Other countries were enlisted to go to war with us against this evil dictator who was sponsoring terrorism and was believed to supply weapons of mass destruction to Al Qaeda. When people in this country objected to going to war against Saddam Hussein, who had no direct connection to the World Trade Center attacks, once again the blame was turned toward the questioners and they were called unpatriotic. When they challenged the existence of weapons of mass destruction, they were called uninformed or blind and evidence was produced to warrant the declaration of war.

Over time, the delusion, dishonesty, and illegality on the part of the American government came to light. The war was entered into under false pretenses and the need to blame someone. As it dragged on and on, we became more and more alienated from the world, even from our former allies. We squandered the compassion that had been shown us, and we became more distant from our supporters as country after country pulled out of the Iraq coalition or denounced us from the sidelines. Through our behavior, we seemed to validate all of the negative qualities attributed to us by Bin Laden. We became more estranged while he gained more power and recruits.

But probably the most disturbing thing, from a systemic perspective, is the fact that no one has been held accountable for the deception and the system as a whole has not asked itself the question, "How could this have happened here?" Not how the Trade Center attacks could happen, but, "How, in the United States of America, with its systems of checks and balances, could a president wage war under false pretenses, wasting precious lives, money, and global goodwill? What is it about how the system as a whole works that allowed this to happen with absolutely no accountability?"

When Barack Obama became president, the Bush administration, the media, and the electorate could have been held accountable. A thorough investigation and discussion might have led to new laws that might have changed the system to prevent this happening again. But at that moment, the country happened to be in the middle of the deepest financial crisis since the Great Depression while simultaneously fighting two wars. This made it very easy for Obama to say, "I'm not interested in looking backward. We need to go forward and fix what we are faced with now." All of that might have been true and necessary to demonstrate his intention to be bi-partisan and collaborative, but the fact remains: America was able to simply blame others and avoid looking at what might need to be changed in our own behavior or in how our leaders are allowed to declare war. Our system preserved its identity, its rules, and its way of doing things in the world.

At this point you might be thinking, "Oh, now I get it. The system is to blame!" No, it's not, although that is an easy mindset to fall into, namely us against the system. The system is the cause of its own behavior, but who comprises the system? We do. If we blame a given system, we distance ourselves from a specific whole of which we are a part. This separation allows us to believe that we are outside that system. We shift the responsibility to the system and become victimized by "them." *But we are "them."* As the cartoon *Pogo* was fond of pointing out, "We have met the enemy and he is us."

When we blame the system and make ourselves into victims, we objectify and therefore disempower ourselves. We believe we have no choice. We deaden ourselves and cut ourselves off from our collective creativity that could offer positive solutions. The fact is that we are parts of the system and therefore responsible for both the problems and the solutions.

CALVIN AND HOBBES © 1992 Watterson. Reprinted with permission of UNIVERSAL UCLICK. All rights reserved..

Not all separation is bad

Dysfunctional separation occurs when the pressures of the system push apart or break relationships among the parts of a system which are, by definition and in practice, interconnected – *and then keeps them separate.* In a healthy system there would be a natural rhythm, almost like breathing, of members of the system dispersing in order to interact with the environment, and then re-integrating to share the information they acquired so the system can learn and grow.

Healthy families usually go through a process where the children, at a certain age, have to individuate from the family to experience more fully who they are as beings in their own right, that is, distinct from the system. Sometimes this happens when, for instance, a child goes into the military or off to college.

When the child comes home from the military or from college, she may have changed by becoming more of an adult, more of an individual. Often this happens when she recognizes her own uniqueness within the family. When she is re-integrated into the family, the family is pushed to adapt and grow as this new individual seeks different kinds of interactions and relationships with the other family members. In this case, individuation is beneficial for both the individual and the system.

But sometimes there is a blow-up in the family and the child leaves or is pushed out. Then the system is broken in such a way that makes it very hard for the child to come back and rejoin the family. In this case, the separation is locked into place and both the system and the individual lose something. Sometimes this break is necessary for the individual or for the family, or both. But sometimes the inability to re-integrate is a sign of dysfunction within the system.

The Systemic Forces of Separation

Three of the dynamics of separation within dysfunctional systems that are worth emphasizing are:

- If we are all one interconnected whole, the experience of being outside of that whole is an illusion – a mindset – perhaps understandable, but still, untrue. Therefore, to act out of the experience of separation leads to less effective, and sometimes damaging, solutions to problems which affect us all.
- Changing Life-deadening, dysfunctional systems into Life-affirming ones cannot be done by any one individual, even a CEO, parent, or president. It takes a critical mass of people coming together to effect those changes. As long as the system can keep us separated, it can control us. Without the collective power of its parts working to change their relationships with each other and the system, the system does not have to change and is able to preserve its dysfunctional identity in the world.
- In order to re-unite, understanding how systems keep us apart is essential. Once you see and understand how system pressures push people apart, your responses can be less unconscious and reactive. You can step back from the system, reclaim your will, and act with more autonomy in the midst of those systemic pressures. When you step back, you can see more and become more inventive in identifying solutions to problems that re-integrate various parts of the system rather than driving them further apart.

Barry Oshry's theory of Tops, Middles, and Bottoms (see Chapter Three) is a very practical model that makes it easy to see the forces of separation within systems. His research makes it clear that the predictable behaviors of people at each level of a hierarchy distance them from each of the other levels, from themselves, and from the whole:

- When a Top reflexively responds to the real conditions of complexity and responsibility by drawing more authority to herself she distances herself from the other levels of the system.
- When a Middle reflexively tries to meet everyone else's needs, he gets separated from other Middles and has no real connection to the people he is trying to serve at the top or the bottom of the system. He is pulled in several directions at once and also becomes disconnected from his inner sense of knowing and direction.
- When a Bottom reflexively sits back and blames the system for her situation, she separates herself from the system as if she were outside it and then views herself as a victim. In the process, she disempowers herself, cutting herself off from her own sense of responsibility, volition, and creativity.

Oshry also addresses what happens among the members of the Top, Middle, and Bottom groups or teams when they are subjected to the system forces.[1]

When Tops, as a group, (for example corporate executives or parents) are faced with the constant complexity and responsibility that is inherent in their positions, they naturally and almost reflexively divide up the tasks they are faced with in order to handle all that needs to be done. The group differentiates. In business, for instance, there is the VP of Finance, the VP of Sales and the VP of Manufacturing. At home, one parent is responsible for the bank account, paying bills, house repairs and homework getting done, while the other parent does the laundry and grocery shopping, maintains the family calendar and carpools, and gets the car repaired. This solution is functional, but over time, the individual feels more and more identification with, and ownership of, their own areas of responsibility and less ownership for the system as a whole. The result: "This is my domain. You take care of your business, I'll take care of mine."

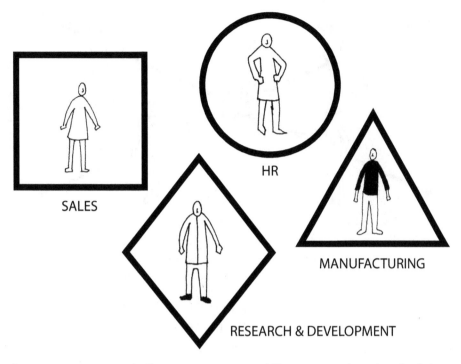

System pressures cause the Tops in a corporation to differentiate in order to handle all their responsibilities. However, in doing so, they run the risk of becoming identified with their domain and lose sight of their responsibility for the whole.

Eventually and predictably, turf wars develop, for example between the VP of Sales and the VP of Manufacturing around budget and quality issues. Maybe the parents fight over which is more important given limited resources: painting the house or car repair. In most cases, the system pressures create *a separation among the Tops* that produces tension, blame, and a loss of respect or trust. It also distances the individuals and the team from their responsibility for the system as a whole because they are identified with the responsibility for their domain only.

The system pressures on individual Middles drive them apart as they try to meet all the needs of the Tops as well as their own teams. They become dispersed throughout the organization and find it almost impossible to regroup and coordinate the activities of the whole.

The Middles can also become competitive and identified with the particular team that reports to them. They blame each other and the other teams when something goes wrong, and because they are so split, they

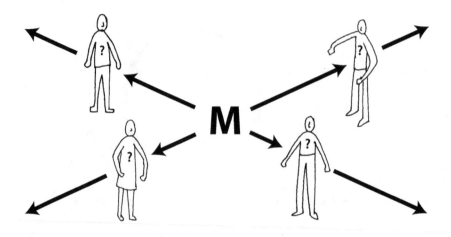

System pressures force the Middles to disperse and lose their individual sense of identity and personal power, as well as any power they have as a group.

possess very little power as a group to make a difference in the system as a whole. An example: parents find themselves in the middle between their child and the teacher who is not satisfied with the quality of the child's homework. Since one parent happens to be responsible for the homework (which the child hates) and the other for the extracurricular activities (which the child loves), they argue about whose fault it is that the child isn't doing well. This, then, separates the couple unit and lessens its ability to work together in a coordinated way with both the teacher and the child.

Finally, Oshry's description of what happens among Bottoms sheds light on some of our most intractable societal problems and why they are so hard to change.*

When Bottoms as a group feel the vulnerability that they are faced with as a result of their position, their natural tendency is to band together, creating an "us and them" situation in relation to those above them in the hierarchy. This causes separation and distance from both the Middles and the Tops. The Bottoms stick together in opposition to those who are, or appear to be, victimizing them within the system. Bottoms feel the need to speak with one voice in order to maintain any semblance of power within the system. For example, unions form to fight for certain rights, or children plot together about how to get their parents to stop drinking or

---

* See Oshry's books *Seeing Systems* and *Leading Systems* for more about these dynamics among Bottoms.

being abusive. Bottoms feel that in order to have any power, they all must be on the same page and act in concert.

The problem comes when Bottoms try to discuss and decide on the best strategy for ending their vulnerability and victimization. The system pressures usually lead to two predictable strategies that Oshry calls "produce" and "protect." The Bottoms who advocate for the "produce" strategy say that the way to get their needs met and become less vulnerable is to do what is expected of them and to do it well. Their solution is to turn out more products at better quality with fewer accidents and to prove themselves too valuable to lay off. Or, in the family example, the children might try to be good, quiet siblings who play amongst themselves and therefore don't attract any negative or abusive attention from their parents.

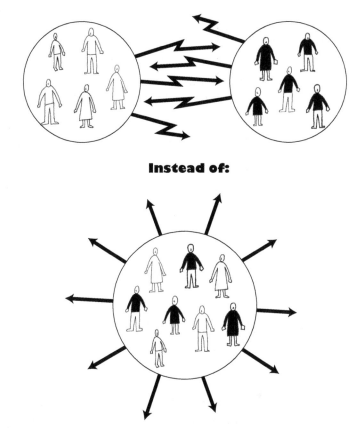

Instead of:

System pressures cause the Bottoms to separate into groups fighting over the best strategy to get what they want. This takes their attention off of the whole system and lessens the power they have when they stand together.

In contrast, the Bottoms who push for the "protect" strategy believe that the only way to get what they need is for Bottoms to look out for themselves rather than be good little soldiers. They believe the Bottoms should demand what they require and not fulfill their responsibilities until those essentials are met. In the family example, the children might tell a grandparent or a school counselor about their parents' drinking in the hopes of getting the adults some help and themselves some protection. In the business example, the workers might go out on strike or stage a demonstration to protest large salary discrepancies between Tops and Bottoms.

The crucial point is that the system pressures cause the Bottoms, who need to be standing together, to fight among themselves about strategy. As long as the system can pressure the Bottoms to focus on their own disagreements, they are not a united whole and will not manifest the power to change the system.

For example, during the late 1950's and 1960's, African-Americans and Jews stood together fighting for the civil rights of African-Americans. But then, in the early 1970's, for myriad reasons, Blacks and Jews began fighting among themselves over political issues and civil rights strategies. In Boston, politicians and bankers used tactics such as redlining and blockbusting to pit African-Americans against Jews (and Catholics) in the Roxbury and Mattapan areas.[2] This preserved certain areas of the city for wealthy Protestants. You could say that was an isolated instance, but now the same system pressures are playing out among Blacks and Latinos and other minorities as they struggle for their place in society. As long as system pressures keep members fighting about what is needed, who deserves what, and the best strategy for getting it, the system does not have to change.

Moving Toward "We"

As you become more acutely aware of how system forces separate you from others, from your deepest self and from Life itself, you begin to develop the ability to step back from those forces in order to re-find yourself and regain your power and volition within systems. Bridging differences and healing divisions are two of the ways to counter the pressures of separation and bring about change in dysfunctional systems, whether they are governments, organizations, families, or teams.

Learning to see and to value our inherent interdependencies as human beings is crucial. Whether it is through what Oshry calls partnership, or through what others might call love or caring or "power with," we all benefit by remembering and honoring our interconnectedness. This can be the motivation to come together with others to build the kind of Life-affirming, creative and empowering systems we want and need. Individuals cannot do this alone. It takes a critical mass, a "We," to affect this type of change.

Part Two will explore how we can come together more effectively to resist the system forces of separation. But first, let's look at one other way that systems gain and maintain power: by asserting that the system's purpose and values are primary, thereby diminishing the importance of one's own personal purpose and highest values.

CHAPTER SEVEN

THE PRIMACY OF VALUES:
INDIVIDUAL, SYSTEM, AND SPIRITUAL

The reality is that most companies are not about any values at all –
they are about making money. It is extremely rare for a business to
stand for anything . . . Ben says to me all the time, it's better to stand
for something. Some people will agree, some people won't agree, but
you're going to connect with the people who agree with you on a much
deeper level than, "Hey this is some great-tasting ice-cream with some
interesting names."[1]

> JERRY GREENFIELD, co-founder of Ben & Jerry's Ice Cream

The last major consequence of dysfunctional human systems is that they often separate you from your sense of the highest good and any larger, more inclusive values of Life by demanding allegiance to the system's values above all others.

A system takes on a life of its own, an identity or 'ego', which then strives to survive in the environments (the other systems) in which it lives. The system, like most people, experiences itself as the center of its own universe. Its purpose, goals, and survival needs are paramount, and the individual people within the system become the means for meeting those purposes, goals, and needs. In order to make sure the members act in accordance with the system needs, it evolves its own rules, both conscious and unconscious, for its people to follow. The human system then exerts considerable subtle, and not-so-subtle pressure on individuals to behave in accordance with these rules and values. Yet the individuals are often not conscious that they are doing so.

Because you participate in so many different systems simultaneously, and because these systems are parts of even larger systems, you are often faced, both consciously and unconsciously, with what I call "primacy of values" problems:

What if your individual values conflict with a system's values?

What if one system's values conflict with the larger systems in which it participates?

What happens when dysfunctional systems pressure you to act against your own deepest values, or what you might see as the higher or more spiritual values of Life?

Conscious and Unconscious values

In their book on organizational learning, management consultants and educators, Chris Argrys and Donald Schön make a distinction between the values that an organizational system holds consciously and the values that it expresses (often unconsciously) in its behavior. They refer to these as the system's "espoused values" and "values in action."[2]

As with individuals, there is often a discrepancy in systems between what the system says it values, and what values it actually demonstrates in its day-to-day actions over time. With the exception of the truly deceitful, I do not believe it is the norm for individuals and systems to intentionally misrepresent their values. I think they consciously believe what they profess. For the individual, the problem is that there are unconscious psychological wounds, conditioning, desires or even biological factors that can shape behaviors in ways that run counter to professed values. Addictions of all kinds are a good example of this dynamic where biological or psychological factors often cause us to violate our better judgment. Parents sometimes become aware of this conflict between values and actions when they hear themselves saying, "Do as I say, not as I do!"

It is much the same for systems. Because of its unconscious rules and/or because of the way a system is structured and/or because of the pressures of the larger systems in which it operates, a system often behaves in ways that run counter to its professed values. Often these systems, whether families, volunteer organizations, corporations and even governments, are not aware of these differences until the feedback from within or outside the system becomes loud enough to attract attention to the discrepancy. Even then, if the feedback is perceived as threatening to the survival of the identity of the system, like an individual, the system will become defensive, rationalize, or blame the people giving the feedback.

In the cult, we gradually came to believe, like so many spiritual fanatics before us, that we were on the side of Love and Light fighting Darkness and Evil. We valued goodness and mercy and the importance of group unity in facing such an adversary. The belief that we were in a cosmic "fight" was controlling more of our behavior than we realized. When someone in the group questioned what we were doing, the simple fact that they were questioning meant, from within the group's belief system, that they were being influenced by evil. This person, then, had to be isolated before they could contaminate anyone else. This never felt merciful or kind, and certainly went against our belief in group unity, but the belief dictated that it had to be done for the person's good as well as for the good of the whole.

Ironically, all of these things that were done for the good of the whole ended up destroying the group. Toward the end of the life of PSI, there were so many members isolated or marginalized, so they wouldn't infect others, that there were not enough members left to do the teaching and work of the institute. Those who were still "clean" spent their time planning on the telephone about how to protect the group, and rarely came together in the same room. So much for being a group, and so much for doing "God's work" in the world. We had completely imploded on ourselves.

But from within the group, everything made rational, coherent sense because we believed that we were in a life-or-death fight between Good and Evil. The stakes were high and we needed to do everything we could to win. It turned out that included, unconsciously, giving up our own sense of right and wrong. We told ourselves that we were doing everything with love and in service to a greater good. We rationalized to ourselves that these horrible things we were doing to each other really were in line with our highest values. It was only after I had left the cult – and stepped back and looked soberly at what we had actually been doing – that I saw how mean, abusive, and divisive we had been. Of course I was ashamed for my/our behavior, and began to ask myself some hard questions: "Where was this shame while I was in the group?" "Why did I not see that I was not practicing my values of love and kindness?" "Why did I not recognize or act on the discrepancy between the values we professed in the group and how we were actually treating ourselves and others?"

There is a reason I am emphasizing this concept of espoused values versus values-in-practice. If the two are not congruent, the system will usually reinforce the unconscious values that are really driving its behavior while believing that it is promoting its professed values. The system will design its structure, rules, and rewards to reinforce its professed values, but since the unconscious values are always at work, they will inevitably be built into the structure, rules and rewards as well.

I have seen many companies profess in their mission and values statements that they care about the work–life balance of their employees. They may create no-questions-asked personal days or allow employees to work from home several days a week. But when opportunities arise for promotion, the people who work long hours, show up at meetings on weekends, and are available 24/7 by cell phone or text are the ones who get rewarded. When this happens often enough, the people in the system learn that the professed values are not real and they succumb to the pressures of what is *really* valued by the system, namely long hours and the sacrifice of one's personal life.

And since most systems profess noble or at least benign values, it doesn't even occur to them to explore the effect of their unconscious values on their members, their clientele, the environment, or the world at large.

Exercises and Reflections

Make a list of values that are most important to you.

- See if you can roughly prioritize these values. This is can be difficult, so give it some thought and don't worry about getting the list in perfect order.
- Now, try to identify the top three values you feel most strongly about.
- Think about a normal day in your life and try to determine how often and where you express each of these values.
- Review the same day again, and determine the things you spend the most time doing. Do these things, and the amount of time you spend on them, say anything about what you might unconsciously be valuing?

Look at a few of the systems of which you are a part, e.g. your family, your workplace, your place of worship or an organization where you volunteer, etc.:

- In which systems is it easiest to practice each of the above values?
- Specifically, how do these systems support the practice of each value?
- In which systems is it hardest to practice each value?
- Specifically, how does the system interfere or mitigate against the expression of each value?

Systems within Systems

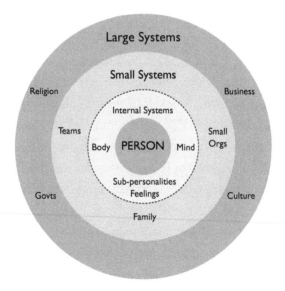

Ben Cohen and Jerry Greenfield, the founders of Ben & Jerry's Ice Cream, opened their first store in an empty gas station in Vermont in 1978. Their goal was to enjoy doing something they loved. As the company grew, it prided itself on having a values-based business model founded on taking care of its workers, doing good in the world, and having fun. Here is a sampling of some of their innovative practices:

- The top person in the company would be paid no more than 5 times the lowest paid worker.
- Milk would only be bought from local dairy farmers at actual, not lower, government subsidized prices.

- They would not inject air into their product in order to cut costs like other ice-cream makers did.
- They would value their workers through profit-sharing and perks such as massages and free ice cream for the packers on the assembly line.
- They set up the Ben & Jerry's Foundation to support social causes and contributed 7.5% of pre-tax revenue each year.

The company was written up in numerous magazines as an example of what a "values-based" business could be. In 1984, because they had outgrown their first plant, the company went public in order to raise the money to expand. Because one of its stated values was, "Business has a responsibility to give back to the community from which it draws its support," they originally only sold shares within the state of Vermont.

In 1983 Ben & Jerry's had expanded to the Boston market with one independent distributor selling to supermarkets. But in 1984, just as they were going public in Vermont, Pillsbury ($4 *billion* in revenue), the makers of Häagen-Daz ice cream, tried to keep their distributers from selling Ben & Jerry's ($3 *million* in revenue).[3] In keeping with the company's value of fun, Jerry conducted a one-man picket line outside of Pillsbury's headquarters in Minneapolis, carrying a sign that asked, "What is the doughboy afraid of?" He handed out information packets and bumper stickers with the slogan, all of which garnered tremendous free publicity for the underdog company and created a grassroots movement to put pressure on Pillsbury. The publicity, along with a good Boston legal team, eventually settled the case in Ben & Jerry's favor.[4] The publicity, coupled with their innovative business practices, the quality of their ice cream, and their inspired flavors and names (Heath Bar Crunch, Cherry Garcia, Chubby Hubby, etc.) fueled the company's rapid growth.[5]

Until this point Ben & Jerry's, as a business system, had been selling nationwide, but primarily participating in the regional, economic system of the state of Vermont. It was a mutually beneficial relationship with the state, which supported the company's growth with State Industrial Revenue Bonds and anti-takeover legislation. In return, the company contributed to the state's local economy through taxes, attracting publicity and tourists, supporting the local dairy and pig industries, and benefitting local shareholders.[6]

As the company continued to grow and expand nationally (and internationally), it began to experience the pressures of the larger economic systems of which it was a part. Although its "second bottom line" – its social action causes and contributions – continued to grow and gather publicity, its business success slowed. By 1999 Ben & Jerry's stock had fallen almost 50% from its peak and some investors were maintaining that the social mission of the company was dragging down profits.[7] Their low stock value attracted interest from outside buyers and there was pressure from stockholders to do something to the raise the value of the stock.

In early 2000, in an effort to preserve the values and spirit of the company, Cohen and a group of investors attempted to buy the company and go private. Because the board of directors felt systemic pressure to maximize shareholder value, they reluctantly refused Cohen's offer. Unilever ended up offering more per share and the assurance that they were interested in maintaining Ben and Jerry's mission and values. Since Unilever was a $45 billion international company based in the Netherlands, no one fully trusted that it would deliver on its assurances.[8] But the board of directors felt that the Unilever deal was the only one that fulfilled their legal requirement to maximize shareholder value, and because three investor lawsuits were filed demanding that they do so, they sold the company.

Ben Cohen and Jerry Greenfield and others felt they were forced to sell and many accused them of selling out. Many thought that the larger system pressures and values had won and the spirit and values of Ben & Jerry's were doomed. However, two interesting outcomes from this clash of values demonstrate the power of Ben & Jerry's advocating for social values as well as business results.

First, Unilever contractually agreed to carry on many of the company's social values:

> The new board included Cohen and Greenfield, and its members, not Unilever, would appoint their successors. Moreover, this subsidiary board had the right to sue Unilever, at Unilever's expense, for breaches of the merger agreement. Unilever also promised to continue contributing pretax profits to charity, maintain corporate presence in Vermont for at least five years, and refrain from material layoffs for at least two years. Finally, Unilever agreed to contribute $5 million to

the Ben & Jerry's Foundation, award employee bonuses worth a total
of $5 million, and dedicate $5 million to assist minority-owned and
undercapitalized businesses.[9]

Unilever also invited Ben to do a social and environmental audit at its headquarters in Holland. If you go to Ben & Jerry's website today, you will see the many social causes they are supporting and the fun and humor for which the company is known. For example, they changed the name of their Chubby Hubby ice cream to Hubby Hubby in support of gay marriage. Of course, no one can say how much more the company might have accomplished had they stayed independent but, in this case, the strongly-held values of the smaller system had some influence on the larger.[10]

The other outcome from the Ben & Jerry's experience was a change in the mindset and the law about the legal obligation of a board of directors to its stakeholders. The board of directors felt the economic pressure of the larger system to maximize shareholder value and the pressure of the legal system to hold them accountable. As Terry Mollner, one of the board members, said at the time, "We think it's horrible that a company has no choice but to sell to the highest bidder or get sued."[11]

In legal analyses since the 2000 sale, it has been argued that the board was not legally obligated to consider only shareholder value and that the social action side of the business could have been a consideration mitigating against selling. These lawyers maintained that it was a mistaken assumption about board responsibilities and fear of being sued that forced the sale.[12] In other words, the pressures of the larger systems forced the change at the company.

Since 2000, in order to not have companies end up like Ben & Jerry's, there has been a large group lobbying for clarity and a change in law. The result has been the creation of new organizational forms that allow, or insist upon, a company's pursuit of social responsibility as well as profit. Ironically, Ben & Jerry's has just become certified as a B Corp (Benefit Corporation) – "a new type of corporation which uses the power of business to solve social and environmental problems." They are the first company that is a wholly-owned subsidiary of a larger corporation to do so.[13]

The evolution of Ben & Jerry's is a prime example of the values of the larger global economic system (growth, return on investment and law) exerting pressure on one of its parts to make those values primary. Ben & Jerry's insistence that social concerns and profit should co-exist in business has served as a model for other companies such as Stonyfield Farm Dairy, Zappos, and Patagonia, that strive to operate in a more sustainable manner in all aspects of their business. These types of companies are growing in number, but they must keep their values constantly in the consciousness of the system in order to counteract the pressures of the larger economic system of which they are a part.

Exercises and Reflections

Think about a system you are a member of, e.g. your family, your work, your place of worship, etc.

- What are the espoused values of this system?
- What are the pressures on this system from the larger systems of which it is a part that either support or interfere with each of these values?
- Specifically, how do these pressures present themselves?
- How does the system deal with these pressures in relation to its values?
- As you look at how time is spent within the system and how it actually works to fulfill its purpose, do you see any things that the system might be valuing unconsciously? Are these values congruent with or in conflict with the system's espoused values?

The Primacy of Values

A system, by its nature, values that which feeds it, keeps it alive, and helps it maintain its identity. A healthy human system recognizes that its being alive is also dependent on the aliveness of the people who comprise it, as well as the aliveness of the larger systems of which it is a part. The healthy human system therefore tries to maintain its values while simultaneously respecting and working with the values of its people and the larger systems to which it belongs.

The world of business is fed, in part, by profit, which is a necessary component of its growth and survival. It is also fed by resources from its environment, such as data, earth-based materials, and employee creativity and energy. Therefore, a healthy business system would consist of individuals helping the system achieve sustainable profitability in a way that is consistent with both individual and system values. That system would also share the profit with its members so that they could live a life consistent with their personal values. The problem arises when a dysfunctional, Life-deadening system tends to see its values as the only or highest values and, subtly or not, pressures the people who comprise it to uphold those values as the primary criteria for inclusion. This is the case with companies whose values-in-practice maximize profit while objectifying its people and neglecting the long-term sustainability of its earth-based resources.

But business systems are hardly the only human system that enforces its values as primary. There are myriad ways to impart values in a family, such as modeling the desired values, preaching, or setting and enforcing rules. The primacy of the parents' values becomes dysfunctional in family systems where the parents impart their values in abusive ways, ignoring the fact that they are dealing with a child (or adult child) who is an autonomous being, developing his or her own values, not an object to be molded to the parents' ends. There is also the difference between the parents' espoused values and their values in practice. This difference gets mirrored back to the parents when they overhear their child making a comment such as, "Mommy says you're supposed to be nice to everyone, but she yells at daddy all the time."

It goes without saying that this process of a larger system imposing its values is demonstrated when a repressive governmental regime imposes its values on its people. Sometimes the people resent this and rebel, or have to go along for their own survival. But the most damaging is when the people are pressured enough over time that they come to believe the system values are their own values and forget that they felt differently at one time. Some call this pressure brainwashing, which can come in the form of overt, forced indoctrination. This pressure took the form of fear in Nazi Germany, of rigid conformity in China under Mao, and of criticizing one's "spiritual development" in our cult.

It is only after the larger system has fallen apart, or you have escaped, that you are able to get enough distance to ask yourself, "How could I ever have believed that? How could I have become such a person?"

Colliding with the System's Unconscious Values

Many values of these larger systems are subtle, even invisible. Still, they are very powerful, in part because you unconsciously assume they are givens, such as the value of the two-party system in America or the importance of the insurance industry. Sometimes the larger system values have power over you because you are enthralled by them and see them as attractive, or as signs of progress, or as absolutely essential. These include the values of consumerism, advertising, or the pharmaceutical industry. I'm not saying that these things are necessarily bad, but they are so ingrained, or so attractive, that it's not possible to see, and therefore consider, the values upon which they are based. These systems are then free to exert their values and influence over the people that comprise them, thus perpetuating the system's values. When these values are questioned, or even explicitly mentioned, and therefore brought to consciousness, the resistance from the system to preserve the status quo, its identity and its unconscious values, is often overpowering.

In the cult, when anyone would point, even unintentionally, to the discrepancy between what we said we valued and what we were actually doing, the reaction was immediate and strong. At one point, as one of the leaders of the group, I felt that we were working very hard and needed to come together in some type of fun group gathering. Proposing to the executive council that the whole group celebrate Thanksgiving together seemed like a good way to do this. In the discussion, members felt that it would be frivolous and take too much time from our work of teaching, protecting the group, and doing "process" with members who were contaminated. I pointed out that we could consider this as part of the work. It would give us a chance to come together to thank God for supporting us while we were doing His work. It would also give us a chance to be thankful for, and appreciate, our support for each other in our individual and cosmic struggles.

"Would everyone be invited, even those in isolation?" some people asked.

"Why not?" I answered. "This will be a celebration of thankfulness to God and to each other. The ritual will invoke so much love and light it might actually help heal them; certainly there will be enough of us to be protected from their bad energies." (As crazy as this sounds, this is a good example of what 'reasoning' looked like from within our twisted belief system.)

At this point, the group leader chimed in: "After all our work together, don't you see what the counsel is saying to you? When we create that much light together, we attract even *more* evil. We become an even bigger target."

I should have stopped right then, but this resistance to my idea, as was often the case, wasn't making sense to me (even from within our belief system). "Are you saying that we can't ever come together again because we would be too easy a target? Wouldn't we be safer together than alone?" I asked.

"You know I am not saying we can't ever come together again!" He was very angry at this point, "We *are* a group. But our work together is as much on the spiritual planes as it is on the material. It doesn't require that we be in the same room. Are you willing to risk exposing the whole group over a trivial holiday? What's going on for you? Why are you pushing this so hard?"

That was the signal that I was about to be "processed" by the group to see what part of my "desire nature" was opening the door to negativity in me and in the group. So I ended up giving up what I valued – coming together, friendship, fun, and giving thanks – for the good of the group (and to save my own skin). Needless to say, we didn't celebrate Thanksgiving.

It all sounds crazy doesn't it? It does until you think about proposing healthcare for everyone in America. . .

I Know There's a Wall Here Because My Head and My Heart Hurt from Banging into it

Americans spend twice as much as residents of other developed countries on healthcare, but get lower quality, less efficiency and have the least equitable system. . .[14]

In its ranking of worldwide healthcare systems in 2000, the World Health Organization ranked the United States' system 37th out of 191, behind the healthcare systems of countries such as Colombia, Cyprus, Greece, Oman and almost all of the other developed nations. On the other hand, we were ranked number 1 on healthcare expenditures per capita,[15] but only 24th in terms of healthy life expectancy.[16] In addition: *"Every other system covers all its citizens, the report noted and said the U.S. system, which leaves 46 million Americans or 15 percent of the population without health insurance, is the most unfair."*[17]

Clearly, the accuracy and meaning of these statistics can be debated. But the question remains: Why has it been so difficult to overhaul the expensive and inequitable healthcare system in this country? And why has the fight about overhaul been so bitter? In the last 30 years both the Clinton and Obama administrations have met with massive opposition to overhauling the healthcare system and extending coverage to the uninsured. People in other countries wonder what the fuss is about. "Why wouldn't you want to make the healthcare system more efficient and cover all of your people?" a friend in Russia asked. And yet the resistance to change is tremendous.

When the Obama administration was able to pass, from my point of view, a few important but very small steps to regulate the healthcare industry, lower costs, and increase coverage, the outcry was immediate, forceful, and toxic. Whether you agree with me or not, I invite you to try to step back from whatever point of view you hold about the specifics, and try to get a sense of the battle, the virtual impasse, and the resistance to change. Every time the issue of healthcare reform comes up, you can feel the caustic urgency of this conflict which, interestingly, is often cloaked in terms of good and evil. What is this really about? I don't have an answer, but I do know that we need to look at this question if we are ever going to reform our healthcare system.

If you overheard a couple in the midst of an extremely nasty fight about whether or not it was time for their son to get a haircut, you would know that this fight was about more than just a haircut. It was only after I left the cult, learned about the dynamics of human systems, and started analyzing our behavior from that perspective, that I began to see what the Thanksgiving discussion was really about. By that point in the group's history, the dysfunctional system forces had generated a great deal of separation and objectification among us in order to maintain the group's existence. The idea of bringing us together was pushing against these system forces of separation and objectification. A Thanksgiving gathering would have re-affirmed our humanity, our love for each other, and our gratitude to something larger than the group, namely God. It would have brought the re-humanizing, re-uniting power of love back into the group. Such a move would be threatening to a dysfunctional system because it means that there is something more important, something to value more than the group and its values. Love would potentialy have put the group back into right relation with the largest whole of which it was a part. And that, ironically, was the Largest Whole whose work we espoused to be doing in the first place.

Re-visiting Espoused Values Versus Values in Practice

So what is this healthcare reform battle really about? It is hard for me – and I imagine that I am not alone – to get a clear sense of the answer because, a) the different sides of the debate are so identified with our individual positions, and b) the arguments tend to be so heated and irrational, e.g. Sarah Palin's comment about Obama's proposed reforms: *"The America I know and love is not one in which my parents or my baby with Downs syndrome will have to stand in front of Obama's 'death panel' so his bureaucrats can decide, based on a subjective judgment of their 'level of productivity in society,' whether they are worthy of health care. Such a system is downright evil."*[18]

It would take a whole book to do justice to the argument about healthcare equity so I won't try. But clearly there is something systemic going on, given the hyperbole of quotes like Sarah Palin's and the resistance that was faced by both the Clinton and Obama administrations. It seems to me that we are in a struggle to see what values should be primary in the system we call America. One of the major problems is that we have not been able to distinguish between the various parties' espoused values and their values in action.

Again, in a dysfunctional system, the espoused values and the values in action are not congruent, and the values in action exert much more pressure on the individual than the espoused values of the system: "Oh yeah, that's the value statement we hang on the wall, but let me tell you how we really do things around here."

Both the espoused values and the values in action are based on mindsets or mental models about how things are and should be. The problem is that the mental models behind the values in action are usually unconscious to the system and to the individual. Therefore they are very hard, if not impossible, to see unless you step back from the system far enough to soberly look at what beliefs might be causing the system to behave in a certain way. All of the "isms" like racism, classism, sexism, etc. are examples of unconscious mindsets driving actions. Consciously, we say that all people are created equal, while some other belief is causing us to act like the whites, the males, the wealthy, and the beautiful are really a little more equal. We say we value all people as God's children, but yet some other belief allows us to treat Muslims and homosexuals as if they are not. All of our religious beliefs say that we should care for the weak and those that are in need, but some other belief allows us to support, and/or be blind to, a healthcare system where the ones without care are the single mothers, the children and the poor.

So I come back to similar questions to those I asked myself when I left PSI and began to see more clearly: "Where is our shame when we treat people this way?" and "Why do we not recognize the discrepancy between the values of love and kindness that we profess in this country and how we actually treat ourselves and others?" To these I would add, "What keeps me, or us collectively, from truly acting in accordance with our highest values?"

Clash of Values Leading to System Change

A dysfunctional system insists that its values always take precedence over the values of its members or of the larger system(s) of which it is a part, as in my group's Thanksgiving example.

A healthy, Life-affirming system, however, would use the clash of values between it and its parts, and between it and its larger environment, as feedback to help determine whether or how to make another step in its growth – its self-organization. I know this from my own family.

As the oldest son, it was quite a blow to the family system when I decided not to go into the family business. For two generations my family had been mid-western, middle-class business people. When my father returned from World War II, he went into business with his father-in-law. My father worked hard to build the business for my brother and me to join and eventually take over. I was the first one to graduate from college, and when I decided to pursue a career in psychology, it caused a lot of pain in the family. My father saw it as a rejection of him and his values and, since it was 1969 and I was an anti-capitalist hippie, he was partially right. He also didn't understand what psychology was and when I tried to explain, he saw no value in it: "It's all mind over matter. You can do anything you make up your mind to do. People are just weak."

This, coupled with the fact that I was not living in Kansas and had married someone from a New York family of medical and psychological professionals, put my nuclear family system through a multi-year process of opening up and expanding its identity. The strain on relationships challenged us to accept and respect each other as people and not just because we were related. Gradually, we succeeded and the family took on a new, more inclusive identity that consisted of other than just businessmen and Kansans. My father eventually went to Dale Carnegie courses to learn the psychology of winning friends and influencing people, and I eventually used my psychology to do family business counseling and then corporate consulting.

A dysfunctional system, however, experiences a diversity of values as a threat to its homeostasis and even its very existence. Pushing back, it uses its structure, processes, and conscious and unconscious rules to mandate and enforce its values as primary. Wanting to maintain certain values isn't necessarily bad within the context of the environment in which the system is living. Wanting, for example, to teach one's family the value of "pride in the freedoms we have in the United States of America" is neither a good nor a bad thing. It is simply something you might want your family members to value highly. The problem comes when "pride in my country" comes up against other values such as "respecting diversity and the opinions of others" and then leads, as it did in the Vietnam era, to the very rigid, exclusionary value, "my country, right or wrong," or "America – love it or leave it."

Dysfunctional Systems and the Larger Whole

When a system rigidly enforces its values over those of its members' out of fear for its own survival, it also cuts itself off from the larger systems of which it is a part. It behaves as if it is the most important system, and it begins to act as if it is the Largest Whole. Therefore, its rules, values, and goals should, of course, be the rules, values and goals of all its parts and of all other systems.

For instance, America sometimes behaves as if it has the only valid system of government when it tries to encourage democracy in other countries without considering the cultural and political systems of those countries. The mission of almost all radical, fundamentalist movements is to impose their values on all people, not just the members of their particular belief system. Mao and Stalin, acting as if they were gods, tried to impose ways of thinking and behaving on their people even if it meant relocating or killing a large number of countrymen within their own system. This hubris also exists in the Catholic Church when it hides and/or defends its child-abusing priests and its image at the expense of some of its own highest values.

This behavior played out as well in dysfunctional corporations such as Enron, AIG, British Petroleum, and Lehman Brothers, for example. Their values, success and survival were the highest priority, no matter what the effects were on others or on the global financial system.

"At Enron.com, the company's Web site, one learns that as a "global corporate citizen" Enron intends to conduct itself in accord with four capital-V Values: Respect, Integrity, Communication and Excellence. This is fairly standard stuff, but a more detailed reading may provide some insight into Enron's corporate psyche.

Take respect: "We treat others as we would like to be treated ourselves." Fair enough. But Enron elaborates: "We do not tolerate abusive or disrespectful treatment. Ruthlessness, callousness and arrogance don't belong here." Oh my. Who brought up ruthlessness, callousness and arrogance? . . .

Well, at least Enron's leaders thought it important to produce a statement of values. Imagine what they might have done had they found themselves without this moral compass."

JAMES S. KUNEN, "Enron's Vision (and Values) Thing"[19]

In October of 2010, GlaxoSmithKline pharmaceutical company agreed to pay a $750 million settlement to the United States government to end civil and criminal complaints that "the company for years knowingly sold contaminated baby ointment and an ineffective antidepressant"[20] along with "20 other drugs with questionable safety." How does one of the world's largest pharmaceutical companies justify such behavior? "GlaxoSmithKline released a statement saying that it regretted operating the Puerto Rican plant in violation of good manufacturing practices." What about violating the larger principles of our common Life together, such as not committing fraud or not knowingly (or unknowingly) endangering the lives of others?

If there is any question about whether Glaxo was putting its values first and preserving its system identity and integrity, you should know that Cheryl Eckard, the company's quality manager (and later, the whistleblower in this case) repeatedly warned Glaxo of the problems and recommended recalls of contaminated products. She was fired. She tried to be true to her own as well as the corporation's espoused values, but Glaxo did not respond to this internal feedback. Instead, their values-in-action demonstrated the primacy of profit and survival at all costs.[21]

And what about man-made ecological disasters? The *New York Times* ran a story based on a leaked internal report after the Deepwater Horizon oil well sank and sent tens of millions of gallons of oil into the Gulf of Mexico. The article states that, according to government records, in May of 2008 "Transocean (the managers of the Deepwater Horizon) was forced to evacuate more than 70 workers after problems with the ballast system flooded part of the rig, causing it to list to its side . . ."[22] It goes on to say, "Transocean's equipment documents reveal that the company was aware of the consequences of the problems. . . referring to at least 36 pieces of equipment in ill repair on the Deepwater Horizon that 'may lead to loss of life, serious injury or environmental damage as a result of inadequate use and/or failure of equipment.'"

Given the severity of the problems, why weren't they addressed? "Some workers said the company was systematically deferring maintenance to save money. 'This rig is getting $550,000 per day; unless it's a sink that needs fixing it isn't getting fixed,' said a worker from the Marianas about the maintenance concerns. "They won't send the rig to the shipyard for major refurb that is required in certain areas."

And it turns out that these same safety concerns applied to three other wells operated by Transocean for British Petroleum. So what values-in-action were BP and Transocean demonstrating as their highest priority by deferring essential maintenance and risking "loss of life, serious injury or environmental damage"? Whatever those values were, they led to massive economic and environmental damage to the larger systems (human, economic and environmental) of which these companies were a part.[23]

There are a multitude of examples from the financial crisis of 2008 where companies acted as if they their values took precedence over the common good. One example of this hubris was AIG, the huge insurance company that played a significant role in the implosion of the derivatives market which led to the 2008 collapse of the global economic system. While the company was pleading for the U.S. government's $75 billion bailout, the board of directors was simultaneously rewarding its executives millions of dollars in performance bonuses. President Obama raised the issue of the arrogance of a system acting as if it is the most important system in the hierarchy when he forcefully commented, ". . .this is not just a matter of dollars and cents, it's about our fundamental values . . . All across the country, there are people who work hard and meet their responsibilities every day, without the benefit of government bailouts or multi-million dollar bonuses. [This is] a corporation that finds itself in financial distress due to recklessness and greed. Under these circumstances, it's hard to understand how derivative traders at AIG warranted any bonuses, much less $165 million in extra pay. Now, how do they justify this outrage to the taxpayers who are keeping the company afloat?"[24]

All of the above examples of hubris, these egocentric attempts at being "Masters of the Universe" in Tom Wolfe's terms,[25] caused disastrous effects on the very universe they were trying to be masters of. All of our man-made, human systems, with their particular goals, values, and rules, participate in the larger Whole of Life with its own principles, values, and laws. I believe that one of our tasks as human beings is to seek and to discover, if possible, what these principles are and what they mean for how we live our individual and collective lives. Then we will be able to participate in and nurture them instead of continually violating them. Not living in harmony with these principles inevitably confirms that we are not, and never will be, Masters of the Universe.

CHAPTER EIGHT

CONSIDERING BOTH
SELF AND SYSTEM

In a large system, such as a society or a corporation, the properties of the system predate the participation of the individuals currently part of it . . . **But it is nonetheless the case that the properties of the system cannot be maintained unless the people in it maintain it.**[1]

PAUL WACHTEL, psychologist *(emphasis added)*

I f the system forces are unconsciously pressuring you to behave in certain ways and accept particular values, what difference does your individual personality make in all of this? Do a person's unique fears, strengths, or values make any difference in the dynamics of a system?

Traditional systems theory does not take much notice of a particular individual part within the system, nor does it usually study why a given part behaves the way it does. An individual part is less important than the relationships among the parts that make up the whole. Given that systems are made up of so many diverse parts, this makes sense. For instance, understanding the particular psychological make-up of Mark Horowitz might give a little understanding of the family system I have helped to create, but it does not shed much light on understanding the political system of which I am a part.

However, especially in the study of human systems, I think there is value in asking and researching questions such as:

- Are there certain developmental psychological dynamics that make us more or less susceptible to the power-over dynamics of a hierarchical system? For example, is there a certain type of person that is more likely to rise to the top or fall to the bottom of a dysfunctional system?
- Are there specific developmental experiences that we all share that contribute to the perpetuation of dysfunctional systems?
- Are there certain personality characteristics of people who can help create or maintain Life-affirming systems?
- Is there a level of personal development that one needs to achieve to be able to disidentify from a system, reclaim one's self and reconnect to Life?
- How can the individual qualities and skills that support Life-affirming systems be taught or drawn out of individuals within the larger culture?

Some of these questions about personal development in relation to systems are being explored in the field of leadership development. Peter Senge's book, *The Fifth Discipline*,[2] was pioneering in its inclusion of both personal mastery skills and system dynamics skills as two of the five disciplines essential to a successful leader. William Joiner in *Leadership Agility: five levels of mastery for anticipating and initiating change*[3] puts forth a framework for understanding the developmental stages of leadership and the characteristics and worldviews of each stage. Robert Kegan in *In Over Our Heads: the Mental Demands of Modern Life*[4] also talks about how unprepared we are developmentally for many of the tasks we are faced with in the family, educational and organizational systems we inhabit.

However, much of the other leadership material separates the developmental and skill aspects of the leader from an understanding of the systems that they inhabit or lead. Most leadership theory does not address questions such as: Why is a leader successful in one system but not another? Why does a leader's personality serve her in a church organization, but limit her at her workplace?

Self-Awareness and Relationship Awareness

These questions are important because, as you will see later in Part Two, my prescription for transforming Life-deadening systems into Life-affirming ones involves learning how to be in new types of relationships with one another. These revitalized relationships start with the individual and therefore require self-awareness skills. Because you are an essential component of the relational equation, it is critical to be aware of those aspects of your personality that inhibit entering into relationships with others, or that determine how you behave in those relationships.

Skills in relationship building and maintenance can be and are taught in seminars on networking, communication skills, team building, parenting, etc. These types of skill training are necessary but not sufficient. This is because the successful practice of a given skill is as dependent on your level of self-knowledge, your maturity and your worldview, as it is on your ability to replicate that skill. If you have not developed self-awareness, it is hard to be truly successful in relationship.

The systems thinker might protest that I am focusing too much on the individual who is relatively unimportant in the system's overall dynamics. However, I think a more integral perspective of group behavior should not focus on *either* the individual *or* the system, but on *both* the individual *and* the system. On the one hand, it is crucial that we learn to see more systemically. On the other hand, we need to develop a deeper understanding of and respect for the complexity of the human being who is participating in these systems. Why? Because there is the opportunity for Life-affirming systems and healthy individuals to reinforce each other's wellbeing, rather than dysfunctional systems energizing our wounds and reinforcing the worst in us.

> *If, because of whatever experiences they encounter – a shortage, a common experience of disappointment, even a persuasive book – they begin to change their values and assumptions, they will perforce begin to change the system as well. In mutually prompting each other and in interacting with others who have not yet changed their view, they can begin to create and to stabilize a new structural arrangement with different consequences for everyone within the system.*[5]
>
> PAUL WACHTEL

Life and Self

My particular human systems perspective arises from my studies with Abraham Maslow and his theories of a hierarchy of needs and self-actualization,[6] and from my studies with Roberto Assagioli, the founder of Psychosynthesis.[7] For over forty years I have taught the latter's psychological and developmental theories of the personal self and its direct, experiential relationship to a Higher Self, a greater energy or force in the universe. This greater source is known in various traditions as the One Self, Life, Higher Mind, Spirit, God, Atman and Yahweh.

Without going into the specifics of either of the above theories, I believe that each human is a unique being with awareness and volition, an integral and interconnected part of the larger Life and therefore, like all Life, miraculous and sacred. I believe that we all have fundamental needs in life, and that, as the basic ones are met, we are moved from within to pursue higher aspirations. As we do this, we grow and develop into fuller and more integrated expressions of who we truly are. We seek to actualize more and more of our self.

Even though this process is called self-actualization, it cannot be done in isolation. I believe that most self-actualization happens in relationship. All of us are on this path of learning and growth, some consciously and willingly and some unconsciously. However, whether we are willing or not, Life keeps presenting us with opportunities to grow and develop. Sometimes we need to learn something new or develop a different quality in ourselves in order to overcome obstacles or hardships. Sometimes the opportunity for learning is presented by a difficult person that we are required to deal with. Sometimes it is another person who helps us to learn, either through their example or by challenging us to reach further than we thought possible.

As we travel on this road of self-actualization we begin to realize that we are not alone in another sense. We begin to understand that we are participating in, and at the same time, expressing something larger than our individual self. We begin to realize and experience that we are an integral part of a larger Life that is expressing through us. Assagioli and others have referred to this as Self-realization (with a capital S). We begin to see that our unique self is a note in the symphony or a color in the palette of that larger Life and therefore essential to its expression. In this sense it can be said that we each contain that larger Life or Spirit and that larger Life contains us. We begin to comprehend that we are both drawing energy from that Life force as well as contributing to it through the full expression of who we are. By helping each other to self-actualize we are also collectively actualizing the potential of the human species and, therefore, Life.[8]

Systems, then, can either consciously facilitate self-realization and the affirmation of Life, be blind to these urges, or worse, unconsciously work against them. Systems can be either Life-affirming, benign, or Life-deadening.

Seeing and Being Seen (Part 1)*

> *"I see you, Jake Skully."*
> *"I see you, Neytiri."*

This is the greeting of the Na'vi people in the 2009 blockbuster movie, *Avatar*.[9] With their large yellow eyes making eye contact, and with great presence in the moment, the greeting conveys much more than a mere "hello." It seems to say, "I see *you,* your essence, which is deeper than whatever surface behavior you are exhibiting in the moment or whatever thoughts I may be carrying about you."

This greeting might serve as a model to mere humans reminding us that there is something in each of our essences that is deep, similar, connected and sacred. It is similar to the Hindu greeting "Namaste" which means, "The divinity within me salutes the divinity within you," and in the moment reminds the greeter that she has that divinity within herself as well.[10]

We have all had the experience of not being fully seen or understood and the frustration, hurt, or anger that arises in us in those moments. Not being seen (or heard) can take many forms, such as:

- Someone holds a mind-set, a mental image of you, and then fits all your behaviors within that pre-existing picture, thus reinforcing it. (It is important to note that this could be a positive as well as a negative image of you. Neither really sees **you**).

---

* *Seeing and Being Seen (Part 2) is in Chapter 12 on Love*

- You are trying to express something and the other person keeps hearing the parts he wants to hear but misses your full message. Or, he is so attached to his message or belief that he refuses to even listen to yours at all.
- Someone makes demands on you based on her needs, but does not consider that you have needs as well.
- Someone relates to you as an instrument, an object, for fulfilling tasks, not as a human being with volition and feelings.
- Your parent treats you as their child, with hopes, dreams, and expectations of you, but does not see you as a separate being with hopes, dreams, and expectations of your own.
- Because someone doesn't like your behavior, choices, or beliefs, they see *you* as a bad, stupid, or uncaring person, rather than as a person with behaviors and beliefs that are simply different than theirs.
- An individual is rushing around managing to-do lists and doesn't take time for real contact with you as her child, friend, co-worker, or partner.
- The company does not acknowledge how hard you work on a project, or the sacrifices you make in general, and just rewards you (or not) according to some seemingly arbitrary reward system.

We are not good at truly seeing each other. This may explain why in many of our lives, there is such a yearning to be seen. We strive to have others see who we are, and when they don't, we feel lonely, angry, or hurt. As Mother Teresa said, "*There is more hunger for love and appreciation in this world than for bread.*"

Seeing and Systems

Why is being seen so important in our lives and why is it a focus in a book on systems? It's worth repeating: it is important for us to explore the relationship between individual human psychology (the part) and systems (the whole) in order to learn what we might do to make the systems we inhabit less deadening and more Life-affirming. When systems treat people as objects, and when we treat each other and ourselves as objects, we are neither seeing nor treating each other as unique human beings. Therefore, any psychological issues that we have around not being seen are usually exacerbated by dysfunctional systems. This leaves us feeling even less acknowledged and more insecure.

Why is being seen so important to us as human beings and what kind of issues arise when we are not seen? A great deal of research has been done on this subject in the field of human attachment theory which investigates the early bonding experiences between parent and child and their effects on growth and development. Researchers such as Bowlby, Winnicott, Kohut and Firman and Gila have pointed to the importance of the parents' presence, attention and empathic love toward the child as essential to the child's formation of a sense of self and identity, and to the child's overall sense of safety and well-being in the world[11]:

> . . . a finely tuned understanding by another individual gives the recipient the sense of personhood, of identity. . . Empathy gives that needed confirmation that one does exist as a separate, valued person with an identity.[12]
>
> CARL ROGERS, psychologist and father of "person-centered" therapy

> However, in addition to "nature" is "nurture" — those things needed from our environment that allow us to include, develop, and express the layers of potential as they unfold. And among the most crucial of these are being seen, understood, met, and loved as we truly are.[13]
>
> JOHN FIRMAN & ANN GILA, Psychosynthesis psychotherapists

So, being lovingly seen for who you are communicates that you exist in Life, that you are connected to others, and that you are not alone in the universe. Being seen means having your self "mirrored" back to you without judgment or interpretation. Being seen also points you toward your true self and helps build your sense of identity, what Firman and Gila call the "authentic personality."[14] Again, the development of a sense of self and feelings of safety in the world happen in relationship to others.

As you grow and mature, people, places, groups or systems that encourage this self-actualization are therefore also self-affirming. This means that Life-affirming systems that recognize and respect who you are can contribute to the healing of any early wounding around not being seen, thus adding to the aliveness of the individual and to the Life of the system as a whole.

Psychologists John Firman and Ann Gila go beyond the attachment theorists and say that in the process of seeing and mirroring another, the individual or system doing the mirroring is not only helping to reinforce the other's personal identity, but they are also giving the person who is seen a glimpse of a larger whole. They say that all loving empathic relationships are tangible experiences of the relationship between the personal self and the larger Whole or Self, what I am calling Life.[15]

So when I am being empathic and truly seeing you, I become a channel for Life to flow through me and affirm the Life in you. In the process, as Life flows through me, I am also affirmed. In this mutual affirmation, we both experience that we are connected as parts of something larger than ourselves: Life or Spirit or Being. As the philosopher Martin Buber wrote, *"Egos appear by setting themselves apart from other egos. Persons appear by entering into relation to other persons. . . .For as soon as we touch a Thou, we are touched by a breath of eternal life."*[16]

So why are we not touched by eternal life in more systems?

Fear and Loathing in Systems

This need that we all have to be seen and loved for who we are is one of the main areas where personal psychodynamics and system dynamics meet.

As most of us who have been in intimate relationships know, our need to be validated can easily trigger our partner's fear of not being seen. "You say I don't see you. What about you seeing me?" This can exacerbate the fear of both people in the couple and separate them as they each strive to receive what they most fundamentally need. This struggle to be recognized and accepted is also exemplified by siblings acting out in order to attract the most attention from their parents, or by the heated and ruthless competition for recognition that goes on within every organization's hierarchy. The personality we form as an attempt to get what we most essentially need, recognition and love, is what Firman and Gila call the "survival personality." It is based on a deficit worldview that makes it seem as if there is not enough love and validation to go around: "If you are seen and accepted by others, I'm afraid they won't see me." This win-lose worldview drives a multiplicity of behaviors that usually obscure our deepest self, and also keeps us from recognizing another's need to be seen.

The individual's survival personality is always at play trying to cope with what it perceives as hostile environments. Dysfunctional systems consciously or unconsciously feed these fears: "This organization is my provider. My life depends on it even though this organization is treating me like an object for its own ends." Under these conditions people vie to be seen, protect their vulnerabilities, and present themselves in ways that the system demands. The prospect of being ejected from the system feeds the fear of not being seen and receiving the validation I need. The fear says: "How will I survive? Who am I if I am not a part of this group? Will I exist outside of this system?"

The result is a culture of fear, control, and reflexive behavior. People do as they are expected. It is as if they are in what Firman and Gila call the thrall or trance of the organization.[17] They operate without awareness of either the system pressures or of their contribution to the continuation of those pressures. As Firman and Gila write, "The more we are dependent on such an environment, whether as a child in a family or as an adult within larger systems, the more powerfully and unconsciously this oppression operates."[18] The ultimate experience is one of feeling trapped in the system: if you stay you are treated like an object, but if you leave how will you survive?

This is usually one of the dynamics at play when abused children deny the abuse and protect the parents, or when battered women stay with their abusive spouses. There is the very real fear of death at the hands of the abuser if a woman leaves, but there is also the fear of not being able to exist outside of the relationship. So she tries even harder to be the good wife, trying to deliver what she thinks the abuser wants.

Arthur Deikman, in his book, *Them and Us: cult thinking and the terrorist threat*, echoes this point about fear within business systems:

> *Compliance with a group increases with one's psychological and economic dependence on it... Sociologist Diane Margolis studied managers at a large corporation and found . . . economic and social segregation played an important role in the corporations becoming, for many managers, the chief source of self-esteem, companionship, and personal expression. . . To leave the company would mean all that sacrifice has been in vain; security must be given up . . . with few connections to the outside world that world can easily appear less desirable–and the Corporation more valuable–than it is.[19]*

My need to be validated and my fear of not being able to exist outside of PSI kept me there in spite of the extreme strain and abuse that I felt, witnessed, and perpetrated. In doing "God's work," I felt connected to something larger than myself and in working with such accomplished colleagues, I felt a sense of belonging as well as feeling seen. But from within the cult, it was very difficult to see how strongly my behaviors were being driven by the fear of being singled out and isolated or, even worse, of being expelled from the group.

It was only upon leaving the group that I could see how much of my true self I had buried, denied, or deluded in order to remain in the group. I had to deny the abusive way we were treating each other by rationalizing that it was for the others' spiritual good. I was forced to cut off relationships with my nuclear family, friends outside the group and, eventually, with my wife because of the group belief that they might contaminate me with negative energy. And most detrimentally, I stopped seeing others as unique human beings with strengths and weaknesses just like me, and instead saw them as vehicles for good or evil. They were either allies or enemies.

If I was doing "God's work" in the cult, then if I left who would I be serving? I would be cut off from the source of all love and light in my life, both God and the group, and banished to a realm of darkness. Because I had cut myself off from all of my friends outside the group, and in some cases saw them as evil, how could I exist outside of the group? Some of this fear was conscious, but much of it was the unconscious fear of my survival personality. It told me that if I could be just a little bit better carrier of spirit, or if I could tolerate just a little bit more pain, then I could continue to be validated by belonging to such an important group.

As Firman, Gila and Deikman point out, it would be wrong to attribute my participation and persistence in the group as entirely my own neurotic psychodynamics or *as only* the systemic pressures of the cult. There was an interplay going on between my fear-based, survival personality and the pressures of a dysfunctional system trying to preserve its identity and existence.

As I've said, it would be easy to write my experience off as an extreme anomaly, but one might consider some of the atrocities that have been perpetrated by good people in the name of religion, as their way of earning validation and a place in heaven. The lying, deceit or frauds, carried out every day by normal people in order to not lose their job, are also examples of feeling trapped by the system. These are just a few examples where the personal psychodynamics and system processes and pressures interrelate and magnify one another.

The Need for Practice

More could be said about the relationship between individual psycho–dynamics and systems, but that is not the purpose of this book. I am writing about it here because I want to begin the discussion about seeing, being seen, and empathic love that we will explore further in Part Two.

A dysfunctional system can never be a good mirror to its members because it sees them as objects and therefore does not affirm and advance the individual's overall growth. By not seeing the individual as a unique human being who is an expression of Life, the dysfunctional system confirms their fear of not being seen. This exacerbates the individual's survival personality and they behave in ways that are not productive or healthy for the individual or for the system.

This brings me back to the fact that personal development, as well as Self-realization, is done *in relationship*. It is unrealistic, I think, to expect that any system – nuclear family, marriage, church or organizational system – will completely fulfill its members' needs to be nurtured, seen, and held with empathic love. But I do believe that seeing others, and making ourselves vulnerable to being seen, are worthy personal goals and worthy lifetime practices not only in our closest relational systems, but also in the larger systems in which we participate.

There is value, for all involved, in practicing not being reactive to surface behaviors and stepping back from your own fear-based personality in order to see the unique being in front of you. Treating that person with respect, even though they may have hurt you or you may disapprove of their beliefs or actions, acknowledges them as a fellow human being. It also reconnects you to your most authentic self when you are able to salute the divinity within others–especially when it is not visible.

At this point you might be thinking, "This is hard enough to do in my marriage and family where I have considerable incentive because of the commitments we have made to each other. Why would I want to make this kind of effort in the larger systems I inhabit when we don't have these same commitments to each other? Why would *I* make these efforts if everyone else isn't making them too? And why would I make these efforts if the system is not making them toward me?"

Whether or not another responds to your seeing him as a whole human being and treating him with respect, and whether or not the system changes, there are still benefits in practicing empathic seeing or loving:

- By practicing being a better mirror, you remind yourself that the other is a human being, not an object. In so doing, you remember this about yourself. This is one of the first steps in re-humanizing a system.
- By not succumbing to system pressures to objectify yourself or others, you are liberating and exercising your will. It models to others the possibility that they also could choose not to play by the system's rules.
- And finally, when you can see another as a unique human being who deserves respect simply because he is a part of Life, you bring something larger into the system you both share. You become a channel for that Life, that aliveness, to enter the system.

These practices of seeing, acknowledging and affirming contribute to the creation of Life-affirming systems. Such a system recognizes that the well-being and development of its people are crucial to the system's overall health and development. The system also acknowledges the need of its members to be seen and appreciated for who they really are. These systems create ways of letting people know they are being seen as unique individuals. Even small actions like trusting people to make their own hours, or to work from home, can contribute to them feeling seen as responsible adults. Letting children (or others) take on challenging projects where they might fail and then helping them learn from their mistakes lets them know that you see them as capable people who want to do their best and who want to grow and develop.

If the need of individuals to be seen, acknowledged and affirmed is a crucial area of interaction between individual psychodynamics and system dynamics, it can also serve as one of the key points of leverage to bring about systemic change. That is why the importance of seeing and being seen is a thread that runs throughout Part Two.

CONCLUSION PART ONE

IS THERE HOPE?

None are more hopelessly enslaved than those who falsely believe they are free.

JOHANN WOLFGANG VON GOETHE[1]

Looking at life as a simple occurrence, where people interact in linear, cause-and-effect ways, causes problems. Doing so is like seeing ourselves as lines of dominoes standing around with no volition or responsibility. One domino falls over and hits the domino next to him; she then falls and knocks over three others, and so on, until a domino falls and finally asks, "Who knocked me over?" When the situation is analyzed from a linear, cause-and-effect perspective, you point to the person next to you and say, "It's your fault."

It may never occur to a person to step back and ask: "What is going on here? Why are we all standing so close to each other? How did this way of standing in lines get created? When did the first block get knocked over and how? Is there a better way to organize ourselves so this doesn't keep happening?"

Seeing in a linear, causal way can be useful in some cases for evaluating events and making changes to either reinforce desirable consequences or to minimize undesirable ones. This is only one way of seeing, however, and it has limitations. A more useful way of seeing is to look at a whole system and the qualities and characteristics that emerge out of the mutual-influence relationships of their parts. This is a perspective that sees the system as if it were a living entity, striving to maintain its life like any other living organism.

A systemic way of seeing will help you to become more aware of how the larger wholes in which you participate are influencing, or perhaps pressuring you to behave in certain ways that are beneficial to itself. Learning to see systems also helps you to be aware that your actions can and do influence any whole of which you are a part. Without your input and action, the whole does not have the benefit of all the information it needs to grow in a way that benefits both it and you.

Seeing the interconnected, interdependent wholes of Life will help you to realize that "we are all in this together" and that all of your actions produce multi-directional consequences. These consequences are then fed back as information about the health of the system and about the next steps needed in the direction all of us are travelling together. This way of seeing removes linearity, blame, and powerlessness from your analysis of situations. Instead, it encourages you to ask, "What are our individual and collective choices in this moment? What can we do now, together, to make sure we are going in the direction we have chosen for ourselves?"

Healthy and Dysfunctional Systems

Systems are not inherently good or bad; they just are. Natural life seems to be organized in larger and larger systems or wholes that are nested inside of each other.[2] Each larger whole possesses capabilities that exceed that of the parts that comprise it. Atoms comprise molecules that, in turn, make up cells that come together to create organic entities. Human systems tend to mimic this nested hierarchical structure: individuals, families, communities, cities, nations, etc. In healthy, man-made human systems, as in healthy natural systems, there is a mutually beneficial, co-dependent relationship between the larger whole and its component parts. The parts work together to assure the survival, health, and growth of the larger system, while the larger whole provides for the needs, health, survival, and growth of its parts. In a healthy human system there is a mutual recognition and honoring of this co-dependent relationship. These healthy systems are Life-affirming in that there is a natural flow of energy in the form of feedback and information that allows for and encourages the growth and development of both the whole and the people in it at all levels.

Problems arise in human systems when this mutually beneficial relationship breaks down. One type of breakdown comes when the parts become more concerned with their own short-term survival or growth and ignore or neglect the life of the larger whole. There were many examples of this in the financial crash of 2008 where a number of investment businesses were so focused on their own greed they destroyed their own companies and nearly destroyed the global economy. It is also visible in our non-sustainable use of the earth's resources that contributes to global warming and its threat to our species.

Another type of breakdown comes when the system's natural process of taking on a life of its own becomes rigid and the system focuses more on its own survival than on the survival of its parts. In this type of dysfunction, the system pressures the parts to behave in ways that become Life-deadening for the parts, and ultimately for the whole itself.

These dysfunctional, Life-deadening human systems disempower and control individuals and groups of people in four key ways:

1 Treating people as objects and in doing so, causing us to sacrifice our humanity by treating ourselves as objects and seeing and treating others as if they were merely resources to fulfill the system's purpose.
2 Separating people from each other and groups from groups, thereby ignoring or rejecting the fact that we are all in this (system) together and that we are one interconnected, interdependent Whole.
3 Killing creativity by dampening our aliveness (see a and b) and by stifling the flow of energy and information within the system.
4 Demanding allegiance to the values of the system over individual or more inclusive values. This cuts us off from our own personal highest values. It also cuts the larger system off from the even larger systems of which it is a part, and ultimately from the largest whole, which is Life.

Turning Dysfunctional Human Systems into Life-affirming Ones

In order to re-find ourselves and our power, and to stop perpetuating disempowering systems, we need to learn, or re-member, how to:

1 Reclaim our humanity and stop treating others and ourselves as objects.

2 Come together, lessen the distance among us, and start practicing behavior that recognizes and affirms that we are all interdependent beings within the Whole of Life.

3 Increase the flow of meaningful information by such acts as including all relevant voices in conversations, and promoting recognition of the benefits of diversity and creativity.

4 Learn to be mindful of what we are valuing; ask ourselves "What does this decision or action in this moment, say about what I/We are valuing right now?" Reach for more inclusive or higher values in our individual and group decisions and actions.

Is There Hope?

Systems exert power over people. When we don't understand this power, we tend to cling to naive ideas about how easy it will be to change what we don't like in the systems or, alternatively, we don't see a path toward change and we feel hopeless. If the human systems we participate in are so dysfunctional, is there any hope? Can systems be changed?

I believe there is hope.

I believe systems can be changed.

Part One is designed to help you make the first steps in the change process: learning to see systems, and realizing just how powerful they are. As you begin to develop a realistic sense of what is involved in system transformation, you will realize that you cannot change these systems alone. You will need to stand together and work collectively with others to make these changes. This is a difficult task because it requires not only new ways of seeing wholes, but also new ways of seeing others and yourself. It also requires new ways of being with yourself and with others, as well as new ways of acting together.

Although these new ways of seeing, being and doing are difficult and take practice to implement, you will see that they are not as foreign as you might fear. In Part Two, I will show that these new ways are really quite old and have been around for a long time. We've just lost touch with them or do not believe they can be practiced in a modern context. I will also show that some of us are already re-discovering these ways and experimenting with putting them into practice in organizations and systems around the world, which is both inspirational and cause for optimism.

PART TWO

RECLAIMING LOVE, POWER
AND SELF IN SYSTEMS

Radicals and exiles typically delude themselves that dictatorships are based exclusively on coercion. This is not true. Long–lived dictatorships engender their own characteristic subculture and their own peculiar normalcy. They create a type of man unused to freedom and truth, ignorant of dignity and autonomy. .. For every dictatorship, the critical moment arrives with the reappearance of human autonomy and the emergence of social bonds that did not enjoy official sanction

ADAM MICHNIK, Polish dissident,
Letter from the Gdansk prison, 1985

CHAPTER NINE

DISIDENTIFICATION: BEING *IN* THE SYSTEM BUT NOT *OF* THE SYSTEM

On the one hand is the exercise of human agency and autonomy; on the other hand are the social structures and social constraints within which these actions are played out. How much autonomy do we have? And how much of our lives are constrained by the conditions into which we were born? . . . To what degree do these social, institutional and cultural structures constrain the exercise of individual agency?[1]

PETER SEIXAS, founding Director of the Centre for the Study of Historical Consciousness, University of British Columbia

How much agency do you have in your own life? When you are not conscious of being controlled by system forces, you believe that you are acting on your own volition and making your own choices. The truth is that you are unknowingly succumbing to the subtle and not-so-subtle pressures of the system. On the other hand, when system forces consciously control you, such as in totalitarian regimes, or overbearingly strict families, you believe you have no choices. In either case, you are cut off from your own agency, or power.

The first step in reclaiming your self, will, and spirit in the system is to be aware of how the system forces are determining your behavior. Until you are aware of the system forces moving you, there is little freedom in how to be, see or act. This is why individual and group mindfulness is so important within family, organizational or corporate systems. Awareness is the important first ingredient of "stepping back," or disidentifying, from the system forces in order to re-establish your freedom to act.

But awareness is only the first step; while it is necessary, it is not sufficient. We've all had our own version of being aware of, and yet being unable to control, a personal weakness or situation. For example: You are aware that you hold a piece of chocolate in your hand, that this is the third piece, and you know that this much chocolate is not good for you, even as you put it into your mouth. Or, as a corporate employee, you are aware that the system is pressuring you to act in questionable ways, and you don't know what to do. You realize you are afraid of what will happen if you lose your job. It feels like you have no choice, but you know this can't be true.

The internal and external system pressures can be very powerful, so you also need to liberate your power–call it initiative or will–and muster the courage to use it. When you do, you will be *in* the system with your own power but not *of* the system, that is, you will not be controlled by it.

Individual Identification and Disidentification

In order to be in the system but not of it, we need to be able to disidentify from the system's pressures on us. Let's look at the terms identification and disidentification from three perspectives. The first is in your personal life. The second is what it means for an individual to be identified with, and to disidentify from, an organizational system or system of ideas. Finally, there are the degrees of freedom groups of individuals experience in what seem like totally oppressive situations like abusive families, concentration camps, or dictatorships.

> *Disidentification means . . . the cessation of taking something to be you, or to belong to you, or to define you.*[2] – A. H. Almaas, author, spiritual teacher, founder of the Diamond Approach

> *We are dominated by everything with which our self becomes identified. We can dominate and control everything from which we disidentify ourselves.*[3] – Roberto Assagioli, M.D.

Assagioli, whose theory of psychosynthesis I will refer to a number of times here, believed that every person has an essential self. This self is distinct from, and yet immersed in, the contents of one's conscious and unconscious mind. Assagioli believed that through careful introspection one can begin to experience oneself as a contentless "center of awareness and power"[4] which is capable of unifying and directing all the various aspects of the personality toward one's chosen goals or purpose. An important part of the process of psychosynthesis is to draw out the self and to free it from various limiting identifications with aspects of its personality. These identifications might be with certain roles we play like the father, boss, teacher; or certain parts of our personality (which he called subpersonalities) like the critic, the victim, the princess; or with aspects of our self such as our feelings, body, or mind.

The point of disidentifying from each of these is to enable self, our truest nature, to have access to all, not just some, of these aspects of the personality as the means for experiencing and expressing itself in the world.

As I was growing up in Kansas my family had the traditional Midwestern 1950's notion that boys should be strong and competent and not show any weakness. "Big boys don't cry," was an admonition I heard whenever I was physically or emotionally hurt and could not contain my feelings. This, coupled with the praise that I won for succeeding in school, winning awards, and generally over-achieving, led me to repress my feelings and become more and more involved in the life of the mind. "I am smart," I told myself with pride. "I" became synonymous with being smart. But being identified with only a part of myself eventually caused problems. When I didn't understand something in school – like trigonometry – I thought that there must be something wrong with me. "I" was no longer smart, or at least not as smart as I thought I was. Suddenly I would be afraid: "Who am I if I am not smart?" And because I had repressed my feelings, I didn't let myself feel my fear. Instead I tamped it down and became depressed, numb or withdrawn until my next achievement when "I" became smart again.

Of course, none of this was conscious to me at the time. That is part of the problem when you identify with something and are not aware of it. All the thoughts, feelings, points of view and actions flow from this identification without any realization that there might be other perspectives on life or alternatives for action.

Identifications are Natural and Can Either Serve or Limit

Being "a chip off the old block" when you are younger can serve you in that it helps you develop certain qualities of your parent and of adulthood that will prove useful later in life. But at some point being a chip off the old block becomes too limiting. It doesn't include all the parts of you that you are discovering. At some point, you have to become your own person in order to continue to grow and develop your full potential, which will naturally be different from your parent's. Similarly, being identified as a soldier, for example, forms a sense of brotherhood and camaraderie that can lead to one's real sense of safety and willingness to fight for and protect one's fellow soldiers and one's country. But if being so identified as a soldier means covering up atrocities like Mai Lai or Abu Gharib, so that "we" soldiers won't look bad, then one may be denying one's own values in order to uphold the code of honor of the Army.

What Identification Looks Like

One way to begin to recognize when you are identified with a particular part of your personality, or with a particular perspective, occurs when you feel like you don't have any choice, that your response is automatic and as if you are not in control. (And, in fact, you are not. This part that you are identified with is in control.) From this identified place, you cannot see creative alternatives for action. You feel stuck in one way of seeing the world, which is the "right" way. You don't understand how others could possibly see it any other way. Another way to tell when you might be identified or hooked in a particular role or position is when you feel defensive or ashamed or the need to prove that you are right. You can't let go or step back and look at your own behavior or allow that there might be something valid in the other's point of view. Psychologists Firman and Gila emphasize this aspect of identification when they say, "*Trapped in a particular identification, you can only make choices from within the perspective of that single part of you. If you are trapped in a constricted people-pleasing role, for example, you only make choices that are pleasing to others, and will perhaps have difficulty making choices to be candid, spontaneous, or self assertive.*"[5]

I began bumping into the limitations of my identification with my mind as I began being interested in girls. I could talk to them about school. I could joke and be witty with them. I could lust after them. However, there always came a time when they wanted to know how I "felt" about our relationship. Gulp. My response that, "I 'think' we have a good relationship," just didn't seem to cut it with them. "But how do you feel about me?" was the inevitable question I was asked. "I 'think' you are really nice," was my standard answer. I just didn't understand what they were looking for. There was a large part of myself between my head and my penis that I needed to discover. In order to do that I had to become aware of when I was thinking about things, step back or disidentify from those thoughts, and ask myself, "What am I feeling right now?"

Asking this, however, was very scary, for two reasons: first, I would ask the question and I wouldn't know what I was feeling. I'd look but I just wouldn't know. I couldn't find any feelings. Second, when I finally learned where to look in my body, I was overwhelmed by what I found: "I feel warm when I'm with you. I care about you and about whether you care about me. I am scared you might go away. I'm scared you might think I'm stupid or immature. I can't tell whether I like you or just want to have sex with you. This is so overwhelming! How does anyone live in this world? It makes me crazy. I can't think straight. Mr. Spock had it right, "Geometry is logical, Captain. Feelings aren't."

Exercises and Reflections

List some things you think you might be identified with, for example: your looks, intelligence, how much money you have, your artistic talents, strengths, weaknesses or fears, a local sports team, or your company, or country. Remember, identifications can be either 'positive' or 'negative.' Thinking, "I am dumb" can control you as much as thinking, "I am smart." Don't judge; just make a list and be aware of these aspects in your life. Can you look at them objectively? Which are the strongest and which are the easiest to step back from?

When one begins to disidentify, it isn't all roses. It opens you up to new parts or aspects of yourself and the new perspectives of these parts. Disidentifying means learning about these aspects of yourself and integrating them with the other parts you are already comfortable with.

It's a process, sometimes painful or chaotic at first, but when you are able to do it, more of your self is available from which to experience the world, plus you gain more agency and a wider variety of ways to express yourself.

The Process of Disidentification

Disidentification can happen in many ways. It can come through bumping into the same problem over and over again and using introspection to discover what identification might be limiting your perceptions or actions. It can also come naturally with different life stages that go smoothly. At some point you step back from being a care-free adolescent and realize that there is more to life than only having fun. You begin to grow up, become an adult and take on more responsibility for yourself and others.

Sometimes, however, disidentification is forced on you by life circumstances. For example, an accident forces you to step back from your unconscious identification with being able-bodied and you need to learn to incorporate limitations into your new sense of self. Or your spouse dies and suddenly you need to expand your sense of self and realize that you possess the ability to do much of what you were depending on him or her for. In each of these cases, you could stay identified with the original part and feel like the victim of circumstances. You could feel that, "I am no longer able-bodied. Now I can't do anything. I'm a helpless person. Life is cruel to do such a thing to me." Or you could eventually accept the new circumstances as givens, step back from the old identification, and ask, "What are my choices here? I've been dealt a blow where my wife has been taken from me. I am no longer a married man. I am single and alone. What choices do I have in this situation that would help make my life as good as possible?" Again, disidentification frees up the will and the ability to act.

The above are fairly significant examples of the process of disidentification that we go through as a natural process of development or that are thrust upon us. But the process of stepping back can be learned and practiced in our everyday interactions if we are able to recognize when we are identified. Some examples of signs that could alert you that you are identified might include:

- If you are overly stubborn in an argument, and angrier than the discussion might warrant, it could mean that you are identified with a part of you that needs to be right.
- If your stomach knots up and you are afraid to speak a divergent point of view in a meeting, it might mean you are identified with a scared little boy part.
- If you blurt out something that you've been feeling even though you've told yourself you weren't going to say it, it might mean there is a part of you that needs to be heard.

These are just a few examples of identifications with parts of yourself that might pop-up in particular interactions. It is possible to learn to notice these signs of identification with a part, and rather than acting from that part of yourself, you can step back and choose what you, not the part, want to do in the moment.

Exercises and Reflections

What are the signs for you that you might be identified with a part of yourself? Do you feel something in your body like muscle tightening or cheeks flushing? Do you have certain feelings or thoughts or the need to defend yourself? Do you talk faster or louder, or do you simply withdraw? Look for your particular clues that you might be identified with something. Being aware of these signs is the first step toward disidentification.

Individual Disidentification from a Human System or Ideology

Since a key step in reclaiming your sense of self and your power is to be able to step back from, be aware of, and not succumb to the pressures of the system, let's look at the experience of being identified with a group and its perspectives and what it means to disidentify from them.

My Awakening

One morning in 1965, early in my first semester at college, I awoke both literally and figuratively. I woke up, and while laying in bed and looking around my dorm room, I suddenly had the thought, "How did I get here?" This was an existential question, not a logistical one, and it was very disconcerting. As I began to think about it I realized that, in a certain way, I had been sleepwalking through my life and therefore following, without questioning why, a path of expectations that had been laid out for me by my family. I was expected to do well in grade school, be a Bar Mitzvah, achieve as a Boy Scout (my father was an Eagle Scout), and get A's in high school so that I could go to a good college. After graduation (with honors, of course) I would come home to participate in the family business, marry a nice Jewish girl and produce grandchildren.

"Whoa!" suddenly I saw it all so clearly—and I was right on track! I felt stupid for being so unaware and just blindly following along. And even my acts of rebellion, like choosing Brandeis University in Boston because it was the farthest away I could get from my home in Kansas, were still being made from within the system that was pushing me toward college. I had never even considered not going to college.

While I felt sad, angry at myself, and stupid, I also felt a great sense of liberation. Now I could ask myself: "What do *I* want to do? Do *I* want to even be in college?" "What do *I* want to study if I do stay here? Business? *I* don't know – but I do have a choice now!" and on and on. I remember walking around for days feeling both excited and troubled. There was so much to figure out, so many decisions to make, and so many opportunities to explore. Also, I realized that making my own decisions might not be so easy. I was responsible for my own life now. That was both exhilarating and scary. "I can do anything! But what if I don't choose the right thing? If I don't have to go into the family business, what *will* I do? What will my parents say?"

I didn't know how to explain this experience at the time. I see now that it was part of the process of disidentifying from my family system and becoming my own person. It is also a good example of what it means to be identified with, and then step back from, a system of which you are a part. When you are identified with a system:

- You are unaware of just how much of your behavior is being controlled by the pressures from the system and therefore, how little agency you have in your own life.
- You don't realize that your perspective of the world is being dictated by the system.
- Your sense of self is constricted or gets lost completely.

As you begin to disidentify from the system of which you are a part, and become *in* the system, but not *of* it:

- You become aware of system pressures and begin to have some choice in your life. You free up your will.
- Your sense of self broadens or fills out, e.g. "I am a member of my family, but I am also more than just a family member."
- Your perspective or worldview widens. You can see that there might be other viewpoints and you can see more possibilities for action.

Disidentification from an Even Larger System

At one of my college reunions, I spoke with a close friend, Rebecca, about the effect the exciting '60's had on us and whether we had learned anything from those times. She told me two stories that were very similar to my awakening.

In 1968 and 1969, during the Vietnam war, some of the bumper stickers we'd see, or the slogans that would be yelled at us as we protested against the war, were, "I'm an American and proud of it!" or "My country, right or wrong!" or "America: love it or leave it!" Rebecca told me that she never understood how people could believe what they were yelling. She felt ashamed of what America was doing in Vietnam. How could these people be so proud of it? "They were saying that they stood with their country even if it was wrong. That just sounded plain stupid to me," she said. Rebecca thought she had risen above being only a citizen of the United States and saw herself as a planetary citizen, capable of being objective about America and seeing it as just one of many countries in the world all deserving equal respect and scrutiny.

She said, "In some respect, I did step back from my identification with my country – a little, only not as much as I thought. I did have a slightly broader perspective than those who were even more identified with America. They needed to see it as always good and always right or they would somehow be flawed."

In thinking about it, Rebecca said she had the sudden realization that she, too, was actually identified with being an American. "Otherwise, why would *I* feel ashamed? It was the country doing these things in Vietnam, not me!" And the fact that she wanted to leave the United States so that she would not be associated with those atrocities showed just how identified she really was. "Maybe not as strongly as those I was calling 'stupid,' but I was still taking some of my identity from being an American just like they were." Rebecca's perspective of America and the world was affected by her identification. In that way, she was not unlike the flag wavers. "The fact that I was feeling ashamed of my country kept me from seeing the things that were good about it, just as they couldn't see what was bad about it." She told me that this was a real eye-opener for her about issues of identity, perspective and beliefs, and prepared her for what she experienced a few years later.

When Rebecca went to Europe for the first time in 1971, at the age of 24, she was confronted with how identified she still was with being an American and how that effected her view of the world. "First, I remember reading the *Boston Globe* on the flight to England and then buying a London paper on my way to the youth hostel. When I read the London paper reporting on some of the same stories I had read in the Boston paper I was shocked. How could the *London Times* get the facts so wrong?" After being in Europe for a month, and reading news in England, Holland, France, and Italy, it finally dawned on her just how American-centric her view of the world really was. "This was a real mind-expander." Unknowingly, Rebecca had taken a huge step back and was now able to look at the United States from the outside in and not just from the inside out. "From over there, I was able to see the U.S. as a whole entity, like a person with a personality. But, my sense of America's personality was definitely not how the Europeans were seeing *us!*" She was eventually able to let go of the defensiveness and was able to have "an amazing, new experience" of being able to love America and be critical of it as well. "America didn't have to be so extremely black or white to me anymore. It had good and bad qualities – just like me."

This example points out other limitations of being identified with a system of which you are a part:

- You are so "entranced" with your beliefs that you are not even aware that there are perspectives or values other than those of your system.
- You tend to see other perspectives as wrong, misguided, or dangerous. This perpetuates separation between systems or systems of thought.

- You become defensive, feeling the need to defend that which you are identified with.
- You blame other systems out of defensiveness, or as the source of your systems' conditions.

As you begin to step back and disidentify from these larger systems of which you are a part, there are multiple effects:

- You wake up to new worlds and new perspectives. It can even feel like veils have been lifted and you can see more clearly.
- You become able to look at your own system from outside without being defensive or self-blaming. You are able to see both the good and the bad.
- You experience and learn how to hold the cognitive dissonance, and therefore, the tension of multiple perspectives. This is difficult to do and not always comfortable.
- You stop labeling the "other" as wrong, bad, evil, or ignorant. You realize that others just have different perspectives and the objective becomes to understand, rather than to blame or disparage.

Exercises and Reflections:

Have you ever "woken up" and realized that you were behaving automatically? What was that like? If you look back, was there a trigger that helped wake you up?

Do you ever experience stepping out of a system – family, church, country, etc. – and being able to look at it more objectively? How were you able to step out of the system? What did you see? What did you learn?

Changing Perspectives as a Way of Disidentifying from a System

When I left the cult, it was made clear to me that I had failed at a life of service. I had let God down, and I was destined to end up penniless in the gutter and then in hell. I spent three months travelling, visiting friends who were never in the group, and reconnecting with my parents, all in an attempt to put the group experiences behind me. At the end of the three months, I returned to San Francisco determined to start my life anew, but was at a loss about where to begin. Depressed, I couldn't think straight.

One day I found myself sitting in my easy chair at dusk in a darkening room and realized that I had been sitting there all day. This scared me. I didn't realize just how depressed I was. When I started looking at this more closely, I saw that it was clearly about having left the group. What was paralyzing me as I tried to start my life over?

I realized that I had accepted as true the group's declaration that I had failed God. I had not been able to stay in the group and suffer through the difficulties required of God's servants. I was inadequate to the task and doomed to a life of meaningless work and existence. Even when I tried to think about it rationally, it looked like they were probably right in some ways. If I couldn't handle the difficulties of long hours, aloneness or looking honestly at my painful short-comings how was I ever going to join the Peace Corps, or work in a hospice or prison, or even teach psychology again?

Something deep inside of me, however, knew there was something wrong with this picture. I was stuck, but didn't know how to get unstuck. Then it occurred to me to use a technique we used often as therapists to help someone disidentify from a particularly rigid part. It involves taking a different perspective and looking back at that part. So I decided to look at my sorry self through God's eyes. I had been attributing all these things to God, but how was God really seeing me?

So I imagined that I was God looking at Mark sitting forlornly in his big chair. Two things happened almost immediately. As God, I felt an overwhelming sense of compassion for Mark, and my sense of humor instantly reappeared. God speaking to Mark: "*You poor, sad little puppy. Why are you being so hard on yourself? What kind of a God do you think I am? Do you think the omnipotent One would be silly enough to create a system where you only had one strike and you're out of the game? That if you screwed up trying to do good, I'd kick you out of the universe? First of all, there is no out of the universe to kick you to, and secondly, I need all the help I can get to make the world better. You get all the strikes and all the mistakes you need!*"

With that, I just burst out laughing and crying at the same time. Of course! What was I thinking? Suddenly everything looked different to me. By quite literally shifting my inner perspective to that of an imagined God,

I was able to disidentify from the group and its ideology that had been paralyzing me. I was able to reconnect to *my* "higher" or more inclusive values – including valuing *myself!*

And as my perspective shifted, so did my degrees of freedom of action. The paralysis lifted and I realized that there were people who had left the group before me whom I could call to discuss all of this. I did so immediately. I also remembered that some students thought I was a good teacher and that I had maintained a few connections at universities in the area. And on and on. . . I had finally been able to disidentify enough from the group to be able to regain my sense of self, my autonomy, and my agency in the world.

I was lucky. Cliff Baxter, one of the central figures in the Enron fraud case, was not. Shortly after Enron went bankrupt, he committed suicide. At the end of the documentary, *Enron: The Smartest Guys in the Room,* his colleagues pointed to his strong identification with the company when remembering him: "I think Cliff's suicide note tells it all, you know, 'where there was once great pride, now there is none. . . . a lot of who Cliff was was tied up in how he had succeeded at Enron. It is hard to look at your life's work and say, it's failed."

Exercises and Reflections

Have you ever had the experience of being able to change the perspective from which you were considering a problem? How were you able to change perspectives? Did you put yourself in someone else's shoes? Did you imagine looking at the problem from a different location, e.g. from above or further away?

What was it like to change perspectives? How did it feel? Did it open up different avenues for thinking or action?

Leaving a System as a Form of Disidentification

In the movie *The Truman Show,* the audience within the movie, as well as the viewers in the movie theater, cheered when Jim Carrey walked out of his fictitious, controlled world that was treating him like an object to be manipulated for others' entertainment. He had regained his will and his freedom. Sometimes leaving a system is a very effective way of disidentifying from its system forces and being able to see the system more clearly.

At the end of the Enron documentary, several of the senior managers commented on what they could see about the system from the outside that they couldn't see from the inside:

"But you have to take a long, cold look at yourself and say, who was I? Who did I become? And realize that you may have seen your shadow."

"Enron should not be viewed as an aberration, something that can't happen anywhere else, because it's all about the rationalization that you're not doing anything wrong. We've involved Arthur Andersen, we've involved the lawyers, the bankers know what we're doing. There's such a diffusion of responsibility, [but] everyone was on the bandwagon, and it can happen again."

"I think the largest lesson was what Enron asked of its employees, which was to ask why? And, you know, I didn't ask myself 'why' enough. I didn't ask managers 'why' enough. I didn't ask my colleagues 'why' enough."[6]

On the other hand, for me, even after leaving the system I was not able to disidentify from it. I was no longer in the system, but I still carried it with me and therefore I was still *of* the system. It took something external to me, something larger, to truly liberate me from the system forces of the cult.

Leaving as a form of disidentification or liberation from the pressures or abuse of the system is a very complex subject. I can't do justice to the topic in one chapter, but I would at least like to point out some of that complexity here.[7]

Whenever I teach about dysfunctional, power-over systems and how to change them into Life-affirming ones, the question inevitably arises, "Should I put effort into trying to change an abusive system or should I leave?" Or, someone will say, "I've tried and tried to change the system, but *they* just won't listen, so my only choice is to leave." Or, "The system is just too big. I have no power to change it, and I'm trapped. I can't leave because we need the income."

This points to one of the complexities of leaving a system as a way of escaping its abusive pressures: sometimes it is literally impossible to leave. How do you escape from a dictatorship when there are no passports and the borders are closed and patrolled? How do you abandon an abusive family when you are eleven years old? How do you exit the systems of racism, classism, homophobia, violence or poverty? Unfortunately, and ironically, in extremely dysfunctional systems some members feel like the only way out, the only way to be free from the oppressiveness of the system and to reclaim their autonomy, is through suicide. One only needs observe the high suicide rate among young homosexuals in this country, the extreme rate of suicides in the mega-factories in China, and the rising suicide numbers in our military as examples of this extreme.

These issues of feeling oppressed, trapped and helpless are ones that need to be addressed when looking at dysfunctional systems and how to disidentify from them. We should not be too quick to judge those who are wrestling with them, or too quick to encourage them to stay in the system or leave, because the situation seems so clear to us from outside the system. We need to remind ourselves that we do not understand or experience the system pressures they are under in their world.

There is a fine line between encouraging people to try new behaviors, or to explore what degrees of freedom they do have, and blaming them for not being able to act on their own behalf, that is, blaming the victims of abusive systems for the situations they are in. From one point of view, we always have some choice in, and responsibility for, our situations. But we also know that some systems, like those of poverty, racism or dictatorships are so engrained and powerful that they can overwhelm and paralyze the individuals within that system. The conscious and unconscious rules of such systems are also strongly stacked against the oppressed. The fact that some individuals can rise above the rules and the paralysis and reclaim their self and agency, doesn't discount the power of oppression in such a system.

"If I Can't Leave, What Choices are There for Regaining Some Sense of Self and Agency?"

When one of my coaching clients asks how to disidentify when he feels trapped in a system, I usually explore two paths. First, I question whether it is really true that he can't leave the system. Sometimes it is the system itself that convinces you that you can't leave, because it would disturb the system's balance and identity. In the cult I was part of, we convinced ourselves that we were the only group doing real service in the world and that everyone outside the group was bad. "Do you really want to go join those people?" was often the question posed to those of us on the verge of leaving. But I have also seen similar fears in embattled top executives in corporations and in women in abusive relationships. They need help from someone outside the system to step back just far enough to explore their true options, not only their scary imagined options.

Secondly, when it is true that the person can't leave a dysfunctional system for whatever reason, I often ask him to try a creative visualization exercise. I ask him to imagine standing outside the system and seeing himself in the system in order to look at what degree of freedom he does have individually and collectively with others. I might say something like: "Look from the outside at Samuel in this system. Yes, in most ways Samuel is a victim. But what if that is not all of who he is? He believes he has absolutely no choices. Looking from the outside, are there any choices he does have in this situation that he just doesn't see? If he got really creative, what options might he come up with?"

Disidentification, Self and Agency in Extreme Situations

The following stories about the Nazi concentration camps and the U.S. Japanese internment camps are included as examples of what can be done in even the most extreme situations. Not only are they inspirational; they demonstrate disidentification as well as some of the other behaviors that I will be discussing later in the book. These examples demonstrate the human possibilities of reclaiming self and agency by disidentifying from the system pressures in extremely oppressive situations.

> *The experiences of camp life show that man does have a choice of action. There were enough examples, often of a heroic nature, which proved that apathy could be overcome, irritability suppressed. Man can preserve a vestige of spiritual freedom, of independence of mind, even in such terrible conditions of psychic and physical stress.*[8]
>
> VICTOR FRANKL

Victor Frankl was a Viennese psychiatrist who spent a total of three years in four different concentration camps, including Auschwitz. The Nazis murdered his wife, parents and brother. Out of his own suffering and that of his fellow prisoners, he was able to develop a coherent theory of psychology and psychotherapy called Logotherapy. Frankl believed that what kept him and others from giving up in the camps and, ultimately helped them survive, was a belief that life had a sense of meaning or purpose "beyond," or in spite of, their current horrendous situation.

The meaning that he speaks of is unique for each person, and comes out of what that person feels he or she is being called to do or be in life. It is a purpose that is a response to something beyond themselves and the system of which they are a part:

> *This experiential evidence* [from the camps] *confirms the survival value of "the will to meaning" and of self-transcendence – the reaching out beyond ourselves for something other than ourselves. Under the same conditions, those who were oriented toward the future, toward a meaning that waited to be fulfilled – these persons were more likely to survive.*[9]

The people in the camps *were* victims. They were trapped in the most abusive and objectifying of systems, and yet it was this sense of meaning that allowed them not to be *of* the system and to hold onto their humanity, values and a semblance of autonomy.

There are many stories from the concentration camps of people coming together to resist the system's attempt to destroy their humanity, spirit, creativity and the will to live. They formed schools, choirs, orchestras, and infirmaries. They did all that they could to maintain human relationships and not allow the system to disconnect them from each other.

The same triumph of self and agency was true in the Japanese internment camps within the United States. In 1942, President Roosevelt ordered the forced removal of 120,000 Japanese to 10 internment camps in the U.S. This was 90% of the ethnic Japanese population, two-thirds of whom were American citizens.[10]

Delphine Hirasuna, whose parents were interned in one of these camps, published a book in 2005 called, *The Art of Gaman: Arts and Crafts from the Japanese American Internment Camps 1942–1946*.[11] In it she chronicles, in pictures and in words, the works of art and craft that helped the prisoners survive their hostile conditions. She translates the Japanese word *gaman* as "to bear the seemingly unbearable with patience and dignity."[12]

American Craft magazine published an interview with Hirasuna by Julie Hanus, in which she echoes many of the themes and scenes that Victor Frankl described from his own experiences in the German concentration camps.

"In the past when people wrote about the camps, it was all about the imprisonment; they wrote about people as victims. . . What The Art of Gaman *did. . .was that it showed the resilience these people had and the dignity with which they conducted themselves. It recognizes the internees as people with personalities, with skills, with hope."*[13]

In other words, they refused to let the system of the camps oppress their creativity and they made objects of beauty in order not to be objectified themselves and lose their humanity.

Hirasuna expected that men and women who were already artists before they were brought to the camps would have created much of the art and craft she uncovered.

What I wasn't prepared for was the average person and what they created. And that they created these objects out of found materials, out of scrap. Oftentimes they had to forge their own tools. When people first went into camp, they couldn't take any metal objects, so they would sharpen butter knives and melt down scrap metal to hammer out tools. They would crush glass and glue it onto paper to make sandpaper. . . [Some of them, like many of the carvers,] had no formal training, and when they got out of the camp they never carved again.[14]

Carvings from scrap lumber by Akira Oye who was interned at Rohwer, AR.

Creativity and beauty was in constant tension with the horrors of the camps, and served as a way of helping the internees to separate themselves from their conditions. The act of making, and the beauty of the results, lifted their spirits and helped them step back and see themselves as more than mere victims or prisoners. It reminded them that Life was more than just what was being imposed on them in the camps. It affirmed their agency and autonomy. Hirasuna:

> *Someone told me a story about how there was one camp where the women formed a suicide watch. In all of the camps, people got depressed; suicides were above normal. When these women heard that someone was depressed, they would find something of beauty and take it to that person. So making art and sharing beautiful and well – crafted things became a way to give emotional strength. What that says about the role of arts and crafts in bolstering the spirit is pretty powerful.*[15]

Carved birds from scrap wood by Himeko Fukuhara interned at Amache, CO, and Kazuko Matsumoto interned at Gila River, AZ..

CHAPTER TEN

POWER: THE EXPRESSION
OF SELF IN THE SYSTEM

. . . you are a unique, never-to-be-repeated event. Your parents could make love a million times and never again reproduce the same genetic pattern. You are the only chance this planet has for your unique contribution. Will others' expectations, rules and roles be your focus? Will you be only what others think you should be? Or will you occur?[1]

GEORGE SHEEHAN, physician/author

I've sometimes said that when we pray to God we acknowledge our dependence on some force bigger than us and that when we actually change and grow we're acknowledging God's dependence on us. The life force in the universe may need us in some way to keep growing as much as we need it.[2]

ROBERT KEGAN, psychologist

Becoming Subject in Our Lives

Dysfunctional systems treat their members as objects to be used to meet system goals. One of the ways to create Life-affirming systems is by not allowing yourself to be treated as an object nor to objectify others. This means becoming subject to your own life and helping others do the same. This is one of the first steps in over-coming the disempowering, self-denying aspects of dysfunctional systems.

Being subject in one's life means standing at the center of one's being and realizing that you have volition and are causal. It means realizing the power you hold to shape your own life and its direction and accepting the responsibility for that power, as well as for the direction of the systems you inhabit. This does not mean that you have total control over your life. This does not mean that you caused everything in your life – your cancer, your divorce or your child who is acting out. As we have seen, within a system there are multiple causes and effects. What you do have is a choice about how you deal with the "what-is-ness" of your life, that is, how you respond to those conditions which life presents to you.

As you begin to recognize the power that system pressures hold over you, that awareness allows you to begin to disidentify from those pressures and to reclaim your self, thereby liberating your autonomy and volition, namely your power. Roberto Assagioli was one of the first to talk about disidentification. He talks about three stages in the process of disidentification:

> *The first [stage] is the recognition that the will [power] exists; the second concerns the realization of having a will. The third phase . . . is that of being a will (this is different from having a will). He perceives that he is a "living subject" endowed with the power to choose, to relate, to bring about changes in his own personality, in others, in circumstances.*[3]

Rather than being controlled by the system, a person who has disidentified from it realizes that he/she is in the system but not of the system. As the examples in the last chapter demonstrate, at that point one has some personal choice even in those systems that are most dysfunctional or oppressive.

But what does it mean to reclaim our self and liberate our personal power? To have power in the conventional understanding usually means the ability to make happen what *I* want to have happen, or having power *over* someone or some thing. But as we have seen, wielding power over someone turns that human being into an object while at the same time objectifying oneself. To exercise this type of power just reinforces the dysfunctionality of the systems you are trying to change.

So let's look at what I mean by power and why it is crucial if you are to create Life-affirming systems.

The Incredible Persistence of Life

"Just to be is a blessing. Just to live is holy."

ABRAHAM JOSHUA HESCHEL

To understand what I mean by "power," and to clarify the context for the rest of what follows in Part Two, I will make a brief side-trip to consider Life, the largest Whole that we inhabit.[4] I believe that Life is the source of our true power.

Although there might be difficulty in definitively answering the question "What is Life?" it is possible to abstract some of its principles or qualities. I want to highlight a few qualities of Life, such as vitality, creativity and diversity, to name a few, that I consider relevant to creating more Life-affirming systems.

Below is an exercise I do in my classes to give my students an experiential (not just cognitive) sense of what I mean when I talk about Life and being and power. I encourage you to read the exercise slowly while trying to experience it at the same time. An alternative would be to read the exercise through once and then sit quietly and try to take yourself through the experience.

Life: A Guided Imagery Exercise

Sit quietly and focus on the rising and falling of your breath for several breaths

- Recognize that you are not making yourself breathe. Your breath keeps rising and falling even when you are not focusing on it. The same is true for your heart. It keeps beating and pumping blood through your system without your effort or awareness.
- You are a living being. Life is flowing in you, through you. Usually we are not paying much attention to this fact. Like our breath and our heartbeat, we take it for granted.

- I'd like you to pay attention for a moment to the experience of being alive, of being a living being – whatever that means to you.
- What is that like? Take your time to notice how you experience this?
- Try not to qualify it as good or bad, weak or strong, happy or sad. See if you can focus on that which you would call "life" in you. Take all the time you need to feel into your sense of what you would call "life."
- Now I'd like you to expand your awareness outward a little bit to include the room you are in and become aware of any other living beings sitting with you. Life is present in each being and in all of us.
- Imagine your family and friends or people that you work with and see if you can become aware of the aliveness that is in all of them. Become aware of that which is moving in and through you and through all people.
- Now expand your awareness outside of this room to include ALL living beings: people, trees, grass, flowers, animals, insects, fish, and on and on.
- Become aware of Life pushing ever outward and manifesting itself in an amazing diversity of living beings. And Life is present in every one of them. Not just different species, but the diversity even within the species ... the number of different kinds of birds, or butterflies, or flowers, or people. And there is something that is Life in every one of them and in all of them collectively.
- Take your time to experience what this is like for you.
- Now I'd like you to expand your awareness even more to take in the aspect of time. This process, this force that we call Life has been going on for millions and millions and millions of years – and will continue to go on well into the future in some form, long after this current configuration of living beings is gone.
- Try to get a sense, an experience of Life that flows through all of these beings and across all of this time. Sit with this experience for a few moments.
- Now, once again, slowly bring your awareness back to your own body, in this chair, in this room. Once again let yourself experience Life in you, right here, right now.

When you are ready, open your eyes and make some notes about the experience you just had. Take a moment and think back to where you started in the exercise and where you "went." Make a few notes about any words or phrases or images that came to you as you did the visualization. If you want, draw these images or write these phrases on a bookmark that you can refer to as you continue reading this chapter.

My experiences and insights from doing this "What is Life" exercise for myself follow. See if they fit with your experience, or how they might differ, or how you might elaborate on them.

When I go inside and contact the experience of being alive, of being a life, it is an experience of tingling, pulsing, energy. Separate from any qualities of happiness, sadness, low or high energy, weakness or strength, there is a sense of something in me that is the energy of life. Some have called it *élan vital* or life force; others have referred to it as energy or spirit or soul. I experience it as something moving or flowing in and through me. It seems that as Life flows through me, I give it substance or shape by the unique way I express it through who I am. I give it a particular color, like light flowing through a tinted lens, or a particular note, like breath flowing through a flute. When I am in this experience, this unique note, color, or shape feels like my expression of Life and my most fundamental reason for being alive. It is my contribution to the Largest Whole. If I do not come into being and express it, that color will not be in the palette or that note will not be in the symphony. The picture will still be painted, the symphony played, but not as fully nor as brilliantly as could have been possible. The yogi, Radhakrishnan says, "*The peculiar privilege of the human self is that he can consciously join and work for the whole and embody in his own life the purpose of the whole . . .*"[5] (See the Appendix, page 303, for an exercise designed to help you experience what your own note or color might be.)

When I imagine my personal expression flowing outward, adding to and complementing the expression of others, I see Life growing, merging as well as diversifying, and becoming ever more complex as it moves onward through time. In my imagination, when I try to grasp this sense of the totality of Life, it seems as if it is one "entity" or source that is infusing and energizing all living beings. I am also struck by the power and incredible *persistence* of this energy of Life. The small weed that pushes its way through concrete, the seed that sprouts in a bare rocky outcropping, or the heart that keeps on beating when all other systems have failed, are to me, manifestations of this persistence of Life. As we mature, we understand that individual living beings, including ourself, may die, but that Life in this larger sense goes on.

When I try to understand what people who talk about evolution mean, I see it as this larger Whole of Life that is evolving, flowing forward or outward from this source, along many dimensions of quantity, quality, diversity and consciousness.

On the larger scale of evolutionary time, Life also seems to persist and flow on with force. This path of evolution has been compared to tree roots branching, multiplying and spreading out as they push further down into the earth. If the roots hit a rock they grow around it. If the roots hit a whole ledge, other roots spread out further where they can. When Life meets an Ice Age, whole species are destroyed, but somehow Life adapts and pushes on with even greater complexity and diversity. As Nietzsche writes in *Thus Spake Zarathustra*, "Life herself spoke unto me: 'Behold, I am that which must ever surpass itself.'"[6]

The Elegant Power of Simply Being

The source of personal power is this force of Life expressing itself through you. Being powerful, as I am defining it here, means being authentic. It is the *power of* being fully who we are, our fullest expression of Life, at any given moment, in the world. "Becoming more powerful" then refers to the ongoing process of uncovering, developing, and sharing more and more of our unique expression of Life over time. Power is the inner drive toward what Abraham Maslow called "self-actualization,"[7] or what Adam Kahane in his wonderful book, *Power and Love: a theory and practice of social change*, calls ". . . *the drive to achieve one's purpose, to get one's job done, to grow.*"[8] Power is, as my friend Tom Yeomans says, "informing the world with your being."[9]

Martha Graham, the dancer and choreographer, beautifully describes this force flowing through us:

> There is a vitality, a life force, an energy, a quickening that is translated through you into action, and because there is only one of you in all of time, this expression is unique. And if you block it, it will never exist through any other medium and it will be lost. The world will not have it. It is not your business to determine how good it is nor how valuable nor how it compares with other expressions. It is your business to keep it yours clearly and directly, to keep the channel open.[10]

Exercises and reflections

- Think about those times when you felt most alive. What was that like? What did you do to contribute to that happening? What are your words for that experience? For example: "I was in the flow or the zone," or "Everything happened effortlessly as if I was being helped along," or "I felt overjoyed, or blessed."

- Not all times of aliveness are happy. Sometimes you feel closest to the Life within when you are in the presence of death. Think about times of sadness or loss or fear when you've also felt alive. What was that like? What are your words for that experience? What did you do that helped you to experience Life flowing through you in those moments?

Power to Do and Power of Being

To actualize means to act, to do in the world. But while power does relate to *acting* and *doing*, there is a distinction between *the power **to*** and *the power **of***. Power ***of*** is the power of *being* that flows through you while you are expressing yourself in the world. You may not achieve your goal but you always have the power that comes from the wholeness of your being.

We've all met people that exude strength just in their being. They don't need to be doing anything. These people are described as people of substance. This is what I mean by the *power of* one's being. It is the strength that comes from standing securely in yourself and recognizing that you are subject in your life.

> "There is no need to run outside
> For better seeing,
> Nor to peer from a window. Rather abide
> At the center of your being;
> For the more you leave it, the less you learn.
> Search your heart and see
> If he is wise who takes each turn:
> The way to do is to be."
>
> LAO TZU[11]

Yet power, in the way that I am defining it, is not passive. Reconnecting with your power might include sitting on a cushion, meditating, and simply being. This may be a necessary practice because it helps you to be mindful of when you are identifying with partial aspects of your self and need to step back into a fuller sense of yourself and Life. But power requires some form of expression of who you are in the world. That expression, however, does not necessarily mean creating something or making something happen. You might be expressing who you are by remaining calm and quiet as you stand in the power of your being in the midst of verbal assault from another, and that is not being passive. The power of being is expressive in that it is always *in relationship* to others, to the events in your life, and to the systems of which you are a part.

Self-awareness and Presence

Another way to describe the power of being is to say that a person has presence. The person is right there with you, present in the moment, attending to you or to what needs to be done. The outcome of what he is doing is not nearly as striking as his being-ness while he is doing it. It might be someone delivering a speech who is deeply authentic in sharing her experiences while also being able to meaningfully connect her personal story to the audience's lives. You might notice presence in a co-worker who is focused on solving a specific problem rather than on making someone bad or herself important; or in a child who is fully immersed in the pure joy of singing a song.

In order to be present, with the power of your being, you need self-awareness. You need to know yourself well enough to know when you are not all there and how to refocus in the moment. Self-awareness is a form of mindfulness about self. Are you present and in relationship with what is in front of you *right now* – whether that is writing a book, running a business meeting, protesting an injustice, or giving your child a bath? How present you are, to a large extent, determines how clear a channel you can be for Life's energy to flow through you in that moment.[12] Self-awareness is necessary to realize what is required to liberate more of your power and to be an even better channel for Life. Self-awareness also allows you to discern when you are up against an internal, rather than external, obstacle that is keeping you from expressing your power.

Then, as you liberate more and more of the power of your being, self-awareness and mindfulness also help you observe and learn from the effects and consequences of the expression of that power. Power without self-awareness and mindfulness of others can easily become power *over*, that is, hurtful and oppressive. Self-awareness allows you to express who you are, observe the consequences, and learn how to do it better next time. Owning your power is an ongoing process.

Exercises and reflections

- Do you know anyone who you would describe as "having substance" or "presence"? What is it about that person that makes you think this? Is it because of what they do, or because of who they are – or both?
- Have you had the experience of standing in the power of your being – of being the fullest 'you' that you can be? What was that like? What would your words for this experience be?
- Think about times when you have been fully present. What was your internal experience of presence like? How did other people respond?
- The next time you are in a conversation with someone, try to remember to notice if you are present or not. Are you thinking about other things, like what you are going to say next or do next? Are you attending to that person? If not, what do you need to do to bring yourself back to being present?

Why is Expressing the Power of Your Being So Important?

Expressing the power of your being is not just for your own growth and development. It is also for the sake of the larger systems of which you are a part. A healthy, Life-affirming system is one that nurtures the expression of the power of its members, but the system also receives something in return.

The system needs its constituents to be expressing the power of their being as fully as possible for several reasons. First, when the power of its members' purposes is aligned with the direction of the whole, the system has the maximum energy of Life available to it to fulfill *its* purpose.

Second, the healthy system relies on the expression of the power of its members as a form of feedback to learn about itself. When members are fully expressing themselves, information – the system's lifeblood – is made available to it. The system then learns such things as what resources it has available for its purpose and where the obstacles are to the effective and efficient implementation of that purpose. For instance, are workers getting the tools, resources and support they need? It is often the workers on the front lines who first recognize problems in the system. If they are not expressing themselves or are not being heard, the system loses important data. The system also learns whether its purpose, or its structures or processes, need to adapt because they are no longer meeting the needs of its members. As a teenager starts to establish his own identity and express the power of his being, maybe in unexpected ways, that is information that the parents and the whole family system can use to understand the teenager's unfolding direction and how the family system might have to adapt to incorporate his needs and purpose.

Third, when the system learns from its members' expression of their power – their creativity, their thoughts and feelings – the system itself grows and evolves into a fuller expression of all that it can be. The more the people fully express who they are, the more the whole fully emerges out of those parts. In this way, the power of the individuals and the power of the system mutually reinforce each other's development. When you study the emergence and evolution of a musical group like the Beatles, for instance, you can see that as each member shared more of himself, either through his playing or songwriting or both, the fullness of the group's potential emerged more and more.

And fourth, when you express yourself fully, you are re-humanizing the system by overcoming the dysfunctional pressures of objectification. Expressing yourself, individually and collectively with others, makes you the subject in your life and restores to the system the aliveness, the energy, and the creativity that flows through your unique being.

Re-humanizing the dysfunctional system, by refusing to let the system objectify you or cause you to objectify others, is one of the first steps of the change process. You don't do this by changing the system so that you can express yourself. Instead, you express yourself authentically so that you can change the system. When you express yourself as fully and as authentically as possible, you remind yourself, other members of the system, and the system as a whole that you are human beings and that you have purpose as an expression of Life. This helps you to further step back from the myopic and egocentric vision of the particular system and remember that you, individually and collectively, are part of an even larger Whole.

The Individual and *Life*

> *I live on Earth at present, and I don't know what I am. I know that I am not a category. I am not a thing – a noun. I seem to be a verb, an evolutionary process – an integral function of the universe.*
>
> BUCKMINSTER FULLER[13]

This leads to the final reason why it is important to express your fullness in the world. When you express the power of your being, you are doing so for the largest Whole, which is Life. As Abraham Heschel beautifully puts it: "The souls of men are the candles of the Lord, lit on the cosmic way, . . . and every soul is indispensable to Him. Man is needed, he is a need of God."[14]

Life, or the universe, or God needing us as much as we need it might be discounted as a rather abstract or spiritual belief that cannot be proved and has no practical value. I believe otherwise. At those moments when you remember that, as a human being, you are participating in a whole that is larger than just our manmade systems, you also (re-) experience that that Whole of Life is holding and influencing you as well. As systems thinker and Buddhist, Joanna Macy says, "*To see the universe [as] both embracing and transcending our separate selves, is of the nature of a religious perception and one in which we might find benediction. It means that we subsist in an overarching pattern of relationships, integral to our nature and 'out of which we cannot fall'*"[15]

This Largest Whole, contains information, resources, and Life-energy that we are able to draw upon, especially at those times when we most need courage to deal with the dysfunctional systems of which we are a part.

In the last chapter we touched on the examples of how individuals in the German concentration camps and the American Japanese internment camps drew on something "higher" or "larger" to be creative and survive in intolerable situations. This was also true for both Mahatma Gandhi and Martin Luther King. Both men drew on these higher forces in their struggle to overcome oppressive systems. Gandhi drew strength from what he called *satyagraha*: "Its root meaning is holding on to truth, hence truth-force. I have also called it Love-force or Soul-force."[16] Dr. King often invoked scripture and encouraged his followers to draw strength from God in the midst of their struggles, "if the inexpressible cruelties of slavery could not stop us, the opposition we now face will surely fail. We will win our freedom because the sacred heritage of our nation and the eternal will of God are embodied in our echoing demands."[17]

Purpose: the Power of Being in Healthy, Life-affirming Systems

In a healthy, multi-level system, Life – the "power of being" – flows in all directions, from the whole system to its component parts, from the parts to the whole, and among all of the parts.

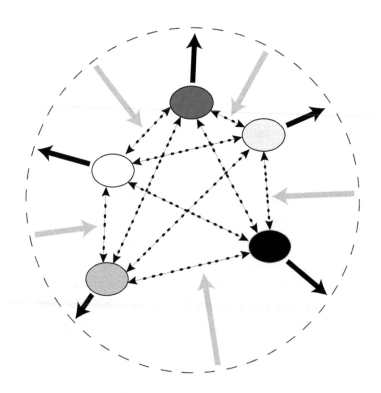

A healthy system is one in which an essential aspect of its purpose is to learn and grow as a vehicle for the expression of Life. In addition to its stated goals, such as raising children or benefitting shareholders or feeding the poor, the healthy system also considers other aspects of its purpose, such as:

- Why are we pursuing this particular goal? What is the meaning of what we are doing here?
- How can we fulfill this purpose in such a way that also energizes individual members and the relationships among our members?
- How can we help our members fulfill their individual purpose as they are fulfilling the purpose of the system?

This can be seen as the real *power of the system*, the drive to actualize its purpose as an expression of Life.

As a consultant, I was facilitating a meeting where representatives from a pharmaceutical company were developing a mission and purpose statement. When I asked them, "So what is it that you do?" the first statement was, "We make drugs to treat asthma, stomach ulcers, cancer and related illnesses." There was not much energy in the room after that response. When I asked, "Why do you do this?" there were puzzled looks on many faces.

"In order to give our shareholders a good return on their investment," someone said.

"That's not why I do it. I do it because it is a real challenge." This comment seemed to make people think more deeply about their motivations:

"I do it because my mother died from asthma."

"I agree, these are serious diseases. We are saving peoples' lives."

"And giving them a better quality of life while they are alive."

Suddenly the room became energized as they began discussing what I would call the larger purpose of their work. Yes, on the level of the medical and financial systems their purpose was to develop drugs and to give shareholders a significant return on their investment. But those systems are parts of an even larger whole of Life. They were beginning to talk about how their more concrete goals fit within a larger purpose. This was very exciting to them and brought aliveness back into the room.*

A Life-affirming system creates space for the discussion of its purpose and opportunities for its members to choose whether and how to align their purpose and the power of their being with the purpose and power of the system. When that alignment happens, Life flows through such a system in amazingly energetic and creative ways.

You can see this attitude of working for something larger in companies such as Google, Apple and Patagonia. You can also see this in government programs or non-profits, such as the Peace Corps, City Year, or Teach for America, where the mission is clear and the people have chosen to be there because the program's purpose aligns with their own.

If a system is healthy, one component of its purpose will always be to intentionally support the *power of being* of its members. The healthy system recognizes that it is most alive and the best possible channel for Life when its component members are being all they can be. (See Chapter Four, page 84.)

For example, in a healthy family the children are each recognized as unique beings, different from each other and their parents. Each is accepted for who she/he is without pressure to be, for instance, more outgoing or to be more like the parents or an older brother or sister. Everyone, children and parents, are encouraged to develop who they are fully within the safely structured and nurturing family system. If mom feels the need to return to school or take a dance class, she is encouraged to do so and the family as a whole will look at what it needs to do to adapt to this new situation in order to support her growth. By including the children in the discussion, a) they feel a part of the system, b) they understand that mom's decision will affect them, and c) they learn that there may be new expectations of them, or new family rules or structures to support mom's decision. They might not get a vote about whether mom goes back to school, but they will be members of the system who will need to find ways to adapt to her growth.

A healthy system is a safe container in which to experiment with the expression of who you are because the structures and rules and decision-making processes of the system are as clear as possible to all. It is also safe

---

* *Of course most of us have also had experiences of companies with lofty 'higher' espoused purposes who do not express that purpose in action.*

because when any member's being-ness-in-the-moment collides with the boundary of the container or with another's being-ness, everyone looks at his or her responsibility in that collision. Each member also asks, "What can I and what can we learn from this? Do I need to develop some quality or learn to adapt to the behaviors of others? Does the system need to grow and adapt? Or both?"

And if the mother goes back to school and is overwhelmed with all her responsibilities, becomes irritable, and wants to quit, the family is willing to look at this dilemma together. The mother is willing to look at whether, given the conditions of the family and her abilities, a full course load at school is appropriate. But the other members of the family are also willing to look at whether they encouraged her and said they would support her but didn't actually deliver on that support. Were they sharing the cooking and cleaning and running their own errands? Did they help her with her homework? Do they really respect her desire to be in school and grow?

In a healthy, multi-level, hierarchical system such as a business, the power of flows up and down the hierarchy as well as among individuals at the same level. The CEO is being as authentic as possible within the system. She is learning and growing by receiving feedback about her behaviors, decisions, and directives from those at all levels.

She also recognizes the unique power of individual members and tries to create opportunities for the expression and development of that uniqueness. In Barry Oshry's words, leaders in a healthy system "create games worth playing,"[18] – giving people opportunities to use their uniqueness and grow rather than assigning them dull, repetitive and meaningless tasks. I once consulted to a company that gave each customer service representative the power to satisfy a customer's complaint in whatever way they deemed appropriate. The company allocated up to $500 for the representative to do so without getting a supervisor's approval. The customer service representatives felt respected and empowered and did a phenomenal job of passing that respect and caring on to the customers.

Also, in a healthy system, the individual members recognize the value of diversity and the power of individual uniqueness. Members draw on each other's strengths to balance their own weaknesses without belittling themselves or others. Members are willing to learn from each other's uniqueness as well.

And in a healthy system, members are willing to speak the power of their truth or experience to each other as well as to the leaders. They are willing to give feedback to, and receive feedback from each other in a way that holds each responsible for her behavior and performance without impugning her being and judging who she is. And because it is a healthy system that is trying to promote the expression of Life, the feedback is delivered within the spirit of promoting the growth and development of the individual and the system. The feedback is given in a way that *increases* the *power of* the other and the system, rather than diminishing it.

Why is the Power of Being So Hard to Express?

If so much good comes out of the expression of who you are, both for yourself and the systems you live in, why is it so hard to do? Sometimes it seems like there are so many internal and external obstacles to the expression of one's fullness that it is too overwhelming to even try.

In the next chapter we will look at what it takes to have the courage to be fully who you are in spite of those obstacles.

CHAPTER ELEVEN

COURAGE: EXPRESSING POWER *OF* AND POWER *WITH*

When we walk to the edge of all the light we have and take that step into the darkness of the unknown, we must believe that one of two things will happen: there will be something solid for us to stand on, or we will be taught how to fly.[1]

PATRICK OVERTON

In a society based on power-over, that work (of drawing out the power-within) must inevitably result in conflict with the forces of domination, for we cannot bear our own true fruit when we are under another's control . . . Given a world based on power-over, we must remake the world.[2]

STARHAWK

Why is it so hard for some of us to express our power in the world, to be authentically ourselves at any given moment? In this chapter we will talk about some of the internal and external systemic obstacles that get in the way of fully sharing who we are with the world.

Internal Obstacles to the Expression of One's Power

Roberto Assagioli's Psychosynthesis and Richard Schwartz's Internal Family Systems Theory,[3] as well as other areas of psychology, recognize the internal multiplicity of parts of ourselves and the interaction between these parts.

Most of us are familiar with the many "voices" inside our head that argue over decisions we have to make: Do I or don't I? Why or why not? Should I order broccoli or French fries?

Assagioli talked about these parts of ourselves as subpersonalities, with their own qualities, needs, wants and fears. Each subpersonality originally developed to help us cope with aspects of life in our formative years. For instance, my macho man part helped protect my more vulnerable feelings in a family where big boys aren't supposed to cry. The problem was that whenever I felt vulnerable, Macho Man took control of my personality, helped me suppress my feelings, and started running the show. But as I matured and wanted my feelings to be more present, the Macho Man came into conflict with my vulnerable little kid subpersonality (which had been in hiding all of these years) about whether it was safe to show those feelings.

According to Assagioli, part of the process of psychosynthesis is to integrate all of these various subpersonalities around a strong central self, or "I." This "I," which has awareness and will, can choose to use the qualities of these parts in the expression of that self. One of the reasons for working on this synthesis is to be a better, more full expression of what Assagioli called the universal Self, or what I am calling Life.

It is fairly easy to see how these subpersonalities, with their own alliances, oppositions and mutual influence relationships, form an internal system of forces that exerts pressure on you to behave in certain ways. Just as you are able to learn to disidentify from external systemic pressures in order to regain more autonomy and agency, you can also learn to step back from these internal systemic forces. The more you are able to step back, the more you experience your core self and the awareness and will that are inherent in it. In other words, the more you are able to disidentify from the various aspects of your personality that control you, the more you are able to step into the power *of* your being. And the more you stand in this inner power, the more able you are to orchestrate the various aspects of your personality to express the uniqueness of who you are and, therefore, your fullest expression of Life.

In Part One of the book we talked about some of the system pressures that objectify us and cut us off from our power or that separate us and cut us off from our love. There are very real outside pressures that keep us from expressing the fullness of our being. But there are also very real inside pressures doing the same. As you will see later in the chapter, there is a resonance between these inside and outside pressures. That is why it is necessary to be mindful of which is which so that you don't blame the system for things that you need to change in yourself, or try to alter yourself when it's actually the system that requires changing. Usually it is a combination of both. To be a fuller expression of Life often calls for both internal and external changes.

Exercises and reflections

Subpersonalities can inhibit the expression of love as well as power. While you are reading this section, ask yourself: "What subpersonalities do I have that might be getting in the way of my expressing my power or my love fully?" If something comes to mind, make notes about it while it is fresh.

The Behavior of My Inner Circus in Dysfunctional Systems

A few of my subpersonalities that I have encountered as I have tried to express more of my power in the world are: "Mr. Competence," my "I'm-the Rock-to-Lean-on," my "Critic/Perfectionist," my "Inadequate One," and "Mr. Nice Guy." In my experience, many of these inner parts seem to be fairly common. Let's look at a few of these internal parts and how they effect my expression of power.

The Critic. This voice tells me I am not good enough, and I have to be perfect before I can show who I am. This part tells me that I can't say what's on my mind in a meeting because it might not be right, or that I can't point out a problem unless I know how to fix it. This is also the part that tells me that the woodturning or piece of furniture I've built isn't good enough to share with others.

When I am in a dysfunctional system with a lot of pressure for very high standards of performance, and where there is strong blame when people don't meet those standards, my Critic gets very energized. He is hypervigilant and watches everything that I do to make sure that it is good enough to avoid blame or humiliation. He is always trying to figure out what my boss or my peers want so I won't be criticized. The Critic keeps me from considering what I think is right to do or what I want to express because it is afraid I might attract the wrong kind of attention to myself.

So I end up expressing or doing what I think others want rather than what I want. What I want is actually an aspect of who I really am and would be useful information for the system. However, I get lost in the system. "Who am I, what do I want, and what do I have to offer?" are not questions I consider when my critic is running the show.

The Inadequate One. Sometimes I refer to this subpersonality as my "little boy" part. Essentially he believes what the Critic is telling him, which is, "You're not good enough and nothing you do is ever good enough. You should do better and improve yourself. You're incompetent." Under this kind of internal pressure, the Inadequate One tells himself, "I can't express what I think and feel. It's too impossible. Everyone can do it better than I can. I should go away." In high pressure or highly critical and blaming systems, the Inadequate One gets energized, and I try to hide and not be visible at all.

Mr. Nice Guy. This is the part that developed in early childhood to cope with the anger and abuse that was in my family and at my schools. Mr. Nice Guy says, in reaction to these power *over* environments, "If this is what power looks like, I had better sit on mine so that I don't hurt others like I am being hurt." Mr. Nice Guy is the accommodator who says, "I don't care; whatever you want is okay with me." When people see from the outside that I am feeling something or seem upset and ask, "What's going on for you?" Mr. Nice Guy says, "Me? Nothing, I'm fine!" It took me a long time to figure out that Mr. Nice Guy was so afraid that I would hurt someone with my anger that he would shut down *all* my feelings and I would become numb or withdrawn. As a teen and young adult, when girlfriends would ask me what I was feeling, I'd look inside and not find any feelings. "I don't know," I would reply, and sadly, that was the truth.

Exercises and reflections

Do any of these subpersonality descriptions sound familiar to you? If you have similar parts, do you have names for them? Sometimes naming them is the first step in disidentifying from them. Take a minute to write down any of your subpersonalities that you thought of while reading the previous section that might be keeping you from expressing your power or your love. How do they operate? What do they tell you? With what 'tone of voice' or energy do they convey their messages?

Life Force

Essentially these parts are all telling me, "Don't express yourself because people might not like what they see or you might hurt them." These parts exert internal pressure to reign in the power of my being. When I unconsciously succumb to the pressures of these parts, I lose touch with who I really am and what I really want to express. Trying to hide by separating myself from others, I become invisible, unavailable, and unknowable to others.

But Life is trying to express itself through us at all times and it exerts a force or a pressure in us as well. The power of Life's energy creates an internal pressure to get through whatever blocks are in its way so that it can be expressed. Think of it as energy flowing through a wire that is too thin or water flowing through a pipe that is too small. Pressure builds up or things overheat. In my case, it builds up slowly in my gut as I experience more and more frustration at not being seen. I start blaming others or the system for not seeing me, when in fact, I am withholding who I am for fear of being blamed for not being perfect, or I am hiding because I feel inadequate. But eventually the internal pressure becomes too great and the parts of me that want to be seen erupt and demand attention.

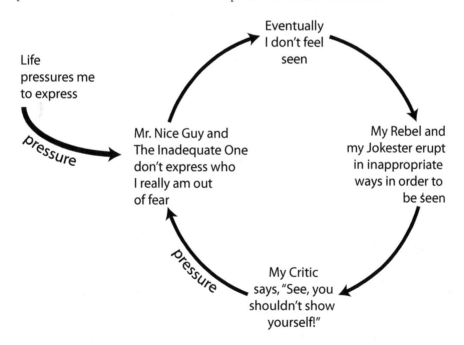

Unfortunately, this often happens in counter-productive ways: my Rebel might act out in an angry way or my Jokester acts out in inappropriate ways to attract attention. In both cases, Life is flowing outward, through me, into the world again, but in distorted or incomplete expressions of who I really am. Of course, this energizes the Critic all over again and he says, "See! I told you to be careful and to not show who you really are!"

Mutual Influence Relationship between Inner and Outer Systems

Liberating your power and love necessitates making changes in the beliefs, structures and rules of your family and organizational systems. At the same time it requires looking at the internal beliefs, structures and rules that keep you from expressing your love and power. If you don't, you accuse the external systems of oppression and don't see how you might be oppressing yourself. This is not an either/or arrangement, but a both/and situation. It is one of the areas where internal psychodynamics interface with external system dynamics, and where I think more research and exploration could be done. Many psychotherapists don't take into consideration the systemic forces impacting their clients' psyches and most systems thinkers don't believe that individual psychodynamics have much relevance to systems theory.

I think, however, that there is a resonance or mutual influence relationship between an individual's internal psychology and the system she inhabits. When, because of internal psychodynamics, individuals can't access their own power or love they are more likely to help create, feed, or condone external systems that don't express love or empower their people. And when a system objectifies its people and exerts power *over* them, it energizes those internal subpersonalities or parts that its members developed to cope with threatening external environments.

However, the opposite is also true. When we as individuals can begin to disidentify from those parts that keep us from expressing ourselves fully, we begin to liberate our individual and collective power and love and that begins to change the systems we are part of. A Life-affirming system can also help call forth the Life-affirming parts of its members (such as "The Artist" or "The Optimist") and acknowledge them as valuable. A healthy system can also help the individual liberate the positive qualities of formerly troublesome subpersonalities. This, in turn, helps the individual integrate that part into the whole of their personality and, indirectly, contribute to the long-term healing of early wounds. For example, when I participated in a supportive system that encouraged learning from mistakes, over time my Critic was able to relax a little. As it did so, I began to notice that the Critic, that was so belittling of me or judgmental of external situations, also had the positive qualities of discernment and discrimination that had been over-shadowed by its more negative qualities. The supportive system helped me to free-up those qualities and use them more consciously without the judgmental energy.

America might not be a perfect Life-affirming system, but many people who arrive here from more oppressive cultures begin to trust, over time, that there really is a level of freedom of expression in our system. It is not always easy, but slowly they begin to realize that they are free to express parts of themselves, like their power and creativity, that were unsafe to show in their former cultures. They realize that, relatively speaking, they can be more themselves here.

Subpersonalities, Mindfulness and Learning

The first step in being able to disidentify from these internal voices that keep you from expressing who you are, is to become aware of them and how they affect you. Just as you can learn to be mindful of external system pressures and how they affect you viscerally, emotionally and mentally in order not to be controlled by them, so too can you learn to identify internal pressures.

As you observe your behavior without judgment and listen more mindfully to these internal voices, you begin to learn how they operate. You can name them, become familiar with them, and, as psychotherapist, Abby Seixas says, "learn to befriend them." All of this means that you are stepping back from the internal obstacles that block your expression and regaining more of your autonomy and power. You are able to hear, but not act on what these internal voices say as they try to keep you from expressing yourself. You are able to feel the various subpersonalities in your body, but because you are aware of this, it gives you more choice: "Oh, I feel the knot in my stomach. That means my Rebel is about to explode. Thank you, Rebel, for letting me know that I am angry about not being seen. Now what do *I* really want to say or do here?"

As you befriend these inner parts, you also learn what they offer as you do begin to express more of yourself. For example, my Rebel has a lot of creative ideas about how to rebel and a lot of power in its anger. My life would be better, however, if these qualities were directed more by me and less by him. (See the Recommended Readings and Resources, page 306, for more about Psychosynthesis and how to work with subpersonalities.)

Remember, my definition of power is, "*the power of being authentic, of being fully who you are at any given moment, in the world, while simultaneously trying to uncover, develop, and share more and more of your uniqueness over time.*" Power is *being* fully whoever you are in the moment while at the same time *becoming* all that you can be. Power envolves *learning* to actualize your full potential. You cannot learn unless you are willing to make mistakes and get feedback from the people and environment around you.

We will make mistakes. In my experience working with others and on myself, I developed what I call the "rusty faucet" theory. When a rusty faucet has been stuck in the closed position for a long time and then gets opened, the first water that comes out has all the junk and contaminants – the dirt, the rust, and the smelly stuff that has been backed up. It seems to be similar with our inner parts as they first begin to express that which has been repressed – all the junky stuff comes out first. As my Critic and my Rebel stop fighting and I begin to liberate my true power, it often comes out with all the cultural distortions of power – anger, power over, intransigence, etc. At that point it is essential that I learn what the real power of my being is and how to express it in ways that are productive. As I first begin to liberate the real love and kindness that is hidden in "Mr. Nice Guy" it can come out first as too soft, too accommodating, or too smothering of others. Then it is necessary to learn more about what love really is and how to combine it with true power (See Chapter Fourteen). Again, I learn these important lessons by expressing and getting feedback from my environment about what does and doesn't work.

A person requires feedback in order to adapt or grow in its environment, just like any other whole system. That feedback is what helps you uncover, develop, and share more of your uniqueness in the future. The feedback helps you to evolve and more fully *actualize* your self. Feedback is information that facilitates learning and therefore, the fuller expression of who you are. But you can't get the feedback from your environment if you don't have the courage to express yourself in the first place and to make mistakes.

Courage

For most of us at first, even in Life-affirming systems, it is anxiety-producing to express our uniqueness and diversity in the face of internal and external systemic pressures. It often takes a small leap of faith, to overcome that anxiety and express the power of our being in the world. This expression of who we are in the world, in spite of our fears of doing so, takes courage. Let me be clear: I am advocating small acts of courage. I am also advocating creating the conditions for, and protection of, the small acts of courage of others.

Yes, there are the large, life-endangering expressions of "who we are" such as standing in front of a line of tanks in Tiananmen Square, or speaking out against the government of El Salvador as Archbishop Oscar Romero did, or being a participant or leader in the civil rights movement in the United States. But one cannot en-courage such acts of another. These acts can only come from deep within the one who is acting on their convictions – the power of their being – in the face of physical harm or even death.

Small acts of courage also come from deep within, from who you are, and also require overcoming fear. Often you feel fear when you are confronted with the choice to fully express your being, and it actually feels like, "If I do this I might die." And while the fear of dying feels quite real, it is usually a fear of humiliation or ego death, rather than actual physical death. I am talking about the courage it takes to overcome that internal barrier of fear in order to speak your divergent truth in a business meeting, or to call the church group's attention to the elephant in the room that everyone is tiptoeing around. It is the courage of a father overcoming fear of losing face or authority with his son and admitting that he, the father, was wrong. It is the courage to share a poem or painting – an expression of one's being – in a classroom of peers. It is the courage to speak up and stop someone from humiliating another. It is the courage to make oneself vulnerable by loving another.

In all acts of courage, you are confronted with either an internal voice or an external systemic pressure that says, "Don't speak; don't act. Something bad will happen to you if you put yourself out into the world at this moment." Yes, it might turn out that you were wrong. Yes, people might make fun of you because they feel awkward or wrong because of the truth you are speaking. But, as the philosopher, Soren Kierkegaard said, "*To dare is to lose one's footing momentarily. Not to dare is to lose oneself.*"

Yes, you might get a reprimand in your company's human resource file, or even be fired – and that could lead to real physical discomfort or harm. In these cases you might have to re-evaluate whether speaking your truth was worth the consequences or whether you really want to work at a place where you cannot express your truths and your aliveness.

On the other hand, you might also have to evaluate from a disidentified perspective whether it was the fact that you expressed yourself or how you did so that got you into trouble. In these cases you are presented with opportunities to learn how to express yourself in ways that can be better seen or heard. The danger would be in believing that internal voice when it returns and says, "Ha! I told you not to speak and not to act! See what happens?"

Audre Lorde, in *Sister Outsider*, after finding out that she had breast cancer, wrote, "*I have come to believe . . . that what is most important to me must be spoken . . . I was going to die, if not sooner then later, whether or not I had ever spoken myself. My silences had not protected me. Your silence will not protect you . . . We can learn to speak when we are afraid in the same way we have learned to speak when we are tired.*"[4]

Jerry's Struggle with Fear and Courage

In my coaching practice I had the privilege of working with Jerry, a training manager in the Human Resource department of a large company. What follows is something that he wrote at the end of our work together:

> I have taught, lectured, and facilitated small and large groups of people for over 40 years. Even though I know (in my mind) that once I start teaching I will most often do a good job and that I am a competent teacher and facilitator, I still feel anxious (in my body) before each event. For many years I felt somehow deficient for being afraid and worked very hard to make the fear go away. I worked on my fears in therapy. I did Rolfing, bioenergetics, EST, etc. but the anxiety still remained.

In one of our coaching meetings, Mark gave me Carlos Casteneda's book, *The Teachings of Don Juan* and I discovered the following quote: *"Death is our eternal companion. It is always to our left, an arm's length behind us. Death is the only wise adviser that a warrior has. Whenever he feels that everything is going wrong and he's about to be annihilated, he can turn to his death and ask if that is so. His death will tell him that he is wrong, that nothing really matters outside its touch. His death will tell him, 'I haven't touched you yet.'"*[5] I decided to try to live with and accept my anxieties and act in spite of them. I was not quite so paralyzed, but the anxiety was still there. I still wanted it to go away, which meant that I hadn't really accepted it.

At that point in our work, Mark gave me a couple of books by Pema Chodron, a wonderful Buddhist teacher and writer, who encourages people to "investigate" their fear, to go into it and get to know it rather than trying to push it away or overpower it. As I practiced this, it allowed me to step back a little from the anxiety and get to know it and all the subtle ways it influenced my life. Eventually I sort of knew it well enough to tolerate it and even to accept it a little. I was able to look at it as just a particular feeling in my gut, like sadness or joy, which visited me occasionally. It was still there, still strong, but it was not all of me. I saw that I also had strong, intelligent, creative and competent parts and that I was able to draw on all those parts even when, or especially when, my fears were realized and something did not go as planned. Somehow I was able to manage those situations and, even in the most disastrous ones where I felt totally humiliated or a failure, *I did not, in fact, die!* So now I have come to accept that the voice and the feelings of anxiety will always be there, but I also think I have gotten better at not believing the content of the voice's messages — namely, that I will die, be annihilated, or somehow become so small out of shame that I will cease to exist.

When Jerry gave me the above, it reminded me of the following quote from the philosopher/theologian, Paul Tillich, in his book, *The Courage to Be:*

The basic anxiety, the anxiety of a finite being about the threat of nonbeing, cannot be eliminated. It belongs to existence itself . . . Courage does not remove anxiety. Since anxiety is existential, it cannot be removed. But courage takes the anxiety of nonbeing into itself. Courage is self-affirmation "in spite of" namely in spite of nonbeing.[6]

When I gave this quote to Jerry, he beamed as he proudly exclaimed, "This is exactly what I meant to say, but it is so much more elegant." "Maybe," I said, "but your explanation is easier to understand!"

The Effects of *Not* Expressing the Power of One's Being

There is only one real deprivation, I decided this morning, and that is not to be able to give one's gift to those one loves most ... The gift turned inward, unable to be given, becomes a heavy burden, even sometimes a kind of poison. It is as though the flow of life were backed up.[7]

MAY SARTON

Like Jerry, observing and befriending the internal systemic resistances to expressing yourself will hopefully lead to the discovery that you will not actually die. However, by observing yourself in these states of fear or anxiety, you may also discover that when you unconsciously *avoid* expressing the fullness of your self, you are often left with a sense of loss or guilt or shame. I am not saying that you should always speak your truth in every situation, or that you should always act when you are afraid. Sometimes circumstances happen too fast and opportunities disappear without realizing it. Sometimes there are blind spots or deep wounds that keep you from expressing without being conscious of this happening.

But sometimes, when you are mindful, you know that you have a choice in a particular moment and choose not to express yourself. You might choose not to confront your partner about something she did or said that hurt you because you would just get into a fight and you are too tired. Or you might avoid speaking out in a group because the issue "doesn't really matter that much." Or you don't say no to a request from a friend because you don't want to hurt his feelings. And sometimes you might choose not to express yourself or act because you are not ready to deal with that particular issue.

In all of these cases you are making a choice and, if you are really mindful, you may notice a small sense of loss. Some deep part of you knows that you have been a little less than you can be. This is also an uncomfortable feeling, just like the fear of expressing is uncomfortable.

When you look at these moments of discomfort or shame for not expressing who you are, you can do one of two things: you can rationalize your actions to make yourself feel better or you can use the discomfort as an opportunity to grow. You can tell yourself that "the issue doesn't really matter much," or that "I don't want to make her mad" and rationalize away your feelings of shame or guilt. Or, you can say to yourself, "I'm not ready to deal with this yet" and ask "What must I develop in myself in order to be ready to deal with this issue?" This latter question acknowledges that you cannot *not* be who you are, you can only express *less* of who you are . . . and that is your choice in any given moment. I am saying that the feeling of discomfort or loss can itself be a spur for learning what is necessary for you to continue to grow and to expand the power of your being.

Power over, Power of, and Power with: Overcoming External Obstacles

Courageously overcoming the internal barriers to the expression of the power of your being is often not enough. It is a necessary first step, but it is often not sufficient to overcome the external systemic forces you may encounter.

Life, like water, wants to flow in all directions at once. So, clearly, when you are expressing the power of your being, there will be many times when you will run into another's expression of uniqueness or up against the forces the system. A Life-affirming system will have processes in place to help deal with these conflicts of expression as they arise. These processes for decision-making, direction-setting, and conflict management will flow out of a larger systemic context or culture that honors, a) the uniqueness of each individual, b) the purpose of the system, and c) Life. This type of culture, with its clearly understood processes, helps to create a safe and focused container to hold the chaos of multiple expressions of uniqueness and, like an alchemical crucible, this container facilitates the emergence of something greater out of that chaos.[8]

Power over

When I am exercising my power–to and I feel myself bumping up against you in exercising yours, and if in this conflict I have the capacity to prevail over you, then I can easily turn to exercising power over you. My drive to realize myself slips easily into valuing my self-realization above yours, and then into believing arrogantly that I am more deserving of self-realization, and then into advancing my self-realization even if it impedes yours.[9]

ADAM KAHANE

Part of what makes a system dysfunctional is that it is unable to create a safe and focused container to hold and channel the power of all of its members. Dysfunctional systems cannot tolerate the chaos of a multiplicity of expressions of the *power of*. This chaos is too unpredictable. These expressions may cause the system to grow in ways that are threatening to its identity, so the system clamps down on the aliveness flowing through its members in an effort to maintain power over its own destiny. We see this dynamic in the uprisings in Libya or Syria, where the repressive regimes

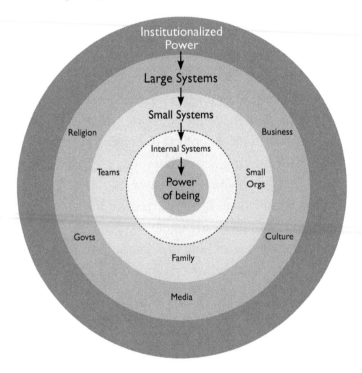

kept trying to crack down on the protesters and exert even more repressive control. We also see it in families where adolescents are forbidden to experiment with alternative ways of expressing themselves like playing punk rock music or getting a tattoo or dyeing their hair purple. However, control by *power over* the *power of* others is like driving a car with the parking brake on. It might get somewhere slowly, but not without a lot of wasted energy and a very bad smell.

In a dysfunctional, Life-deadening system, whether it is a church, a family, a corporation, or a financial system, the power only flows in one direction. The larger system has power *over* its component parts, and those component parts, in turn, have power *over* the systems that comprise it, and ultimately, power *over* the human beings in those systems.

It takes courage for an individual to resist the immense systemic pressure to give up her power in these one-way, power-over, systems. The psychologist Rollo May spoke to this dynamic when he said that *"the opposite of courage is not cowardice; it is conformity."*

There is a classic scene in the movie *Network*, where Peter Finch, playing a newscaster, is being reprimanded for having the courage – born out of anger – to express on air his personal beliefs and fears that the business of TV is controlling peoples' lives. Finch is sitting at the darkened end of an enormous conference table. Off in the distance, in the light, is a corporate bigwig (a white male, of course, played by Ned Beatty) pointing and waving his finger at Finch and shouting as if in a revival tent, *"You are an old man who thinks in terms of nations and peoples. There are no nations! There are no peoples! . . . There is only ONE holistic system of systems, ONE vast and immane, interwoven, interacting, multivariate, multinational dominion of DOLLARS! . . . It is the international system of currency which determines the totality of life on this planet. That is the natural order of things today. . . And YOU have meddled with the primal forces of nature, and YOU... WILL... ATONE!"*

We have all seen this same *power over* behavior from leaders in other large institutions, such as organized religion where rabbis, ministers, priests, nuns or congregants have been silenced for expressing beliefs that are different from the official religious doctrine; or in corporations where whistleblowers have been fired for speaking out about company waste or fraud, or in families where children are punished for speaking about their abuse or their parents' addictions.

Power with

It is important to recognize, with humility, how hard it is to change dysfunctional power-over systems. It is extremely difficult for the *power of* a single individual to overcome such strong systemic forces. That is why dysfunctional systems keep us separated, treating each other as objects. By doing so, the system maintains its identity and its power over us. Therefore, it is imperative to learn how to be in relationship with other beings of power. It takes practice to learn how to express the power of one's being without exerting *power over* the *power of* another's being. In other words, you become more effective systemic change agents when you learn, with others, how to exercise *power with*.

When you can respect the *power of* another's being and exercise your *power with* each other, you also develop a kind of collective courage that comes from knowing that you can count on each others' support. This encourages and magnifies the others' power rather than diminishing it. This kind of support and collective encouragement creates a positive feedback loop that reinforces the power of and the courage of the collective.

On December 1, 1955, when Rosa Parks had the courage to sit in the power of her being and refuse to move to the back of the bus, she gave strength and visibility to a movement. Her act of courage brought even more people together to exercise collective acts of courage such as bus strikes, lunch counter sit-ins and marches. Blacks came together with blacks, and also with whites who believed in the righteousness of their fight. Together they said, "We shall not be moved!" A collective stand, this was an exercise of *power with*.

Nowhere is this collective courage and the exercise of *power with* more important than in confronting dysfunctional systems and the extreme cases of systems of oppression. Sometimes those systems are visible, as in repressive regimes or physically or sexually abusive families. At other times, they are invisible, as in cultural systems of racism, sexism, and classism.

What did Peter Finch's character in *Network* do to evoke such ire from the system? He awakened the masses out of their trance, reminded them that they were human beings, not objects, and encouraged them to stand together and take collective action:

"I don't know what to do about the depression and the inflation and the Russians and the crime in the street. All I know is that first you've got to get mad. You've got to say, 'I'm a HUMAN BEING, God damn it! My life has VALUE!' So I want all of you to get up out of your chairs. I want you to get up right now and go to the window. Open it, and stick your head out, and yell, 'I'M MAD AS HELL, AND I'M NOT GOING TO TAKE THIS ANYMORE!'"

Standing up and exercising *power with* means learning to draw out and respect one another's power. It also requires humility in the face of the strength of dysfunctional system forces. How to practice exercising *power with* will be explored further in later chapters. But first, let's look at the force that bridges and brings together all of these individual expressions of *power of* and makes *power with* possible: Love.

CHAPTER TWELVE

LOVE: REHUMANIZING SYSTEMS

In my experience, as people see more of the systems within which they operate, and as they understand more clearly the pressures influencing one another, they naturally develop more compassion and empathy.[1]

PETER SENGE

When I speak of love I am not speaking of some sentimental and weak response. I am not speaking of that force which is just emotional bosh. I am speaking of that force which all of the great religions have seen as the supreme unifying principle of Life[2]

MARTIN LUTHER KING, JR.

What happens when the eleven people in your business meeting or the six people in your family develop the courage to express their uniqueness – the power of their being – at the same time in the same space? What would allow them to negotiate that dilemma harmoniously?

Power with

When you liberate your individual power and begin to express your uniqueness, you are likely to run into both the force of the system trying to maintain its identity and the *power of* other individuals trying to express their uniqueness. As you try to express the power of your being, the system forces will still be separating you from others. If you are not mindful, the system pressures will cause you to fall back into patterns of *power over* or power against each other

But, by learning to step back and disidentify from these system pressures, you can be more mindful of yourself and your relation to others. You can then see more clearly what is really going on, as opposed to what the system is telling you is happening, and you see that there are more choices and possibilities for action. You are also freer to connect with your own deeper values rather than the enforced system values. As you step back from the system and its dysfunction, you understand that there exists a choice to see and treat others as you would like to be treated, that is, as a unique living being and not as an object.

When this happens, caring enters the system and acts as a bridge bringing people closer together. As Assagioli says in the *Act of Will*, "Love, being attractive, magnetic, and outgoing, tends to link and unite."[3] This caring and respect for self and others allows you to be with other beings of power without giving up your own power. Love and respect are powerful forces that bring us together rather than push us apart and they create the conditions for *power with*.

I maintain that this caring and respect, this love for self, other and Life is the answer to the dilemma of how to harmoniously orchestrate multiple expressions of *power of*. It is love that allows us to express the power of our being, simultaneously and collectively, as *power with*. The easiest place to see *power with*, or multiple expressions of uniqueness in service of a larger whole, is in various forms of well-functioning teams such as an orchestra, a sports organization or a dance troupe. In all of these cases, there is an over-arching vision or purpose that all members are aligned with, whether it is a musical score, winning a game, or the choreography. But within that purpose, there is encouragement for the members to be all that they can be while at the same time trying to draw the best out of all of the others in the group, for the good of the whole. Yes, there are stars. There are higher paid players and there are soloists, but each knows that their status is dependent on the mutual agreement and commitment to their purpose and on the performance of the rest of the group.

However, there are teams that are not comprised of stars, but whose members share the *power of* their unique skills in such a way that what emerges out of their *power with* is way beyond what anyone, including themselves, would have predicted. Consider the jazz combo that features solid musicians but no superstars, where each respects the others' skills and each pushes the others further. You can also see this *power with* when parents in a family respect each others' strengths, accept their own and each others' weaknesses, and work together to achieve a synergy that works for each of them, for the benefit of their children, and for the family as a whole.

The concept of teams and teamwork became a strong trend in business management in the 1970's and has lasted until the present day because of the potential synergy that can be realized by teams. But real teamwork was not as easy to achieve as was first imagined. Organizations had to learn more than just techniques for good teamwork. They had to learn about the principles behind those techniques, primarily the principles of the right uses of power and love and their concrete practice in a business environment. (See Chapter 14 and the Appendices.)

But, before going any further about how love contributes to *power with*, as well as what other purposes love serves within a healthy system, let's look more closely at what I mean by love.

What is Love?

When I first ask, "What is love?" in my systems classes, I get a range of answers, from the romantic – "It's what makes your heart flutter and your brain turn to mush" – to the practical – "Love is the rationalization for sex and sex assures the survival of the species" – to the abstract – "Love is the force which connects us all. God is love." I also give this question as homework to focus my students on their *experience* of love and how it moves them to behave. I ask them particularly to look at love and its relevancy to groups, organizations and systems. The last part of the assignment is for them to think about and observe the positive and negative aspects of love.

Exercises and reflections

Take a few moments before you continue to read to ask yourself the questions. Don't labor over your answers, just give each question a few moments' reflection and see what comes to mind:

- What is love?
- How does love make me behave?
- What are the effects of love on me and on my relationship with others?
- What are the strengths and limitations of love?

After they've completed their homework and we come back to the questions of "What is love?" "How does it move you to behave?" and "What are the strengths and limitations of love?" I hear answers that are more connected to their experience, such as:

- Love pushes or pulls me toward another person. It closes the distance between us.
- Love makes me weak. When I care about someone I want him to care about me and I twist myself all out of shape to please him. I lose my self in the relationship.
- Love makes me look at myself and the other person more closely. It makes me want to know their soul and them to know mine. But then I put myself in their place looking at me and I get scared about what they might be seeing.
- Love is a very powerful force. It is healing or nurturing. When I feel loved, I feel happy. I come alive.
- When I think about love in general and not just in relation to another person, like my love for nature or art, I see that it pulls me out of my own little self and opens me up more. I feel connected to everything and to something larger like the world or beauty or spirit or God, I don't know what to call it.
- When I am feeling loving or caring I don't want to hurt anyone or anything. I want to treat them with care because I understand they feel pain or hurt or rejection just like me.
- Love makes it hard to get things done. My boss doesn't care about me so I don't care about my work, but I don't want to treat my co-workers like that. So I try to show caring, but I don't know how to get them to do what I want and be caring at the same time. It's like I'm too understanding about their other pressures so I don't push for what I need.

As they share their experiences and thoughts with each other, they begin to understand more about why I might ask an unexpected question like "What is love?" in a course about organizational systems. They start to understand the connections I am pointing to between dysfunctional systems and their own experiences of love:

1. If dysfunctional systems dehumanize us, treat us as objects and cause us to treat each other the same way, it is love that reminds us that we are human and that others "feel pain or hurt or rejection just like me."
2. If dysfunctional systems create structures based on *power over* to control us and separate us, then love is the force that "closes the distance between us" and helps us "feel connected to everything."
3. If dysfunctional systems are deadening and kill our creativity, then love is the antidote because "When I feel loved, I feel happy. I come alive."
4. If dysfunctional systems cut us off from our values and make us believe that the system's values are the highest values, then love reconnects us to "something larger like the world or beauty or spirit or God."

The Principle of Interconnectedness

Love is knowing that the interconnectedness of all Life already exists, and living our lives with the recognition that there are responsibilities and consequences to this fact. I call this the *Principle of Interconnectedness*. Love, then, is that force which reminds us and brings us back into these relationships which already exist so that we might discover and express more of their nature. Love is also the force that reminds us of our interdependence and helps us to stay in relationship when other forces are trying to separate or fragment us.

Love attempts to close the distance between us, to move us toward each other, not for the sake of merging, but for the sake of being with and understanding. If I merge with you, no one is left to understand you and appreciate your uniqueness. And if I disappear, I am no longer available to be drawn out and understood by you. "We are all One," does not mean we are all the same. It means that in our myriad diversity and uniqueness we are still interconnected and interdependent. Being in relationship means unique individuals standing in the power of their being together and exploring the nature of that relationship to discover what emerges.

One evening in the summer of 1992, my wife and I entertained a group of Americans and Russians who were participating in a "citizen diplomacy" psychological and cultural exchange program. Everyone was very loving and, like most exchange programs, flush with the feeling of how similar we all are as human beings and as part of one human family. So it came as some surprise when a heated argument broke out over what was the main cause of the fall of the Soviet Union. Our Russian friends attributed the liberation of their country to the person they saw as the greatest American president ever: Ronald Reagan. The Americans, all liberal democrats who despised Reagan, insisted vehemently that it had been the only humane Soviet premier, Mikhail Gorbachev, who had single-handedly liberated his people. The Russians thought Gorbachev was just another party apparatchik and the Americans denounced Reagan as a war-monger who built up massive arsenals in order to bankrupt the Soviet Union. Both sides continued arguing for a long time, backing up their arguments and getting somewhat irritated because the others were telling them what was true about their own president or premier. At one point, as the host, I stopped the conversation and said something like, "It seems we aren't all the same after all. It seems like the world looks a little different from the Russian perspective than the American one. Maybe it is time to take our exploration of each other to another level and explore our differences as well as our similarities." Everyone agreed, so I proposed that we go around the table, with the Russians explaining what the essence of being Russian was to them and the Americans explaining their view of the essence of being American. We went long into the night and came away with a much deeper understanding of each culture than we had at the beginning of the evening when we were only looking at how similar we were.

Is It Necessary to Like Someone in Order to Love Him?

This question always brings the class up short:" Yes." "No." "It depends on which definition of love we are using." "No it doesn't." "Sure it does."

If love is defined as the recognition of our existing interconnectedness or as the energy that awakens us to the unique existence of others, then love becomes a practice, an attitude toward all living beings. Can I be mindful enough in the moment, to hold this person as a unique expression of Life, just like me, and as such, having value and being worthy of respect just like me? And can I stay in respectful relationship to that person knowing that he is an imperfect expression of Life, just like me, and that he is struggling, just like me, to be a better and better expression? This is the basis for all secular and religious understanding of compassion. Bill O'Brien, former president of Hanover Insurance Company expressed it this way:

> By "love," I mean a predisposition toward helping another person to become complete: to develop to their full potential. Love is an act of will . . . you do not have to like someone to love him or her. Love is an intentional disposition toward another person.[4]

Roberto Assagioli also refers to love as a practice and as an act of will, "*To love well calls for all that is demanded by the practice of any art, indeed of any human activity, namely, an adequate measure of discipline, patience, and persistence. All these we have seen to be qualities of the will.*"[5]

Love takes intention, effort, and practice. Rather than waiting for love to happen to us, we can cultivate a loving attitude toward all of Life. When we do this, it moves us toward Life and toward the other rather than succumbing to internal or external system pressures that separate us. When we recognize that we are existentially interconnected, we also understand that one of the effects of this interconnection is that all of our attitudes and actions incur consequences for our self, the other, the system, and Life.

Inevitably, someone in my class always asks, "But what about the terrorists who committed the atrocities of 9/11, or Hitler? Do you expect us to love them, too?" We are human beings, not saints, and of course we do not feel love toward everyone. I stress the word intention to explain what I mean. Do we hold the intention to love, to move toward the other, even if we are unable to do so? Do we cultivate the attitude, even if we do not fully know how to express it, that this person is a human being just like us and deserves to be understood and respected as a part of that larger Life we both participate in? Do we want to be more loving in our lives toward those who are different from us, or who cause us discomfort, as a way to better understand the other, our self, and Life? And, are we able to choose to love another, or do we reflexively recoil or retreat or separate ourselves because of internal or external systemic forces?

Most of us are not going to meet the Hitlers or the perpetrators of 9/11 of this world. But, if this should happen, that is why in the previous two chapters I have also emphasized understanding and using power. Contrary to what the Beatles may have thought, love is not all you need. Power is also essential, and as you will see in the next chapter, it is necessary to learn how to balance love and power in our lives.

In the meantime, are you willing to get better at loving the others that you encounter in your day-to-day life, whether you like them or not?

A Personal Awakening: Seeing is Loving

One morning I woke up to find a strange woman in my bed. She looked familiar, and I found myself staring at her intensely and asking myself, "Who is this woman?" Of course I knew that this woman was Abby, my wife of 25 years, but that morning I had literally and figuratively "woken up" and it was as if I was seeing her anew. In asking myself, "Who is this woman?" I was trying to see and understand who she really was right there in that moment. I had the shocking realization that she was not simply the image of Abby that was in my head. That image was of the girl I had met 25 years ago, overlaid with all the images of her that I had created in my mind during our lives together. Abby was made up of all these images of who I thought she was. But who was she really? I could feel myself really trying to see her without any preconceptions.

This was a scary question to ask for many reasons. What if I didn't like this person I was trying to see? Could I go back to seeing her in the old way, or had I destroyed those images by becoming aware of them? If this was true for me, was it also true for her? Did she really see me, or was she just seeing her accumulated images of me? Then the scariest realization of all hit me: I could never really know her. I would always be making images in my mind of who I thought she was, and the fact was that I would never be able to know her fully as she is. And that meant that she, that no one, could really know me fully as I am except maybe myself, and even that was being called into question.

In that moment, I recommitted myself to the challenge and the practice of closing this existential gap. I decided to make it a Life practice to try to truly see and know others, to move toward them, as well as to make myself available to be known by them. Even if I could not fully bridge this existential gap, it would at least be a worthy experiment. I would start with whoever this woman was laying next to me in bed.

> Once the realization is accepted that even between the closest human beings infinite distances continue to exist, a wonderful living side by side can grow up, if they succeed in loving the distance between them which makes it possible for each to see the other whole against the sky.[6]
>
> RILKE

The Courage to Love

Courage is the ability to stay with anything . . . To tolerate whatever it is, as it is, without needing it to be different.[7]
ELIZABETH STANLEY, PhD, Captain (Ret),
U.S. Army Mind Fitness Training Institute

Fears often arise when you attempt to express the power of your being. There is a moment of choice where it takes courage *to be* in spite of those fears. As most of us have experienced, it also takes courage to love. Love is an act of will, an intentional act to be in relationship with another being *in spite of our fears of doing so.* Consider your conventional intimate "love relationships" and the concomitant fears of being hurt, overwhelmed, inadequate and/or disappointed. These same fears can also arise when you allow any other being to exist in your consciousness as someone of value, someone to be respected.

You might ask yourself: How can I respect someone if I don't know whether or not she will hurt or disappoint me? How can I value someone who might overwhelm me or make me feel inadequate?

I believe that your willingness and ability to cope with these fears determines the degree to which you are able to meet others as equals and to value everyone as an expression of Life.

When I "awoke" to Abby, many things happened in that moment. Some were liberating and some were scary. One thing that took me a while to figure out was this: "If I just woke up with a stranger in my bed, why wasn't I more afraid than I was? Yes, she was beautiful, but still . . . And, even though I might never fully know her or her me, why did this not totally discourage and paralyze me? Why was I so excited, energized, and curious to find out who she was?" What I finally realized was in that the moment I awoke to Abby and all my past images of her fell away, somehow the past images of myself in the relationship also fell away. I was not the person who married her 25 years ago either. I was not the boy who needed to be loved to know I had value. I was not the boy who was out of touch with his feelings and yearned for Abby to awaken them in me. I was not the boy who would die if she were not around. I had grown and changed. Of course this raised the obvious question, "Who am I now, then?" but for some reason, rather than being afraid, I was excited to find out.

Part of my excitement and my lack of fear, I realized, was because I did not cease to exist when my old images of Abby and the relationship ceased to exist. I did not die when my old images of myself died. I did not know *who* I was, but I did know *that I was*. I existed. In that moment, I realize now, I was standing in the power of my being, knowing that images of myself could die and that I would still survive. This is what allowed me to accept the fears that came up about this new relationship and move toward it in spite of those fears. I realize now that by contacting the power of my being, my ability to love expanded.

> From love we learn to ease
> our relentless longing for more
> and to rest in the blessedness
> of things as they are.
>
> From love we learn to heal our losses
> and our fears of loss.
>
> Love awakens us.
> It shows us the truth about ourselves and
> gives us the courage to live this truth.

Love sustains us:
it is our quintessential nourishment.

And love connects us – to others, to
ourselves, and to the source of all being.

Love is our teacher,
and we are love's apprentices.[8]

RICH & ANTRA BOROFSKY

Power and Love Feed Each Other's Growth

I see a reciprocal developmental relationship between power and love in our individual lives: *the more I am rooted in the power of my being, the more I can love; and the more able I am to love the more secure I become in the power of my being.* As I develop more understanding and experience of the true power of my being, the more I am able to love, knowing that my imagined fears of being overwhelmed, lost or hurt will not cause me to die. Also, the more that I am grounded in the power of my own being, the less my identity is dependent on others, and therefore the more able I am to recognize and allow others to be who they are. This is true love. I do not require you to be a certain way for me to be comfortable with myself. Thomas Merton said it well: *"The beginning of love is to let those we love be perfectly themselves, and not to twist them to fit our own image. Otherwise we love only the reflection of ourselves we find in them."*[9]

And the more able I am to love, the more secure I become in the power of my being. This is true in two respects: 1) To love myself is to allow myself to be perfectly who I am in the moment and not what others want or expect me to be. The more I am able to love myself – to recognize my unique value and that I am worthy of respect – the more entitled I feel to express who I really am, the power of my being, without fear of how I will be received; and 2) When I love others and enter into relationship and truly meet them, I also meet myself in the process. The other's mirroring confirms that I do in fact exist as a separate being. He or she also mirrors back to me how I am seen in the world, thereby giving me a clearer sense of who I am versus who I think I am.

Seeing and Being Seen *(Part 2)*

When you delve more deeply into the question, "What is love?" you begin to see a multifaceted force that includes a) being in relationship to another, b) truly seeing another as a unique but incomplete expression of Life, and c) accepting the other, as he or she is, without demands that the person be different in order to be loved.

In order to deepen your understanding of love, consider the following questions:

- What does it feel like to be seen?
- How do you know if you've been seen?
- What do you do as the seer and as the seen?
- How do you know if you have seen someone?
- Why are seeing and being seen important?

What does it feel like to be seen?

The experience of not being seen is much more familiar to us than that of being seen. Yet, most of us know, if only fleetingly, what the experience of being seen feels like. When I ask people what it feels like to be seen, they say things like:

- I feel totally relaxed and accepted just for who I am right in that moment.
- I feel nurtured.
- It makes me feel like I fit somewhere, I belong here.
- It affirms that I am alive, but even more, that I deserve to be alive.
- It reminds me that I am and I have value just because I am.
- It makes me feel a little uncomfortable, too. I feel like someone is seeing my essence, my soul and I feel a little vulnerable.
- It's not like all gooey and with fireworks. When someone really sees me, it's just like – calm. It's like we are really meeting each other like equals or something.
- When I feel seen, I feel closer to the person. We come into relationship.
- I am not invisible. They opened the drapes and are looking in.

Firman and Gila point out that all acts of compassion embody the relationship between personal self and spiritual Self, the Largest Whole, which I am calling Life. "It is as if the light of Self shines through the various lenses of empathic relationships..."[10] Martin Buber points to this as well when he says that "*as soon as we touch a Thou, we are touched by a breath of eternal Life.*"[11]

So when I see you, I am acting as a representative or channel for the energies of Life to flow to you and remind you of who you really are and that you are a part of that Larger Whole. People who have met with various spiritual teachers have described this experience of "'seeing God' in his or her eyes." Of course, this experience is nurturing, affirming, and accepting. It doesn't take a guru, however, to channel Life. It just takes a willingness to be present and to see or meet another. In addition to connecting the person seen to the larger whole of Life, seeing and accepting another also affirms and draws out the best in that person.

As Viktor Frankl says when speaking about the effect of love in relation to another, "*By the spiritual act of love he is enabled to see the essential traits and features in the beloved person; and even more, he sees that which is potential in him . . . Furthermore, by his love, the loving person enables the beloved person to actualize these potentialities. By making him aware of what he can be and of what he should become, he makes these potentialities come true.*"[12]

What do you do as the seer?

How do you actually see another person? What you do or say is important, but probably even more essential is the *inner attitude* or *place* from which you practice seeing. Some of the components of that inner attitude are:

- Intention
- Recognition of mutuality
- Curiosity and the desire to learn and grow
- Discernment and the willingness to see the human being before you as distinct from their thoughts or behaviors.

Intention. Since seeing and loving another are purposeful acts, we have the possibility to enter into each encounter mindfully with the intention to see and love the other. We are able to choose to see and to love.

Recognition of mutuality. Remembering that we each possess inherent value and deserve to be respected as a unique human expression of that larger whole, Life. In other words, as individuals, from the perspective of the Larger Whole, we are completely equal. This is difficult to hold on to in the midst of contentious interactions, but it is essential. This is what I call the *Principle of Respect and Inherent Value*: trying to see the person before you as someone who, like you, is growing and developing and working to actualize his or her full potential as an expression of Life.

Curiosity and the desire to learn. We are equal in value as living beings. In relation to a given situation, though, there are perspectives, opinions, or creative ideas that are more important or more useful. We are equal as people, but our ideas, feelings and behaviors have different value based on such things as our history, experience, intelligence, intuition, etc. However, you cannot discern which idea or perspective is more useful unless you truly understand the other. Try putting yourself in the other person's shoes to really experience and understand this other unique expression of Life. Try to be curious and eager to learn something about the other, yourself and Life.

Discernment. Try to be mindful of and practice this way of seeing even when the other's behaviors, words, or attitudes are challenging. If you can catch yourself getting hooked in the moment, you are more able to disidentify or step back from the part of you that got hooked. You can then remember the inherent value of this being before you and remind yourself that, just like you, this person is distinct from and more than just the ideas and behaviors they are expressing.

In all of the above I used the word "try" because the process of truly seeing another is a constant practice. You will intend to be empathic and understanding but find yourself getting angry or recoiling from the other. Seeing requires constant mindfulness and a continual returning to yourself and what you know to be true, and then becoming present again to the other. This is the practice of mindfulness in relationship.

Since all beings are interconnected and interdependent, completely equal in value and deserving of respect, we will continually confront the uncomfortable tension of respectable people with different points of view. In an unconscious effort to relieve that tension, we usually discount the others or ourself. I am encouraging you to learn to recognize and tolerate that tension, to stay with it and to see what emerges out of the diversity that is before you. Together, you might be able to come up with a fresh understanding or a new course of action to which you all agree. But that will certainly not happen unless you see each other as beings of value and from that perspective try to understand each other's ideas. Even if you do not reach a new understanding or course of action, you will have learned more about yourself and the others in a respectful way that preserves the relationship.

One of my oldest friends is a conservative Republican. I am not. His views and the certainty with which he presents those views often infuriate me. However, he is a true friend who would go out of his way to help me or my family in any way needed. He has a law degree, is a doctor practicing international medicine for the state department, a terrific auto mechanic and is one of the most interesting and brilliant people I know. Because of this, I cannot just dismiss his views, as I do with a lot of conservative Republicans, as "uninformed stupidity." He presents an ongoing opportunity for me to practice staying with the tension of opposing ideas and trying to see past his inflammatory behavior. When I am able to do so, I learn a tremendous amount about myself and about him and his ideas, all of which help me to grow and broaden my perspective on Life.

When you are confronted with people who you find difficult to see or understand and who make you want to scream and run away, you might try asking yourself, "What is Life trying to express through this person? What can I learn if I stay open to seeing and hearing him? What is Life trying to express through me that might be of use here?" Remembering your interconnection and staying in relationship in this way is an act of love. It resists the system pressures, mentioned in Chapter 6, that are trying to separate and create distance between you and others.

Why power is essential to loving fully

One might accuse me of being pollyanna-ish and say that I am giving up my own authority or power by being so concerned with respecting and understanding the other. "What about them respecting and understanding you?" one might rightfully ask. This is why I talked about power before talking about love, and why I have written about the reciprocal development between love and power. The more secure I am in the power of my being, the more fully I am able to love. If I am afraid that I will lose myself in another, I cannot fully love them. If I am afraid that when I fully understand another I will give up my own authority and choice, I can never allow myself to really see them. And if I am afraid that I will judge myself based on what I see in another, I will never allow myself to really meet them. In other words, if I respect myself and am centered in the power of my own being, I am more able to be in relation to another without the fear of being lost, hurt or humiliated.

"But what if the other person doesn't respect me?" you might also ask. "Are you saying that I should still love them?" Yes, I am. We are not saints, though, and this is not always possible, but it can be something we aspire to and practice. Love, respect, and seeing bring us closer together and acknowledge our interdependence as expressions of Life. If just one of us can hold on to this context or this attitude, there is still hope that we can get through a difficult interaction. If both of us lose this perspective, then we see each as "other" and become separated, oppositional parts of something that is, in fact, whole.

The Vietnamese Buddhist teacher Thich Nhat Hahn in his book, *Peace in Every Step: The Path of Mindfulness in Everyday Life,* offers this inspiring example of what we might aspire to in our practice of trying to see and love another. He tells the story of receiving a letter about a young refugee girl, a boat person, trying to escape from Vietnam, who threw herself into the ocean after being raped by a sea pirate. He writes,

> When you first learn of something like that, you get angry at the pirate. You naturally take the side of the girl. As you look more deeply you will see it differently. If you take the side of the little girl, then it is easy. You only have to take a gun and shoot the pirate. But we cannot do that. In my meditation I saw that if I had been born in the village of the pirate and raised in the same conditions as he was, there is a great likelihood that I would become a pirate. I saw that many babies are born along the Gulf of Siam, hundreds every day, and if we educators, social workers, politicians, and others do not do something about the situation, in twenty-five years a number of them will become sea pirates. That is certain . . . all of us are to some extent responsible for this state of affairs.[14]

His compassion for the pirate is evident in these few lines from the poem, "*Call me by my true names*" which he wrote in response to the letter he received.

> I am the twelve-year-old girl, refugee on a small boat,
> who throws herself into the ocean after being raped by a sea pirate,
> and I am the pirate, my heart not yet capable of seeing and loving.

How do you know if you've really seen someone?
- Because I understand them and know how they think.
- When I've really seen someone I stop judging them.
- I see them as just another person, like me.
- I am able to put myself in their flip-flops and see the world from their perspective and feel what they are feeling.
- I sense their pain and/or other feelings they are having.

The above are typical of the students' answers, and they do contain aspects of the process of seeing. But if you look carefully there is something missing. In all of these answers, it is the person doing the seeing who is determining whether or not they have seen the other. I usually have to prompt them further by asking, "Yes, but how can you be sure that you have seen this person?" They usually look puzzled for a moment, and then reply along the lines of, "Well, I guess I can never really be sure." Eventually someone understands the direction I am pointing and says, "I guess we could ask the person if they feel seen or understood by us."

You can never be sure you have actually seen and "met" the other unless you check it out with them and they say that they, too, feel the connection and acknowledge feeling seen by you. This is the basis of all good communication theory: inquire to find out if you have been understood by others and if you have understood them.

It is hard to remember to do this kind of inquiry unless you are working with the principles and from within the context that the person in front of you is a human being, to be valued and respected as a unique expression of Life. You want to see the person and understand him because he is presenting you with an opportunity to grow by learning something about him, yourself, and Life. Without this context, you are not moved to inquire. With this context, you are more motivated to persist in your inquiry until you truly see and understand the other and the other acknowledges being seen and understood.

What do you do as the one being seen?

Here are some of the answers I've heard from students and in corporate trainings:

- I try to make them see me by getting their attention somehow by flirting, ignoring them, talking a lot, or trying to be witty.
- I argue until they give up. I'll repeat my point over and over until they get it.
- I demand that they focus on me and listen to what I'm saying.
- Usually it is necessary to point out that this is what they do in order to be seen. "But what do you do if someone really wants to see who you really are, to know you?" Again, the answers are varied:
- What do you mean? I'm just there. They either see me or they don't.
- I try to answer their questions openly and honestly.
- I get uncomfortable when someone tries to really know me. That's very intimate. Sometimes I withdraw and hide, but sometimes if I really like the person I try not to run away.

- It feels like I have to make myself vulnerable. If I want to be seen, that means warts and all, and that's scary.

It's very likely that you've met people – co-workers, adolescents, sports team members, friends in social groups – who continually act out in order to be seen. It is as if their only focus in Life is to be seen, but the way they are going about it has the opposite effect; it drives people away. All that others see is the person demanding to be seen and it is very hard to see beyond that. And, with this type of person, if you do attempt to see past that part to who he really is, he maintains that you still don't see him.

Often the problem is that the person trying to be seen is not doing anything on their end to show themselves to you. Their psychological wounding has been so great that they are crying out to be seen and hiding at the same time. These are extreme examples at one end of the spectrum, but most of us exhibit our own versions of this dynamic, e.g. I'll show you my strong parts, but I'll hide my weak, bad, or shameful parts; or I'll respond truthfully about some aspects of myself, but obfuscate others, or I'll tell you everything is fine when it really isn't.

The fact is that you are required to make yourself a bit vulnerable if you want to be known. This might be uncomfortable because it feels intimate and, yes, it might even be scary because it means that others might see you, warts and all. This ties back to the definition of power – being visible with who we really are, the power of our being. This takes an act of courage, the crossing of a barrier to be who we are, in the world. Therefore, when someone is trying to bridge the distance between the two of you and to really see you, it helps the process if you can use the power of your being to be a little more vulnerable and visible. The reverse is often also true. If you are willing to use the power of your being to be vulnerable and express who you are, that can often evoke respect and caring from the other for your willingness to be visible. Of course this is difficult to do, but the payoff can be great in the form of a true "meeting" of individuals.

A gay friend captured this dynamic once when we were speaking about the process of becoming friends:

"Mark, I could tell early on that you were trying to get to know me and that you were a sincere and sensitive man. But I immediately came up against my fear. Earlier in my life, every time I would try to be visible about being gay – like with my father, teachers or friends – I would be kicked in the gut psychologically or emotionally, and once physically, by their responses. I desperately wanted to be seen, but these experiences pushed me into hiding. So I really wanted to let you in, but every time I started to be vulnerable in any way, that fear of being kicked in the gut would come up. I would have to tell myself 'Mark is a good person. He won't intentionally hurt you and besides you are stronger now and more confident in yourself' and then I could go through that door and be visible to you. This happened over and over again in the beginning of our relationship."

We had been friends for several years but this was the first time I had heard him describe this dynamic. His vulnerability and sharing moved me deeply and I felt more profoundly his struggle with me and in life. He saw my tears and he knew that I understood his struggle. "I feel seen," he said. In that moment we met each other again.

Why are seeing and being seen important?

From a systems perspective, seeing and being seen is one of the crucial expressions of love within the system. It re-humanizes the system because when you really see another, you are reminded that we are all human beings and that we are all in this together. It also gives the system information that is vital to its healthy functioning. When we see and understand each other, the system has access to the unique qualities, wisdom, creativity, and perspectives of all its parts, not just some. This gives the system the feedback that it requires to develop in the direction of better meeting its purpose while simultaneously nurturing the growth and development of its people.

The opposite of this is demonstrated by dysfunctional systems like oppressive regimes that only care about preserving or maintaining the system and not about the development of either the system or its members. This relationship between the absence of love – of not being seen – and *power over* is described very poignantly in the prologue of *The Invisible Man* by Ralph Ellison:

> I am a man of substance, of flesh and bone, fiber and liquids – and
> I might even be said to possess a mind. I am invisible, understand,
> simply because people refuse to see me . . . It's when you feel like this
> that, out of resentment, you begin to bump people back. And, let me

confess, you feel that way most of the time. You ache with the need to convince yourself that you do exist in the real world, that you're a part of all the sound and anguish, and you strike out with your fists, you curse and you swear to make them recognize you.[15]

It is through loving, seeing and being seen that we come into relationship, call forth the best and highest from each other and remember our common humanity. Doing so re-humanizes our systems. We meet as equals and change the dynamic of our dysfunctional systems, whether they are families, organizations, or society as a whole, from *power over* to the dynamics of relationship and *power with*. Again, it is love that makes this possible.

There is one final reason why expressing the power of our being, truly seeing others and allowing ourselves to be seen are so important. This one is a belief or an intuitive leap, and it is not unique to me. It also seems to me to be a natural extension of all that I have been writing about here:

As a part of Life, each of us is an organ of perception that provides data to Life through our unique perspective. The more we can truly see each other, and thereby see more of what's true in ourselves, each other and life, the more information Life has to use in order to grow and evolve. Some people refer to this as Life knowing itself. You can also think about it as our feedback to the Largest Whole.

The astronaut Rusty Schweickart described this experience of Life knowing itself through us. It came to him as he was outside the capsule on a spacewalk and being awed by the image of the whole, fragile earth floating in dark space: "You realize that this [vision of the whole earth] is not just for you. You are a piece of a total life and it comes through to you very powerfully that you are up there as a sensing element for man . . . You're out there on the forefront and you have to bring that back somehow . . . And all through this I've used the word you because it's not me . . . it's you, it's we. It's Life that's had that experience."[16]

Love of Self, Love of Other, Love of Life

There are three main foci of love – love of self, love of others, and love of Life. In addition to being interconnected with each other, the three are also related to power.

Love of self

> *... so acceptance of oneself is the essence of the moral problem and the acid test of one's whole outlook on life . . . What I do unto the least of my brethren, that I do unto Christ. But what if I should discover that the least amongst them all, the poorest of all beggars, the most impudent of all offenders, yea the very fiend himself – that these are within me, and that I myself stand in need of the alms of my own kindness, that I myself am the enemy who must be loved – what then?*[17]
>
> CARL JUNG

So far, love has mainly been defined as the force that brings us into relationship, the force that pushes me to see you, to affirm your existence as equal to mine. It is the force that draws me closer to you and to understanding you.

Roberto Assagioli, in *The Act of Will*, says that, "The first love is love for one's self."[18] However, it is extremely difficult to feel real love and acceptance for oneself if one has not been adequately loved and accepted by others. The psychological attachment theorists as well as Firman and Gila explain that the self or "I" needs to be "invited out from among the content and process of [one's] personality"[19] by being seen or mirrored by empathic others. Being seen and being accepted gives a sense of security and okay-ness as you express that self in the world – the power of your being.

Unfortunately, no matter how good our parents or our teachers are, the systems that we grow up in are often dysfunctional and treat us as objects to some degree. In such systems we are not adequately seen or appreciated. When this happens, self-love and acceptance does not develop fully enough to provide us with the inner resources we need to cope with the trials and disappointments of life. In addition to family and educational systems, we also develop within social, cultural and political systems that don't fully see and appreciate their members because of deep-rooted system dynamics such as sexism, racism, classism, or political disenfranchisement. All of these system dynamics mitigate against developing an adequate love of self and sense of self worth.

However adequate your sense of self is, it is still true that if you want to be seen, you have some responsibility to make yourself visible. It is much easier to do so when you appreciate yourself as you are. And if you want acceptance from others, it is essential to hold at least enough love for yourself to let the acceptance of others in.

The role of love of self, which is self-esteem, in moving out of systemic wounding toward real power of being could not be said more eloquently or forcefully than did Martin Luther King in his speech to the Southern Christian Leadership Conference in 1967:

> *Psychological freedom, a firm sense of self-esteem, is the most powerful weapon against the long night of physical slavery. No Lincolnian emancipation proclamation or Johnsonian civil rights bill can totally bring this kind of freedom. The Negro will only be free when he reaches down to the inner depths of his own being and signs with the pen and ink of assertive manhood his own emancipation proclamation. And, with a spirit straining toward true self-esteem, the Negro must boldly throw off the manacles of self-abnegation and say to himself and to the world, "I am somebody. I am a person. I am a man with dignity and honor."*[20]

Love of other

> *When she looked at me, she really looked at me, and I knew I existed.*
>
> JOE LAMB, from the movie "Super 8,"
> speaking about his dead mother[21]

Mirroring and acceptance from others is intimately tied to the self-esteem and courage that enables us to own the power of our being in the world. This, then, is the gift that we give to another when we love them and see them. We call them into existence, value them as equals, and simply by seeing them, we encourage them to express their uniqueness and potentialities in the world.

This equality, which is recognized when we truly love, is what allows *power with* to exist. When I love my self and I love you, I feel safe to express the power of my uniqueness and I recognize and encourage you to express your uniqueness. I acknowledge that we can both be powerful selves at the same time, together.

But another dilemma remains: if I am living in dysfunctional systems where I am not affirmed enough and don't feel safe enough to express either my love or my power, where else can I turn?

Loved by Life, Love of Life

In the last chapter we talked about the source of our uniqueness, the power of our being, ultimately flowing from a larger source of energy – Life. All living beings participate in this source, whether we are aware of it in the moment or not. We are one thread in the web of life, the larger fabric of the universe "out of which we cannot fall,"[22] as Joanna Macy says.

Buddhism uses the metaphor of Indra's net to describe this web of life that encompasses all beings. *"Imagine a vast net; at each crossing point there is a jewel; each jewel is perfectly clear and reflects all the other jewels in the net, the way two mirrors placed opposite each other will reflect an image ad infinitum. The jewel in this metaphor stands for an individual being, or an individual consciousness, or a cell or an atom. Every jewel is intimately connected with all other jewels in the universe, and a change in one jewel means a change, however slight, in every other jewel.'*[23] Even at those moments when we feel most lost, least mirrored, most afraid, we are still being held by, and are still an integral part of, something greater than us.

Simply remembering this fact is the first step in disidentifying from despair and reconnecting to that larger source of Life. In reconnecting, you move closer to it and allow it to move closer to you. By recalling the source, you are once again connected to Life and love. And by reconnecting to this larger fabric of Life you no longer experience yourself as totally alone. While it may be true that no one may ever completely see you or know you, it is also true that you are not alone and isolated. You are fully a part of a larger Whole out of which you cannot fall no matter what your current situation or feelings about yourself.

In his book *Proof of Heaven,* brain surgeon Eben Alexander describes his own near-death experience from a bacterial infection in his brain. Because of his extensive knowledge of the brain and its mechanisms, he had always made light of claims of near-death experiences even when reported by his own patients. His own experience, however, convinced him that the realm to which he traveled was "not remotely dreamlike but ultra-real – as far from illusory as one can be." One of the first beings he met in "heaven" was a beautiful angelic being who became his guide. Early in their meeting, she said to him. "You are loved and cherished. You have nothing to fear. There is nothing you can do wrong."[24] In the book, Dr. Alexander writes about the love and power that comes from knowing that you are being held, accepted fully, by Life, spirit, or God. This is the ultimate acceptance, the true experience of unconditional love.

But there is also *our* love for Life, spirit, or God. Have you ever felt amazement and gratitude for the sheer fact of being alive? Abraham Joshua Heschel captures this joy when he says, "*Just to be is a blessing. Just to live is holy.*"

The loving of Life connects us to it and allows us to draw sustenance – love and power – from it. The gratitude for being alive reminds us of our place, our purpose within the Larger Whole. It aligns our individual purpose with the larger purpose of sustaining the continual unfolding of Life. In dysfunctional systems, we lose touch with this larger purpose because the system believes, and causes us to believe, that the system's purpose is supreme. Clearly, this lack of love of the whole of Life leads to much that is wrong in the world today, including environmental degradation, war and poverty.

However, it is possible for each of us to do something, no matter how small, to make the world a better place. You do not have to wait until you, or our systems, are perfect before practicing this kind of love. It is possible to be Life-affirming in how you treat yourself and others, right now, in the moment. It is also possible to be Life-affirming in the structures and processes you use to change systems and to create new ones. When you love, you are reminded that all Life on Earth is already sacred and you act accordingly in your small, everyday behaviors toward yourself, others and Life.

CHAPTER THIRTEEN

THE DANCE OF WE: BALANCING LOVE AND POWER

The danger of untempered will is that it lacks heart ... on the other hand, love without will can make an individual weak, sentimental, overemotional, and ineffectual . . . . One of the principal causes of today's disorders is the lack of love on the part of those who have will and the lack of will in those who are good and loving. This points unmistakably to the urgent need for the integration, the unification, of love and will.[1]

ROBERTO ASSAGIOLI, M.D.

One of the greatest problems of history is that the concepts of love and power are usually contrasted as polar opposites. Love is identified with a resignation of power and power with a denial of love. What is needed is a realization that power without love is reckless and abusive, and that love without power is sentimental and anemic. Power at its best is love implementing the demands of justice. Justice at its best is power correcting everything that stands against love.[2]

DR. MARTIN LUTHER KING, Civil Rights Leader

The Problem

As is clear from the above quotes, there are severe downsides to the use of power without love or vice versa. As individuals, whether by nature or nurture or both, we have a tendency to be attracted to and better suited to use either one or the other. And therein lies the problem. As Assagioli says, *"Love and will are generally present in individuals in inverse proportion. That is to say, those in whom love is predominate tend to possess less will and are little inclined to use what they have, while those endowed with a strong will often lack love or even exhibit its contrary."*[3]

In addition, our society has very little understanding of the concepts of either love or power in the way that I am talking about them here. This means that when you do express your dominant quality, you tend to express the cultural norms of that quality, which are only partial at best, or damaging at worst. When you express power, you gravitate toward *power over* or control and domination of others. You think more of what *you* need or of what *you* are trying to accomplish and see others only as a means to that end. If love is your strong suit, you tend to fall into being overly inclusive and allowing, taking care of others' needs even if it means sacrificing your own or the system's needs. This lack of understanding of love and power, coupled with the lack of balance of the two, has definite consequences in our lives, both for ourselves and for others.

In an article in *Atlantic* magazine, "How to Land Your Kid in Therapy,"[4] psychologist Lori Gottlieb writes about Baby Boomer parents who were so concerned about raising happy children that they smothered them with love and attention and rescued them whenever they ran into difficulty. As a result, these children have not learned how to confront and manage hardships on their own. The smothering love has kept them from experiencing the *power of* their own being. Consequently, she is seeing more and more young patients who feel loved but empty inside.

There are not many good models of parenting from a place of balance between love and power. In addition, many boomers, partially in reaction to the more rigid power-over parenting style of the 1950's and 60's, have a strong tendency toward the love side of parenting, including all of its deficiencies. Because of this, we have not always been comfortable practicing the theories that try to balance love and power.

I remember reading *How To Talk So Your Kids Will Listen And Listen So Your Kids Will Talk*[5] and realizing how sensible the idea of logical consequences was. It allowed me to see my daughter as an independent being who was learning how to negotiate life and make her own choices. Rather than get into interminable arguments or punish her when she did not respond to my advice (really, more like my attempts to have *power over* her), I could just let her suffer the logical consequences of her choices and learn from them. But I couldn't. The first time, at age 4, when she chose not to wear a coat to play in the snow in the middle of a New England winter, I was unable to let her do it and suffer the consequences. In looking back, I'm pretty sure she would have come back to get her coat before she got frostbite. It is not that the theory and practice wasn't good and useful; I just wasn't balanced enough between love and power to either set clear boundaries and enforce them or let her suffer the consequences of her choices.

Adam Kahane writes about the generative and degenerative aspects of both love and power.[6] He says that the generative side of power is, obviously, the *power to* make things happen and get things done. It is also the drive to grow and realize one's self in the world. The degenerative side of power is *power over* and the control of others to meet one's ends. The generative side of love, he says, brings together, unites the separated, and cares for relationships. The degenerative side of love, which Kahane points out is less obvious, is the attempt to create harmony in relationships at any cost. It tries to keep divergent forces together even if it stifles individual or group development. In other words, degenerative love "overlooks or denies or suffocates power."[7]

In speaking of their complementarities and the need to use them together, he says, "Love is what makes power generative instead of degenerative. Power is what makes love generative instead of degenerative."[8] Similarly, love is what makes *power with* possible. One of the biggest developmental steps that I, and many who share my values, need to learn is how to use our power in service of our love.

Most of us feel more comfortable with and better able to express either power or love. Is this true for you? If so, which are you better at? If you are not sure, think about some of the following situations and see if they help you decide. You will note that I have broken each of the qualities of love and power into two categories, 1) examples that are usually considered to be the strengths or more constructive side of that quality, and 2) examples that are usually considered to be the limitations or weaknesses of that quality. Because each of us has our own versions of the strengths and limitations of love and power, this is not an exhaustive list, but rather a sample of experiences to get you thinking.

Those more comfortable in the love arena often experience these positive aspects of love:

- You want to bring people together in various ways, for example: networking; conversations for the sake of better understanding; matchmaking; compromise solutions to problems.
- You are a good listener and you are able to empathize easily with others. People say you really understand them.
- Being civil/nice/kind is a high priority for you. You are a peacemaker.
- You feel great compassion for the disenfranchised and want to do more to help society as a whole include those less fortunate as respected members.
- When you run meetings you want to make sure that everyone is heard, especially divergent voices, even if it takes longer.
- How other people are feeling is as important to you as what they are thinking.
- As a parent you are able to see things from your child's perspective.

Limitations of love:

- You don't like to "make waves." (e.g. You tend not to send restaurant meals back to the kitchen if they are not right.)
- You see the validity of multiple perspectives and sometimes this makes it hard to make a decision.
- It is hard to say no and set boundaries.
- You rush in to soothe your child's disappointments or losses, only to find that you are more upset than they are.
- You have a long to-do list; you spend a lot of time taking care of others and have little down time for yourself.
- Sometimes you lose yourself in another's feelings or in your feelings for another.

- It is uncomfortable for you to express your needs, while at the same time you often end up resenting others for not seeing and meeting them.
- You judge yourself more harshly than others.

Those more comfortable in the power arena often experience these positive aspects of power:

- You know what you think and are able to state your opinions clearly.
- You are decisive and are equally comfortable doing tasks yourself or delegating them.
- You pay attention to power dynamics in a given situation and try to increase others' power without diminishing your own.
- You let other people make their own decisions and learn from their mistakes.
- You are able to persist in getting what you need.
- You make clear agreements and are able to set clear boundaries.
- It is easy for you to say "no" when the situation warrants it.
- You recognize the value of feedback and don't hesitate to ask for it or to give it.

Negative aspects of power:

- People say you aren't listening to them, or that you are stubborn.
- You dislike the consensus process. It is too inefficient and takes too long. You'd much rather get input and make the decision yourself.
- You find yourself in a lot of arguments that don't necessarily get resolved.
- You don't like to compromise. It never seems like the best solution or it feels like a sign of weakness.
- You believe your children should do what you say because you are the adult; your employees should do what you say because you are the boss; your spouse should do what you say because you are right.
- Feelings, both yours and other people's, are sometimes scary, confusing, or overwhelming, and better avoided if possible.

Being more comfortable in one arena doesn't mean that you have mastered that quality. It usually means that you are stronger in both the positive *and* negative side of that energy. In trying to balance these qualities, practice turning the negative side of your strong suit into more positive behavior. At the same time, experiment with expressing the generative aspects of the quality you are trying to develop. My experience, with myself and in teaching others, is that when we first try to practice adding qualities from our weaker side, often we end up expressing the degenerative side of that quality. So don't be surprised if it is uncomfortable at first, or if you make mistakes like hurting someone because you were awkward in how you expressed your power. This is part of the process of learning how to balance love and power.

For most of my life I have been strongest in the love arena, including all the negatives that come with that. As I tried to own my power, I seemed to swing to the other side of the pendulum, thinking that if I didn't get my way then I wasn't owning my power. I started micromanaging everything in a *power over* way; and I stuck to my guns in an argument whether I was right or not. In contrast, a corporate executive and father that I was coaching wanted to bring more love into his life. After we discussed this in a coaching session, he went into a meeting with his team with the intention to practice love and inclusiveness. He led off by saying, "I want us to make this decision together, so what do you really feel about this strategy?" People trusted that he meant it, and as they spoke more and more, there were so many divergent feelings and thoughts in the room that he didn't know what to do. He was paralyzed. Finally, he ended the meeting and went off and made the decision on his own, albeit having been influenced by the discussion. But naturally, his team did not feel like they had made the decision together.

When I saw him next, he was exasperated and ready to give up, "Besides my team meeting, I also really tried to listen to my 10 year-old daughter, but she has so many conflicting feelings and issues that I didn't know how to help her fix them. All I could say was, 'Uh huh' or 'wow' or 'gosh.' I felt totally incompetent!"

This is natural when you are developing a new quality. You feel awkward, make mistakes and learn from them, and eventually you become more comfortable. Also, in the case of love and power, there aren't a lot of good models for the practice of the positive side of either, and even fewer models of people who balance both. The key, I remind my corporate executives and students (and myself), is not to totally let go of your strong side while you are practicing the other quality. Remember, you are adding to what you already possess; you are not starting from scratch.

Exercises and Reflections

- Who is someone you see as a good example of the expression of power? How does this person express it, both in ways that work and don't work? What can you personally learn from them about the expression of power?
- Who is someone you see as a good example of the expression of love? How does this person express it, both in ways that do and don't work? What can you personally learn from this person about the expression of love?
- Who is someone you see as a good example of a blend of love and power? How does he or she express both? At the same time? Sequentially? A synthesis? What can you personally learn about the balance of love and power from this person?

Martin Buber's I and Thou

One of the ways that I like to think about the balance of love and power is based on the writings of Martin Buber. Buber was a German-Jewish philosopher who was born in 1878 in Vienna and died in 1965 in Jerusalem. One of his major works, *I and Thou*, was published in 1923.[9] [Author note: depending on the translation, "I – Thou" and "I – You" will be used interchangeably.] Many people are familiar with the phrase "I and Thou" and have an intuitive understanding of its meaning. Fewer have delved into the complexities of his work because Buber is very difficult to read. This is, in part, because we are working with translations from the German, but also because Buber himself struggled with the language to express the nuances of his thinking, in some cases developing new words or using old words in new ways.

Most people understand the phrase "I-Thou" to mean that I treat you as a unique, sacred being and, as such, fully my equal in our relationship. Most take this to mean that if we are in an "I-Thou" relationship, I should treat you with the love and respect with which I wish to be treated, as articulated in the Golden Rule. But Buber deepens this meaning. First, he says that because all life is relationship ("*All real living is meeting,*"[10] and "*All actual life is encounter.*"[11]) *how* we are in relationship, actually determines *who* we are in that moment. He says that there are two possibilities: we are either the I of an I-It relationship or we are the I of an I-Thou relationship, depending on whether we are treating the other as an "it" – an object – or as a "Thou" – a sacred being. "*There is no I as such but only the I of the basic word I-Thou and the I of the basic word I-It.*"[12]

This means that if I am seeing you as an object, as a "thing" in my life, like "a good barber" or "the cashier" or "mom" or "my boss" – that means something not just about you, but also about me. In that moment, "I" am not the sacred, unique being of *my own* fullness, "I" am the I of the I-it relationship, an object in relation to another object. "I" am "the worker" in relation to "my boss"; "I" am "the customer" in relation to "the good barber"; "I" am "son" in relation to "mom." In all of these cases, I limit the other and myself to partial expressions of our true selves. "*The basic word I-Thou can only be spoken with one's whole being. The basic word I-It can never be spoken with one's whole being.*"[13] For me, this means that not only is how I see you important, but where I am coming from as I try to see you is also important. As Buber wrote, "*When one says You (Thou), the I of the word pair I-You is said, too. When one says It, the I of the word pair I-It is said, too.*"[14]

My definition of power is the *power of* one's being, in the moment, being expressed in the world. So to me, power is equivalent to standing in the "I" of an I-Thou relationship. I can intend to see you as a Thou, but if I am not coming from my fullness in that intention then I turn us both into "Its." For example, if I try to see you as a Thou, so that I can be a better person, then you are a resource for me, an object for my growth, and we are both "its." If I try to see your "'Thou-ness" and see you as an amazing person who is so divine that I can never be like you, then I am not accepting my own sacredness. I am putting myself in a one-down relationship and therefore I am not in the fullness of my being which compromises our relationship. So it is essential to approach relationships from both the "I" side and the "Thou" side.

The Principle of Respect and Inherent Value

My thinking about the mindful use of love and power has led me to formulate what I call the Principle of Respect and Inherent Value:

> *You* **are a unique human being with inherent value as an**
> **expression of Life**
> while simultaneously and equally
> *I* **am a unique human being with inherent value as an**
> **expression of Life**

If I am trying to balance love and power in my life and if I have the intention of creating the space for more I-Thou encounters, then I will try to approach all relationships with the Principle of Respect and Inherent Value. I have value and deserve respect as an expression of Life *while in the same moment, and equally,* you have value and deserve respect as an expression of Life.

This may seem obvious and hardly deserving of being labeled as a principle, but just as some people are better in the power arena and some in the love arena, the same is also true in the I-Thou arena. Some people are more focused on the "I" side (the *power of* side) of the sacred word and some more focused on the Thou side (the love side). But by focusing more predominantly on one side, you can unintentionally turn those encounters into I-It relationships. If you care so much about the other that you forget yourself, then you turn yourself into an object, an "it." If you focus too much on getting your needs met, you turn the other into an object to meet those needs and the other becomes an "it."

In order to balance love and power, it is necessary to be mindful *simultaneously* of both the I and the Thou sides of the sacred word I-Thou. This is the essence of Buber's work. I discovered this the hard way. There was a period of several years where friends were going through painful dying processes or were severely incapacitated. Because I am more comfortable in the love arena, it was easy to put myself in their shoes, experience their physical and emotional pain, and feel compassion for them. I wanted to help make their pain go away. In several cases, I left home to be with them for extended periods of time. My intention was to treat them as "Thous" during their most difficult times, no matter what they were going through or how painful it was for them or me. Each situation required long hours, focused attention, little sleep, and being surrounded by constant emotional and physical pain.

I was able to maintain my attitude of "Thou-ness" for a good amount of time, drawing energy from the love connection to my friends and the other helpers. But in each case I eventually became overwhelmed and burned out, and unconsciously, I resented the situation I was in. I was so focused on the "Thou" side of the equation–valuing, respecting and helping the other–that I totally lost touch with the "I" side of the equation – valuing, respecting, and taking care of myself. Having experienced this multiple times, I am finally starting to learn. Now I try to practice caring for both myself and others simultaneously, thereby trying to put into practice the Principle of Respect and Inherent Value.

I intend for this principle to convey the idea that 'I respect you and myself equally.' However, no matter how strongly I emphasize this, my students and the executives I coach often understand it as: "We should respect and value *each other* equally" or "I'll respect and value *you* if you are respecting and valuing *me*." However, my objective in the Principle of Respect and Inherent Value is to remind myself in the moment that I have the intention to respect and value both of us equally *whether or not* you are doing the same for me. I highlight this because I believe that in trying to hold both you and myself in this way, I remind each of us of, and evoke from each of us, the highest and the best within us – the I and the Thou. It only takes one of us holding this perspective to make a difference in the relationship.

Creating the Conditions for True Meeting

Buber says that the true encounter of another happens between two fully unique human beings *in the moment* – the present – free from pre-conceptions and needs. He says that it happens by grace and not by seeking.

True meeting may happen by grace, but I believe it is possible to have the intention to meet the other and to create the conditions for grace to occur. I believe it is this purposeful act of "speaking the basic word of I-Thou" to another that establishes the opportunity to enter into real communication. It reminds you to be fully who you are, expressing the power of your being, and extends an invitation to the other to meet you fully with the power of his being.

"*The basic word I-You can be spoken only with one's whole being. The concentration and fusion into a whole being can never be accomplished [only] by me, can never be accomplished without me . . . All actual life is encounter.*"[15] Here Buber points to the systems perspective of interdependence. We are always in relationship and we need each other to "actual"-ize, to become a whole being.

Buber equates the world of I-It to the world of egos where everyone is putting themselves first, showing their acceptable qualities, but not relating from the full power of their being. The world of egos is a world of separation, of individual identities vying to be seen for power or for love. Of course, we cannot remain in the I-Thou encounter forever. We are human. Eventually, interpretations, judgments, and needs once again arise and we return to the world of I-It relationships. Buber says that this is the way of life. We move between the two worlds of It and Thou – the material world of its and the spiritual world of true connection. The I-It world is necessary for getting things done and experiencing things, but to Buber it is not the most real or fulfilling world. He says that we cannot live without the world of It, of objects, but to live only in that world means that we lose our essential humanity.[16]

Re-humanizing Our Systems Through I–Thou Relationships

In dysfunctional systems the world of I-It is locked into place by the systemic pressures to preserve the identity, ego, and purpose of the system. In these systems, there is little hope and no encouragement for I-Thou encounters. One of the ways to change dysfunctional systems is to re-humanize them by refusing to treat others or ourselves as objects by practicing the Principle of Respect and Inherent Value. By seeing each of us as a human being with unique value and worthy of respect as an expression of Life, we move from being separated to being in relation. This is part of the power of love. The force which moves us toward each other and reconnects us, love is the hyphen between I and Thou, it is the connecting thread of the web of Life. It is the force that we tap when we truly meet another in our fullness. It re-humanizes us and brings Life and spirit back into the system: "*For as soon as we touch a Thou, we are touched by a breath of eternal life.*"[17]

In his writings, Buber shows a deep understanding of the mutual influence relationships of systems. He implicitly recognizes the relationship of two people as a system, whether it is an I-It or I-Thou relationship. He says that real meeting or encounter (I-Thou) is a mutually-reciprocal dialogue where you have a willingness to be influenced, not just to influence, and an openness to what emerges in that dialogue. In this, he touches on the systemic principle of emergence where a whole is formed that is greater than, and different from, the sum of its parts.

> *Relation is reciprocity. My You acts on me as I act on it. Our students teach us, our works form us . . . we are educated by children, by animals! Inscrutably involved, we live in the currents of universal reciprocity.*[18]

You are constantly influencing others and others are constantly influencing you, whether you are aware of it or not. For this reciprocal influence to be Life-affirming, it helps to approach each encounter with questions such as, "How can I be open to the other? How can I avoid controlling the encounter solely for my benefit or out of my own fears? Do I have the awareness and the willingness to be influenced as well as to influence? Am I willing to allow something unknown to emerge from this meeting?"

You begin to change your experience within systems by treating yourself and others differently. When you try to treat others as "Thous," you influence them, and they in turn affect you by giving you feedback, consciously or not, about how well you did. And through this mutual reciprocity of "Thous" something new emerges in the systems of which you are a part. Together, you begin to change the dominant mode of interaction from power *over* to one of respect and power *with*.

Here is a dramatic example. In December of 1994, a man killed two women and wounded five in two different abortion clinics in Boston. Even within, or perhaps because of, this climate of fear, the Public Conversations Project was able to convene a series of secret dialogues among six women leaders of the pro and anti-abortion groups in Boston. The leaders agreed to keep the dialogues secret so that the people involved could step back from the systemic pressures on them as leaders of a particular stance, and thus, be more likely to talk openly as one woman to another. At the end of almost six years of dialogues, on the eve of the killer's trial, the group went public in the *Boston Globe* about their meetings and what they had learned:

> *These conversations revealed a deep divide. We saw that our differences on abortion reflect two worldviews that are irreconcilable.*
>
> *If this is true, then why do we continue to meet?*
>
> *First, because when we face our opponent, we see her dignity and goodness. Embracing this apparent contradiction stretches us spiritually. We've experienced something radical and life-altering that we describe in nonpolitical terms: "the mystery of love," "holy ground," or simply, "mysterious."*

Their courage – both to express the power of their own being while simultaneously seeing and respecting one another – changed the tenor of the abortion debate in Boston from then on. Months later, when the anti-abortion women heard that an out-of-town group intended to travel to Boston to confront women entering a local abortion clinic, they called the group and told them not to come.

As one of the participants put it:

> *In this world of polarizing conflicts, we have glimpsed a new possibility: a way in which people can disagree frankly and passionately, become clearer in heart and mind about their activism, and, at the same time, contribute to a more civil and compassionate society.*[19]

The Double Golden Rule

Clearly, how I see and treat you affects you and how you see and treat me affects me. This is obvious and understandable. The less obvious part of the equation is that *how I treat myself* or *allow myself to be treated* also has an effect in the system. If you are a boss who wants to promote work-life balance in your organization, but feel stressed and never take holidays or weekends off, your workers feel this and pressure themselves to do the same in order to preserve their place in the system. If you are a mother who protects your children and treats them with love and respect, but who allows your husband to physically or psychologically abuse you, the children see you accepting that abuse and are affected by that as well.

In trying to describe the process of balancing Love and Power or I and Thou, I have formulated what I call the Double Golden Rule:

Do unto *others* as you would have others do unto *you*.
and
Do unto *yourself* as you would have others do unto you.

The Double Golden Rule flows naturally out of the Principle of Respect and Inherent Value. In both cases you remember to include both self and other in your attitudes of love and respect.

The mindful use of love and power will be situational but the following list includes some of the major areas where one might want to practice balancing them. This would mean striving to have both the "I" and the "Thou" columns opposite present in any encounter, exchange, or relationship.

Opportunities to Learn

As I've said, most of us are stronger in either the power or the love arena. This implies that all of us will be faced with learning new abilities if we want to balance love and power in our lives. Life will continue to provide us with opportunities – in adolescence, in love relationships, in work relationships, in marriage, in parenthood, in dealing with aging parents, for example – to hone our skills in the following six areas:

1 *Understanding the meaning of love and power and learning the principles behind balancing them.*

Continue to explore the definitions of power and love in Chapters Twelve and Thirteen, the Principle of Interconnectedness in Chapters One and Eleven, and the Principle of Respect and Inherent Value and the Double Golden Rule in this chapter.

2 *Exploring and learning about your personal obstacles to the expression of love and power.*

This is the interface between the personal and the systemic touched upon in Chapter Eight. This requires looking inwardly at one's blocks to the expression of love and power and at the effects of these blocks on self, other and system.

3 *Developing the intention to balance love and power and to learn to be mindful moment-to-moment of whether you are fulfilling that intention.*

Try to be mindful of the consequences of the lack of or misuse of either love or power in your life, as explored in Chapters Eleven through Thirteen. Choose to achieve a balanced expression of these qualities within yourself. Continually re-choose as your life stages and situations present new opportunities to learn about balancing love and power.

4 *Learning to see how systemic forces are pressuring you to behave in relation to issues of love and power.*

This area is the central focus of all of Part One.

5 *Learning to use love and power together, as power with, to create the "We" that is able change the rules of the system to make it more Life-affirming.*

We investigated **power with** in Chapters Eleven through Fourteen. **Power with** is an on-going dance of love and power that we do together as respected equals. Out of this dance comes what Ken Wilber calls, "the miracle of we,"[20] a very potent force for change.

6 *Learning and practicing the techniques for expressing the balance of love and power in everyday life.*

Skills and techniques are practical applications of the principles presented in Part Two. You could see them as the dance steps of the Dance of We. The skill of mindfulness is presented in the next and final chapter. Two other key skills are touched on in the appendices: 1) How to express love and power in our communications with others, and 2) How to become aware of and step back from our mindsets – the way we see each other and ourselves.

I	and	Thou
My Power	Love	Your Power
	Love is that which is between an I and a Thou. It is what brings us to and keeps us in relationship as two beings of power.	
I am an independent being who is expressing myself authentically. I am informing the world with my being	and at the same time	I see you as an independent being and I am present to your authenticity. I am open to being informed by your being. I am willing to let you be.
I am being visible, open, and willing to be seen	and at the same time	I am trying to see and understand you.
I am advocating for myself, my needs, and my ideas	and at the same time	I am actively listening to you, inquiring and drawing you out in order to better understand you, your needs, and your ideas.
I am expressing my uniqueness as fully as possible	and at the same time	I am drawing out and welcoming your expression of uniqueness and appreciating the diversity you have to offer.
I am standing in the power of my being.	and at the same time	I am standing *with* you, another being with power.
I remember that I am a part of Life, Being, God, Spirit, the source of my power, love and uniqueness	and at the same time	I remember that you are a part of Life, Being, God, Spirit, the source of your power, love and uniqueness.

CHAPTER FOURTEEN

INDIVIDUAL AND
SYSTEMIC MINDFULNESS

Individual Mindfulness

In order to develop either more love or power in your life, and to learn how to balance them, it helps to have awareness in two areas. First, it is necessary to know when you are not expressing one of these forces that may be called for in the moment. Second, it is important to realize when you are expressing either in a negative way. This takes mindfulness. While mindfulness is the essential component of the practice of love and power, it is also, in itself, an expression of both love and power simultaneously.

Many excellent books have been written about mindfulness meditation and mindfulness practice (see Readings and Resources). For our purposes, I will use the term to mean *being aware of and present to, what is happening right here, right now in this moment.*

Most people are familiar with the idea of mindfulness in relation to meditation. Mindfulness meditation involves learning to be still and becoming aware of how our mind seems to have a life of its own that takes us on trains of thought that travel away from the present moment. You might be focused on your breathing and then all of a sudden you realize that you are re-hashing last week's argument with a co-worker. You are totally unaware of having lost focus, much less of how the argument arose in your mind and grabbed your attention. It is as if all of a sudden you wake up and remember that you had intended to focus on breathing. What caused you to wake up and remember your intention? Sometimes it is a nodding of your head, or a pain, or a sound that brings your awareness back and reminds you of your breathing. But at other times, you just remember.

Part of the purpose of sitting meditation is to train you to become aware of when your mind starts to travel back to the past or forward into the future, or when it gets distracted by something else happening in the room. Over time you begin to see just how much your mind controls your life through what it focuses on. You also might notice that certain thoughts are connected to strong feelings so that every time a given thought crosses your mind, you also experience that feeling. For example, every time you think about your children you might feel happy or worried, or every time you think about public speaking you feel dread. You also see over time how some thoughts just come and go with no substance to them unless they grab you and you invest them with energy because you continue to pay attention to them. Eventually, you begin to comprehend just how strong thoughts are and how easy it is for them to take you away from your intention to stay present in the moment.

The focus and presence you learn in sitting meditation is directly applicable to mindfulness in everyday life. Presence is meant to be practiced and strengthened in your ordinary activities and relationships as well as on the meditation cushion. If you want to express more love, it is necessary to be aware of when you are not doing so. If you want to be more in touch with the power of your being, you first must notice when you are being pulled out of yourself either by being overly loving or by trying to control others or events through power over. Bringing these qualities into your life requires that you 1) practice the Life-affirming expressions of love and power using the principles that I have outlined; and 2) practice being mindful of when you are, and are not, doing so.

Mindfulness is itself a practice of both love and power simultaneously. When you are mindful and fully present to what is in front of you, you move closer to what is there, you meet it as it is and enter into relationship with it. This is one of the definitions of love. Remember a time when you were talking with someone while thinking about something else. In that moment you were not really in relation to the person. You were with your thoughts. Then perhaps you suddenly realized that you had not heard what they were saying and you re-focused your attention on them and became present again. Doing this re-connected you and moved you back into relationship.

Remembering the interconnectedness that already exists is also one of the definitions of love. When you become mindful of falling out of relationship, you then have the choice of reconnecting by using your love practices. This is the love component of mindfulness, that is, being present and remembering our interconnectedness, brings us into relationship.

You know those times when you are fighting with your spouse or a colleague and you get so caught up about who is "right" about the content of the argument that you polarize with each other? If you can be mindful in the moment, and realize that the polarization is pushing you apart, that awareness gives you a choice – do you want to continue moving further apart or do you want to try something, anything, that will break the distancing momentum and move you closer together? For instance, you might say something like, "Hold on a minute. I realize that I am getting caught up in trying to be right and that's getting in the way of my hearing and understanding your perspective. Can we start again and I'll just listen and really try to get what you are saying? Maybe if I understand your point of view, I'll be able to be clearer about mine. Would that be OK?"

In addition, to be aware of and present to what is happening right now in this moment demands that you be centered in yourself. Being present requires presence. It means showing up with the fullness of your being to meet whatever is happening in the moment. When you are fully mindful you can be present to yourself as well as the other. What is going on inside you *is* part of the present moment. You are standing in yourself and meeting whatever or whoever is in front of you, as well as whatever is inside you. Standing in the fullness of yourself, whoever that is in the moment, is being authentic. This is the power component of mindfulness: remembering to be present brings you back to the power *of* your being.

Let's say in the previous example, that you have listened carefully to your spouse or colleague, have repeated what you heard them say and they have acknowledged that you now understand their perspective. At this point, if you are mindful and present to yourself, you might say something like: "OK, so now you agree that I understand what is important to you here. I'd like to try again to explain what is important to me because I'm uncertain about whether or not you fully understand it. Perhaps I haven't been clear or I haven't asked you what you are hearing from me, but I'd like to try to explain my point of view again. Would that be OK?"

Being mindful is simply seeing what is there as clearly as possible. For some, it might even evoke curiosity, an impulse to penetrate more deeply into what is in front of them. This is what I felt the morning I woke up and saw Abby as if for the first time, looking at her features and wondering "Who is this person?" It is simply being centered in who you are (power) and being with, staying in relationship to (love), whatever or whoever is there.

Being aware and present simply means accepting what is, as it is, in the moment. It is not judging, interpreting, or trying to change what or who is before you, or what is happening within you. Nor is it attributing cause or allowing your mind to create stories about why or how it is. From a systems perspective, there are so many mutual-influence relationships affecting a given situation that identifying cause is almost impossible and therefore a waste of energy. The important thing is to observe what is actually occurring, without bias or blame, so that you can see the interactions and relationships more clearly, and therefore, discover alternative ways of being in the moment.

Being mindful also gives you choice about how to act in relation to what is here and now. When you are caught up in and being controlled by feelings or thoughts about the situation, you can become lost in your automatic reactions. When you wake up and see your reactivity, you become more present. This is a form of disidentification, a stepping back from your reactions to a more observant and willful place in yourself. Victor Frankl says it elegantly, "*Between stimulus and response there is a space. In that space is our power to choose our response. In our response lies our growth and our freedom.*"

You still experience the situation fully, but you are now aware of your reactivity as well as the situation and therefore you realize that more choices for action are available to you. You can fully engage with what is in front of you, but you are not controlled by your experience of it or your reactions to it. You can now choose not to react. You can choose to just be with what is happening and see what emerges. Or, you can choose to act, to the best of your ability and with more alignment with your intention to express both love and power in this moment in your life.

When I first met Greg, a coaching client in a large pharmaceutical company, his boss and team viewed him as a good salesman with a great sense of humor but who did not take things seriously. He was told that he made jokes rather than addressing difficult situations. He was confused by this feedback because the boss and the team were laughing at his jokes and unconsciously reinforcing his behavior. His problem came to a head when he made an inappropriate joke during a meeting where a customer was complaining about a quality issue. Even Greg could see that the joke landed like a lead balloon and was out of place. When I asked him to think back to what was going on just before the joke he said, "I was feeling like the company was being blamed for the quality problem, and I was afraid that we might lose the client." I asked him if he could remember anything that was going on in his body in that moment. "Yes, " he said, "I felt this knot in my gut that I feel a lot of the time at work."

I asked Greg to start noticing if there was a relationship between the knot in his gut and his jokes. If he felt the knot, was he tempted to make a joke? Or, if he made a joke and looked back in time, was he feeling the knot just beforehand? Greg came into our next coaching session very excited about what he had found. "First, I made many but not all of my jokes when I felt that knot in my stomach. I couldn't always stop joking when I was aware of the knot, but I did become more aware of the connection. Second, not all of my jokes are connected to the knot, so I don't have to stop making jokes altogether! I like to make people laugh. Third, I saw that I don't just do this at work, but at home with my wife and kids as well. And fourth, twice during the week I felt the knot and was able to keep my mouth shut. It wasn't easy, but I did."

Then I asked Greg what happened when he felt the knot and didn't make a joke. "I was very uncomfortable. The knot got worse both times and there seemed to be some tension in the room when I didn't fill the space. One time while I was struggling to keep my mouth shut, Beth made a joke. It wasn't as funny as mine, but people did laugh." At first, as Greg was able to be mindful of the knot in his gut and not make a joke, people asked him what was wrong. He explained what he was trying to do when he felt the knot of discomfort. As Greg withheld his jokes, the group as a whole began to be aware of one of its patterns: whenever the tension built in the room, someone would make a joke, change the subject, or blame an external person or situation in order to relieve the tension. As a group, they began to be mindful of the tension and able to stay with it longer. Because they were now aware of this group behavior, when someone would say something like, "things are getting weird in here" or "I'm feeling uncomfortable. Is anyone else?" the other members were able to use that as a cue to become more mindful and present as a group. By doing so, they were able to explore what the tension was about and to see if anything creative might emerge out of it.

Systemic Mindfulness

So far we have been talking about an individual person waking up and becoming more mindful and therefore having real choice about how to express more love and/or power in a given situation. But this book is about systems, that is, groups of individuals. As we saw in Greg's example, it is possible for a group or system to be aware of itself and its interactions with its environment. It is possible for a group to learn to wake up and become more mindful and see more clearly what is happening in the moment. But, like individual mindfulness, it takes intention to do so and lots of practice to get into the habit of doing it as a group.

Systemic mindfulness is a component of what Peter Senge and others refer to as "organizational learning," or what Tom Atlee calls "co-intelligence."[1] There are many processes and techniques to help a system become more mindful of itself and its behaviors and to learn from them. I list many of them in the bibliography, including Tom Yeomans' Corona process, REOS consultants' Social Labs, the GE Workout Process, David Bohm's Dialogue Process, Women's Circles, the World Cafe, Harrison Owen's Open Space, or Marvin Weisbrod's Future Search Process, just to name a few. All of these techniques help large groups to step back, become more aware of their thought processes, their behaviors and the diversity in the room, and to make collective choices based on seeing the whole more clearly. All of these processes are structured and guided by a facilitator who takes the group through the experience. The group can then learn how to facilitate the process on its own in the future. This is much like a meditation teacher teaching mindfulness meditation and the individuals then practicing it on their own.

In addition, just as the individual is able to learn to identify the signals that he or she is not being mindful in the moment, so too can a group learn to identify when it is caught in its system dynamics and how to wake up in the moment to see what is going on more clearly. What are the clues that the system forces are running the show rather than the group members? And what can we, as a group, do about it in the moment? In Greg's team, the group identified the clues to the group tension: a) long silences, b) jokes, c) changing the subject, and d) blaming external factors. If these clues occurred, individuals learned that they could call a time-out and say, "I think we are in our tension-avoiding dynamic. Let's try to see what is going on." It was not always the same person who called the time-out. As the group took responsibility for itself, the first individual to become aware in the moment would prompt the others. Then they could all explore the tension together.

I experienced the importance of group mindfulness firsthand when I started teaching in Russia in 1995, only six years after the fall of the Berlin Wall and the disintegration of the Soviet Union. The Harmony Institute was committed to bringing western existential, humanistic, and spiritual psychology to Russia. I was asked to teach organizational systems theory to the third-year students in their three-year post-graduate program. I did not know what to expect. I did not speak Russian and would be working through a translator. To complicate matters further, I would be using Barry Oshry's very experiential Organization Workshop to give them a feel for dysfunctional system dynamics and how to create more empowered systems. To my knowledge this workshop had never been done in Russia and I had no idea if or how they would relate to it.

Given all of these unknowns, the three-day workshop went extremely well – until the third day. The students had done the organization simulation and loved it, feeling all of the predictable system pressures on Tops, Middles and Workers. They had understood everything, including Barry's slang phrases such as "Tops suck up responsibility to themselves" and they were excited about what they were learning. Then, on day three, when we were talking about empowered actions that Tops, Middles, and Bottoms could take in the system, everything fell apart. They got confused and were having trouble understanding what I was saying. They were blaming the translator (as I was) and the translator was blaming me (as I was) for not being clearer. All of a sudden these happy, eager people became angry and aggressive. As I was thinking about how I would never teach in Russia again, it suddenly occurred to me that something was going on in the group as a whole (all of the blame flying around was one of the flags for me). I quieted the angry mob and asked something like:

"In the spirit of learning about systems would you be willing to take a time-out from the content I've been presenting to step back and look at what is going on right now in the class as a whole?"

There was eager consent.

"Okay. We've been together for two whole days and you've understood everything I've said, including my jokes, perfectly well. Would you agree with that?"

There was complete agreement.

"And today, all of a sudden, you are confused, you think the translator is doing a bad job, and I am being unclear. Is that your experience?"

There were many nods of agreement.

"So here's my question: If we assume that it is not the translator or how I'm explaining this or your ability to understand that changed all of a sudden, what else might be going on for the group as a whole right now?"

"Well, we don't have a word in Russian for empowerment and that is causing confusion," said a student. Another disagreed and said, "But somehow we understood what Mark meant when he said that dysfunctional systems disempower us. But, still, you might be right that this has something to do with this concept of empowerment . . ."

"When I talk about empowerment, what feelings does that bring up in the group as a whole?" I asked.

Now there was long silence, some confused looks, and a lot of glancing around the room.

"Maybe we can get a sense for the feelings of the group as a whole by sharing what is going on inside of each of you right now as we talk about empowerment. Would you be willing to do that?"

Now there were nods of assent followed by the sharing of feelings of sadness, depression, anger, guilt and being ashamed. These, in turn, were met with many more nods of agreement.

I was very surprised by the feelings that they shared. I had experienced resistance to these ideas before, but not in the form of sadness, guilt or shame.

"There's no excitement, or energy, or sense of possibilities?" I asked hopefully. There were a lot of heads shaking no, and then a long silence. Since I didn't have a clue what was going on, I decided to trust and allow their thoughts and feelings to deepen. Finally (Thank God!) one of the students said, "I think what might be going on is this: When you talk about being empowered and taking responsibility for our automatic responses to system forces, the main system we think of – of course – is the Soviet Union. (People started to sit up, perk up and nod unanimously in agreement.) And when you say that Bottoms should not sit back and wait for the Tops to change, but rather take responsibility for the conditions of their own world, it forces us to ask ourselves, 'Was there more we might have done as empowered Bottoms or Middles within the Soviet system?' I, for one, am scared about what I might find if I ask myself this question."

With this comment the energy in the room lifted and everyone came alive again and there was a lot of rapid discussion among themselves in Russian that the translator couldn't keep up with. Interestingly, as I was sitting there letting their excited Russian conversation flow around me, I realized that this was the same question I had asked myself when I left our cult in California and became aware of my tendency to blame the leader and the group. It was scary to ask, "Is there more I might have done? Could I have found more courage to speak up about what I saw and felt?" These questions opened up the possibility that I might have more responsibility for my actions than I was taking.

I felt a great deal of compassion for the students in the room at that moment. Being aware sometimes confronts us with difficult choices. It seems like it might be easier and less painful to be blind to or repress what is going on in front of us.

I started to feel badly for possibly giving these Russian students the impression that I thought they should have overthrown the oppressive Soviet regime. But if I couldn't speak up in the oppressive system of the cult, how could I be so arrogant to imply that they could have done more? Fortunately at that moment another student spoke up, "It would be easy to blame you for asking such a question or making such a statement since you weren't here and don't know how difficult life was for us back then. But we understand that if we did blame you, it could potentially keep us from learning something powerful about the past, and even more so as we move into the future. Besides, it was not you who connected this to the Soviet Union. It was us. Thank you."

There were no more problems with translation and the workshop ended with much excitement and eagerness to put into practice what they had learned.

As you can see, as a group becomes familiar with the experience of system forces and how ingrained they are, it is often possible for a group member to wake up the group by calling a time-out and thereby helping it to become mindful of what is going on in the group as a whole in that moment. It helps if the system has the intention to learn about itself and grow, and some awareness of the group's particular clues or wake-up calls that remind it to be mindful. The member doesn't have to know what is going on. She just has to have the ability to recognize the signals that point to *something* going on, and the courage to call attention to that fact. (In the above example, I had no idea what was happening, I just became aware of the sudden rise in the amount of blame in the room.) However, it is not always possible for a single person to wake up a group and we need to have some humility about how strong system forces are and how hard it can be to get information into a system (such as our cult, for example) or to change a system (such as the Soviet Union).

The Courage to Be Mindful

It might seem strange to think about the courage to be aware. What does this mean? You probably have had the experience of not wanting to look at something, for example a part of yourself that someone is pointing to, or a gruesome news story on television. We all have the tendency to resist, repress or tune out that which we don't want to be conscious of. Often this aversion or resistance to seeing is unconscious and instantaneous. However, we can learn to notice when we are automatically avoiding something, so that in the moment we can choose to turn toward it and simply see it and allow it to be as it is. But it takes the courage to really see what is there. It might be something that is painful or scary, or it might be something that you can't control. That's what happened when I called the time-out in the class in Russia. I was forced to face my own fear and confusion. I had to be willing to hear that what was going on might have something to do with how I was teaching. Perhaps I wasn't being clear. Or, I might have unintentionally offended the students. Or, I might have been using an experiential exercise that couldn't work in Russia, and so on.

Janice Marturano, the founder of the Institute for Mindful Leadership, in a presentation to the 2012 Mindful Society conference, told a story about a leader who had the courage to see the situation she was in with clarity.[2] The leader – let's call her Mary – was the head of a team that was tasked with working on one of the company's most important projects. Several months into the project, she attended a mindfulness training retreat. At the first meeting after returning from the retreat, she became aware of unease in herself and in the room as team members were reporting on their work. She did not know what it was, but she stopped the reporting in order to address the unease. Mary used a process of going around the room and giving each person two minutes to speak without interruptions about the question, "Is this project worth doing?"

As Marturano said, "Obviously it took enormous courage to raise this question on such an important project after the team had already invested time and energy in it." But after the mindfulness retreat, Mary was committed to seeing clearly what was in front of her, and if the project wasn't worth doing she wanted to see it now and not later. Plus, she wanted the team to see clearly what was going on in the group as a whole. Marturano completed the story by saying that the entire group felt that the project was not worth doing, but acknowledging this allowed them to brainstorm how to improve it. In the brainstorming they ended up creating a project "that was far more groundbreaking." So by having the courage to be mindful and see clearly what was in the room – i.e., that no one believed in the project – they created space for something better to emerge.

But being mindful doesn't always end happily. Sometimes, when you have the courage to simply be with what is in front of you without reacting, going away, or trying to change it, what emerges are painful feelings such as despair, sadness, or anger. These are the authentic feelings that you experience about what you see and, ideally, they would be acknowledged and accepted rather than reacted to. Being mindful does not always feel good, and knowing this, it takes courage to be mindful.

I realized one day while reading the morning paper that I was automatically skipping over the stories of suffering and disaster. One moment I was glancing at a headline, "230,000 die in tsunami" and the next thing I knew I was reading about some puppy rescued from a drainage ditch. I instantaneously and unconsciously moved away from the pain of the first story. When I chose to go back and read the story I was immediately overwhelmed by the magnitude of the suffering – 230,000!

I couldn't even begin to comprehend so many dead people and all the attendant suffering. I noticed all the different urges that were trying to take me away from just seeing and accepting that this horrible thing had happened. I wanted to send money to make it better. I wanted to go there and help. I wanted to stop reading. But I tried to just stay with the pain I was feeling while reading the story.

Then I read about a child who had lost her entire family and was found wandering in shock after the tsunami. At that point I just broke down crying, realizing that whatever pain I was feeling paled next to what this young girl had gone through. I let all of this in as the truth of the moment and wailed. Eventually I stopped crying and noticed that I felt softer, like I was no longer bracing myself against the horrors of the world. My heart had opened a little and I was feeling compassion. I still felt the pain of what was happening, but I could look at it more squarely and more honestly and with compassion rather than resistance. Opening to the event and just sitting with it, rather than resisting it also gave me space to consider what I wanted to do about what I was seeing. Seeing a painful situation clearly and accepting it as it is does not mean *not* acting. In fact, if anything, it allows your actions to be more effective because they are based on the reality of the situation rather than reactively based on how you want it to be or on your fear of how it might be.

The Mindful Practice of Love and Power

Intention

Because being mindful is not easy and often takes courage, it is helpful if we set and reinforce our intention to be mindful whenever possible. Do I, or do we as a group, have the intention to practice balancing love and power in ourselves and in our systems? Do I want to be mindful of what is going on in me and around me, even if it is negative, sad, painful, or infuriating, in order to learn and grow? These same questions can be asked of groups as well as individuals. That is why I asked the group of Russian students if they were willing to look at what was going on when the mood in the room changed. The question gave them a choice and allowed them to reaffirm their intention to see clearly and learn.

Each time you "wake up" and remember your intention, you create an opportunity to choose again to be mindful and to face squarely what is in front of you, without judgment, interpretation or the need to change something. And because difficult situations are usually highly charged, it is good to set and reinforce your intention at other times as well, such as in your meditations or prayers, or when you see someone else being courageously mindful. I believe that reinforcing this intention to be mindful is what helps us to wake up when we are on automatic pilot and forgetting our purpose. The more you strengthen your intention individually and as a group, the more often the awakening comes.

Mindfulness Alerts

Once you are clear about your intention to be more mindful, then it helps if you can identify those cues or clues that might alert you to the fact that you are not fulfilling your intentions.

Being unconscious means not being aware. If you are not aware of a feeling or internal pattern that is controlling your behavior such as fear or jealousy or the need to be liked, psychologists say those forces are operating in your unconscious. If you are not conscious of these forces, you cannot transform them. Becoming mindful of these internal psychodynamics gives you an opportunity to observe them, understand them, work with them and liberate the energy that is locked within them for your benefit.

The same is true of those forces that operate outside of our collective awareness in the systems to which we belong. If we as a culture don't understand systems and can't see systemically, then the unconscious system forces will control us, objectify us and separate us.

Mindfulness cues can serve as "wake-up" calls to be present and pay attention to what is happening in the moment, both internally and externally.

Since none of us can change what we are not aware of, I encourage you to look for the mental, emotional or physical signs that will remind you to pay attention to the ideas and principles I have written about in *The Dance of We*. Identifying these visceral clues or wake-up calls is the very first step in the process of practicing these principles into your everyday life and using them to transform the systems of which you are a part.

Individually and collectively it is useful to have reminders that alert us to the dysfunctional system pressures that might be objectifying us, separating us, stifling the flow of information among us, or demanding allegiance from us. It is also helpful to recognize indicators of the need to do a better job of expressing love or power or a balance of the two qualities in a given situation. It is worth the time and effort to explore – individually and together – what some of the key cues are for you and your systems that would wake you up to the fact that you might be succumbing to system forces and remind you that you can practice other behaviors. For example:

- It might be the strength of the blame you are feeling toward another or the amount of blame in the room, that alerts you or the system to the pressures of separation that are present. You then have the choice to use some of the love practices mentioned previously.
- It might be the anger that arises in your belly when you are treated like a cog in a machine and not seen as a unique human being, that wakes you up to the forces of objectification. This cue can remind you to practice your power moves.
- Or, your group might be frustrated once again with a particular member who is perceived as talking too much. The frustration might signal the group to give the member clear feedback about his behavior – a power move. On the other hand, it could be a signal that the group needs to listen more carefully to what he has to say. This would be a love move and possibly help him to feel heard and recognized.

One of the most powerful experiences for me in Barry Oshry's Organization Workshop (see Chapter Three) was the visceral experience of the system pressures as I inhabited different levels of the system. After the workshop was over and I went back to my everyday life, these visceral cues then became wake-up calls alerting me to when I was unconsciously and automatically reacting to the system pressures and had other, more empowered choices that I could make in the moment. Instead of automatically taking all responsibility onto myself as a Top, for instance, and feeling even more overwhelmed and burdened, I could use the feelings of being overwhelmed and burdened as a wake-up call that I might be taking on too much responsibility. Then I had the choice to delegate more tasks to other levels within the system. Or, the frustration of feeling pulled between two different people or groups could serve as a mindfulness alert to get out of the middle and to remember that it is their issue to work out.[3]

Of course, mindfulness alerts are also essential as we attempt to bring the fundamental principles of Interconnectedness, Respect and Inherent Value, the Double Golden Rule, and Honoring Life into our everyday behaviors. These are important but rather abstract principles. To make them a daily practice, it helps to ask ourselves questions that will highlight cues in relation to these principles as well. For example: what are the signs that our system is practicing these principles and what cues will alert us when we are not? How do I know when I am not valuing myself and what I have to offer? What are the cues that I am seeing or treating someone as an "other?" What are the signs that our system might be forgetting that we are a part of an even larger Whole?

There are many more questions you could ask that would facilitate identifying specific cues to help you remember to practice what you have learned here. The purpose of these sample questions is to start you thinking about and maybe discussing in your systems, how you want to be expressing love and power, how to tell when you are not expressing them in the way you intend, and what to do about it.*

Mindfulness in Action

These principles are difficult to practice because of the degree of mindfulness that is required to catch these more subtle moments when you are not standing in your true power or not holding the other as a human being who deserves love and respect just like you. By subtle moments, I mean that kind of fleeting moment when you have a choice either to see more clearly, to be more authentically who you are, or both. Being aware of these moments, in relationship, while they are happening, and choosing to act on them or not, is a form of mindfulness in action. One of my coaching clients presented a good example of the difficulty and subtlety of practicing these principles.

Rebecca worked in a non-profit organization. She was trained as a psychotherapist and was a long-time meditator. Intelligent and self-aware, she was a joy to work with. One of her best friends, Justine, also worked at the non-profit. During one of our coaching sessions, Rebecca was very

---

* For those of you who want to explore the issue of mindfulness alerts and how to use them to remind you of the ideas and principles in The Dance of We, I have included a more detailed, step-by-step exercise on my website: www.newcontextcoaching.com.

angry with Justine for hurting her feelings by making an insensitive remark. When I asked her what made the remark insensitive, Rebecca said, "Justine should have known better. She's my best friend and should know that I am sensitive about that issue."

"Have you ever discussed your sensitivity around this issue with her?"

"We've talked about the issue many times, so she *should* know that I am sensitive about it."

"Have you ever told her explicitly about your sensitivity? Maybe she was just unaware or unconscious of the issue," I suggested.

"Unconscious, insensitive, what's the difference? She still hurt my feelings."

There was a lot of blame in the way that Rebecca was talking about Justine and a lot of defensiveness when I suggested that Justine might have been unaware. Since Justine was one of her best friends, I assumed that there was something going on in the relational system as a whole, and that Rebecca, as well as Justine, was somehow unconsciously contributing to the dynamic. Because it was a coaching session and not a therapy session, it was not appropriate to go into the reason why Rebecca was so sensitive to this issue. I did, however, take the opportunity to point out a subtle way that Rebecca was contributing to the problem.

"Rebecca, I hear that this is a sensitive issue for you, that you feel hurt, and that you are angry at Justine for doing this to you."

"Yes, clearly."

"Would you be willing to look at what's going on between you and Justine a little more closely? There is a subtle but important point that I think might be helpful to you."

"I guess so."

"You are using the words 'insensitive' and 'she should have known,' which are your interpretations of what she said. They imply causality, that she did this thing to you. She hurt you and you are angry at her for doing so."

"Yes, she did hurt me."

"I know that you feel hurt, but can you see that there is a slight difference between saying 'I feel hurt' and 'Justine hurt me?' If you slow down the interchange you had with her, did it go something like this?: a) she said something, b) you felt hurt, c) you labeled her remarks as insensitive, and d) you blamed her for being insensitive and hurting you?"

"Yes, that's exactly what she did."

"Do you see any role that you played in this event?" I asked.

"What do you mean?"

"When you label her words as insensitive, that is your interpretation, your mindset about her remarks. This mindset then leads to anger and blame as if she did this thing to you."

"Well they were hurtful."

"Yes. You felt hurt. But, again, there is a subtle but significant difference between saying 'I felt hurt' and 'she hurt me.'"

"It seems like you are splitting hairs, Mark." I could see that Rebecca was getting a little more defensive and frustrated with me.

"Would you be willing to try one more thing?" I asked and she agreed. "I don't know if Justine should have known about your sensitivity or not. For this exercise, see if you can hold the idea that "Justine should have known" as a belief. Your mind is set and you believe it is true. But what if it isn't the whole truth, or the only truth? How might this belief be limiting you? Is there anything that it might be keeping you from seeing or doing? Slow the process down a little more. Imagine Justine saying the same words to you, but this time consider that your belief might not be the whole truth. If you are able to do that, what happens?"

"I immediately feel a resistance to doing that. I'd have to let go of my anger and of being right. It changes my view of her to someone who just said some words that I ran with. If I don't immediately label it insensitive, I have to consider other possibilities like maybe she was unaware, or maybe I haven't been as explicit as I thought, or maybe she had a lot on her mind that day. I really don't know what was going on inside of her."

"Yes, and what happens to the hurt?" I inquired.

"The hurt is still there, but it is my hurt, my sensitivity. If I want to make the hurt go away, I have to take responsibility for the sensitivity and look at why it is such a hot button for me. But are you saying she doesn't share in the responsibility for this?"

"Yes, I am saying that you don't share the responsibility like 50-50 or 60-40. I would say that you are each 100% responsible for the exchange. Again, I don't know if she should have known better than to say these things or if she was just unaware. She is responsible for looking at that, if she chooses. But no matter which it is, unconsciousness or insensitivity, you are still 100% responsible for what you do with that."

"Wow," she said as she thought about this more, "that's a very subtle difference in how to hold this interchange, but a very powerful one. I think this would be very hard to catch in the moment."

"It takes practice and the intention to not make up stories about other people's actions and to try to hold them with love."

"I do love Justine and know that she wants the best for me, but that totally went out of my head when I started blaming her for doing this to me."

"For the future, Rebecca, what would be a clue that would help you catch in the moment that subtle difference about how you are holding a relationship?"

"I think the first clue would be feeling hurt and the second would be the blame toward another for causing that hurt. If I could recognize those clues, I guess I could ask myself, 'Why is this hurting me? What button is it pushing in me?'"

"Yes, and in that moment, you are less reactive and more proactive. You step back and are looking at the whole dynamic, including your role in it. That gives you more choices about how to act."

Everything that I have written about in *The Dance of We* is an attempt to bring into consciousness the unconscious dynamics of systems, whether they be two person systems or large multi-person ones. This process of making the unseen knowable revolves around mindfulness.

When we are mindful, we begin to notice internal and external systemic dynamics that were formerly unconscious. Once we bring these dynamics into awareness, we have the possibility for more empowered and more caring choices about how to respond to them: we do not have to objectify ourselves or others or allow ourselves to be objectified; we have the choice to move toward others rather than allowing a difficult situation to separate us; and we have the choice to express our deepest values even when the system is pressuring us not to. Becoming conscious of dysfunctional system dynamics is the first step in breaking the control they hold over us and over the families, workplaces or political environments of which we are a part. Mindfulness is the crucial skill in being able to recognize and change dysfunctional systems into Life-affirming ones.

CONCLUSION PART TWO

THE MINDFUL DANCE OF WE

Why this material is so important to me

When my editor began reading the manuscript for *The Dance of We* one of the first pieces of feedback she gave me was, "Watch your 'need tos', 'musts', and 'shoulds.' Clearly, this material is important to you, but you don't have to push so hard on readers. They'll get it."

She was right. The material in this book is so important to me that I want to shout at everyone, "Don't you realize how important these principles are? Why aren't we practicing them?!" Of course, this attitude violates the very principles that I am writing about. First of all, both of these questions are mindsets that separate me from you: 1) I assume they are as important as I think they are, 2) I am assuming you don't understand this, and 3) I am assuming you aren't already practicing these principles to the best of your ability. Secondly, captured by those feelings of overwhelming importance, I forget that although this writing might be an expression of my uniqueness and purpose, you might not see things in this way at all. My attitude of "you need to get this" sees you as somehow lacking, and as an object, a vessel, into which I have to pour my wisdom.

That is a simple but clear example of why I believe this material is so crucial: I am teaching it and writing about it, and yet I can only get it right a small percentage of the time. "So what?" you might say, "That's life. We're not perfect. We make mistakes." Of course, you would be right. We're not saints; we're human beings. We make mistakes. So as I have been writing I've tried to be mindful of this energy to hammer home the ideas and principles. Where is this coming from in me? What I've found is two-fold: an aversion to pain and a deep personal understanding of how subtle and difficult it is to practice these values in daily life.

Aversion to Pain

I have a high tolerance for physical pain and a very low tolerance for emotional and psychological pain, that of others as well as my own. When I see how much pain there is in the world, it hurts me. I don't want to witness that suffering or feel that hurt. So I retreat, make myself numb, or try to avoid it in any way I can. I am sad when I see us treating each other in ways that add to that pain rather than alleviating it. I am seeking to be better at practicing what Zen master Bernie Glassman calls the "Zen of action, living freely in the world without causing harm, of relieving our own suffering and the suffering of others."[1]

But then the subtleties and difficulties of practice confront me and I discover that I am pushing my readers or making assumptions about someone that has led to misguided or hurtful behavior. At those times, I feel ashamed for adding to the pool of world pain and just want to withdraw. (Of course, I also add to the pool by the pain I cause myself by being ashamed.) I am tempted to withhold the power of my being and become invisible. I have to continually remind myself that these ideas and principles are good and might be useful to others even if I am not able to practice them perfectly.

But it is not just the pain I cause another or myself that is at issue here. Because we live in myriad mutual influence relationships or systems, the pain we cause each other becomes magnified many times over. When parents treat each other with disrespect in front of the children, they not only hurt each other, they also injure the children. The children then copy this disrespect in the systems that they inhabit. When the powers-that-be foster an economic system for the benefit of a certain class, they cause pain to the multitudes that are excluded by that system. This pain is magnified in the educational, medical, and social systems of those who are excluded. This eventually comes back and impacts even those who created and maintain the inequality. When Democrats and Republicans gridlock in an effort to hurt the other party, there is little awareness and seemingly no care paid to the pain and damage they are causing throughout America.

Because I have such a low tolerance for this type of pain, I want to make it go away, either by watching television so I can ignore it, preaching to my students or readers, or shaking people and saying, "Stop it!" So far none of these seem to be very effective.

The best *effective* strategy I have been able to come up with is to try to remind others, and myself, about these timeless principles and to take them on as my daily spiritual practice. Because we live in systems, the good we do is also magnified. When I am able to practice these principles, I believe it ripples throughout the system, both as a model to others and in the way it makes others feel to be seen and valued. While this might not totally change a given system, it will bring a little more power, love and aliveness or Life into the lives of the members of that system.

The Subtleties and Difficulties of Practice

The principles of Interconnection, Honoring Life, Inherent Value and the Double Golden Rule that I am writing about here are not new. They are timeless; there are versions of each in every major religion and work of ethics. They are four of several tenets of what might be called the fundamentals of right relations and there are reasons why they have been around for millennia.

On the surface, they are so easy to understand that we take them for granted: "Of course, we are interconnected. We are all human beimgs." But the deeper implications of these principles in our daily interactions are much more subtle and difficult to comprehend and practice. Obviously, we both have inherent value as unique expressions of Life – I am an "I" and you are a "Thou" – but what does this mean when you do something hurtful, like not really seeing me?

One night, my wife and I were on our way to a movie and parked, as usual, in the lot of a bank near the theater. As we got out of the car we noticed a truck towing one of the cars in the lot. Worried that the bank had changed its policy about nighttime parking, I went up to the tow truck driver and asked if he was towing all the cars in the lot or just that one. He had his back to me as he hitched something under the car and didn't answer. I assumed he didn't hear me so I tapped him lightly on the shoulder. He still didn't respond. When he got up, I asked him again but he just walked right by me without acknowledging me and got into his truck. The rage of not being seen welled up inside of me and I yelled, "You're a real asshole!" as he closed the truck's door. Ironically, I had just finished writing the chapter on I-Thou relationships and balancing love and power. This was not my finest moment of practicing what I preach!

Clearly, we teach what we ourselves need to learn. And to rub in just how off base I was, when the car was towed from the space, I was able to see a small sign on the railing saying to leave the space vacant for patrons of the ATM machine even when the bank was closed or your car would be towed.

I noted the name of the tow company and immediately called them on my cell phone to complain about the rude tow truck driver. I made it clear that he could have saved me a lot of time and emotional energy by simply acknowledging that he was towing only that car. The man who answered the phone was the owner. He said he was sorry, but the tow truck driver was just following his, the owner's, rules not to interact with bystanders. We had several rounds of me explaining how a simple acknowledgement – even just pointing at the sign – would have solved everything, and the owner explaining all the reasons for the rule, which just increased my frustration of not being seen or heard. I could see that I was not getting anywhere and I was worried about being late for the movie, so I just ended the conversation by saying, "I hear you have this rule, but I think it's a shitty rule," and hung up.

As I was walking to the theater I began to calm down and realize how overcome with rage I had been at not being seen, and how that rage made me forget my practice of "Zen in action – causing no harm, and relieving my suffering and the suffering of others." I had, in fact, actually created suffering for the poor guy on the phone, perhaps for the tow truck driver, as well as for myself. I then started beating myself up adding even more suffering to the world.

While standing in the lobby of the movie theater, my phone rang and, even though it was a number I didn't recognize, I answered it. It was the owner of the towing company.

"I didn't answer the phone and patiently explain our rules to you in order to be sworn at," he started.

I thought, "Hmmm, maybe the universe is giving me an opportunity to redeem myself with more practice."

I said, "First of all I wasn't swearing at you personally. I said it was a shitty rule. [I was defensive, but I realized it as I was saying it] But you are right; that was not a nice thing for me to say and I am sorry. You must get a lot of angry calls like mine every night [putting myself in his shoes]."

"You have no idea," he said, "especially on weekends and where the spots are poorly marked like at that bank's lot. We are just trying to keep our drivers from getting into fights with irate people by having them not interact at all."

"Just for you to know," I offered, "sometimes the rule backfires. In this case it made me more angry to not be responded to."

"Yes, I know," he said quite dejectedly. "We can't seem to win in either case. We're doing a job that doesn't make anybody happy." Surprisingly, his comment made me feel heard and then a little compassion arose in me.

"Maybe I should go to the bank and ask them to put their signs on poles so they would be easier to see," I thought out loud.

"Would you? That would sure make my life a little easier."

"I'll see what I can do. I appreciate your calling me back to clear the air. Thanks."

This is a rather obvious example of how difficult it is to practice the principles of right relations no matter how much we believe in them. My wound around not being seen got triggered automatically and instantaneously by the rules of the tow truck driver's system that I had chosen to enter. On the other hand, it is also an example of how to come back into right relations with another if you have, or are able to create, the opportunity to do so.

It is also another example of why the principles in this book are so important to me. It is an example of a small system of mutual influence relationships where a little misunderstanding or misinterpretation generated and magnified the normal pain or frustration that comes from daily living.

I think you can see or imagine how much more necessary these principles would be in even larger systems. PSI, our cult, was a prime example where these principles were not practiced and where the pain that resulted affected many people both inside and outside our group.

Healing Within Systems

The psychotherapy institute in California that evolved into a cult, and that I have been using as an example of a dysfunctional system throughout the book, eventually imploded upon itself and ended. The members of the group were scattered all over the U.S. and Europe. Because we had been such good friends and, at least in the beginning, enjoyed working together, we eventually started seeking each other out in order to process our experience and to try to understand what had gone wrong. Many of us felt the need to apologize for the hurt we had caused each other through the use of power over. In time, most of us also looked at what kept us in the group past the point where we knew something was wrong, in other words, why we had let the values of the group take precedence over our personal and higher values.

In the 35 years since the PSI fell apart, almost all of us came back into right relationship and again became close friends. Each of us took what we had learned from that appalling experience and incorporated it into our work and our teaching and the other institutes we formed. Much of that learning was about what contributes to dysfunctional group behavior and about the potential for psychological inflation in trying to help others and in doing spiritual work.[2]

For me, the experience in the group was humbling as I realized how I had succumbed to the systemic pressures and given up who I was along with my values and volition. It was also humbling to see how I had contributed to creating those system pressures for others. I couldn't just hold the group leader or others responsible. The more I understood about systems, the more I realized that we were all caught up in a dynamic that no one of us would have chosen to create, but that somehow had emerged out of our relationships, beliefs, structure, conscious and unconscious rules, and yes, even out of our desire to do good in the world.

Although I would not choose to go through it again, I am grateful for what I learned. The experience launched me on a search to understand what had happened in our group that eventually led to my writing *The Dance of We*.

The Mindful Dance of We

My primary purpose in writing *The Dance of We* is to bring awareness to the simple fact that we all live in systems. We are all interconnected and interdependent parts of larger wholes that can take on a life of their own. The systems perspective allows for a powerful shift in worldview with significant implications for how we all live our lives. It can help us to reject simplistic, linear, cause-and-effect solutions to complex, multi-dimensional problems. When we grasp the interconnected nature of systems, we know that blame and finger-pointing are irrelevant because we know that no one person or group is the cause of a given situation. We understand that individual and system behavior are the result of the beliefs, structures and rules of the system. And, we also know that even though individually we may not have caused a problem, in a system we are all responsible for its solution.

Seeing systems is the first step in being able to step back or disidentify from them. We begin to see how a given system operates and we begin to recognize its pressures on us to objectify ourselves and each other, to separate us, to stifle the flow of information and to demand allegiance to the system values. As we become mindful of these system forces, and consciously choose not to respond to them, we begin to act from our own volition – the power of our being.

The more we make these kinds of choices, the more we liberate and strengthen our power and our love – two of our most essential human qualities. And, by reclaiming our love and our power, individually and collectively, we begin to rehumanize our systems. We remember our fundamental interconnectedness and interdependence and re-join the Dance of We.

The Dance of We is not an easy dance to learn or execute. It is the dance we do between love and power as we try to liberate, integrate and coordinate these two forces in our lives. It takes a lot of practice, and when we don't practice it is easy to forget the steps.

The Dance of We is the dance of power *with* – its steps enable us to act together, in partnerships and in groups, as human beings of equal value and power. System forces are powerful and when we are unaware of them, they often control us. But, at the same time, as I trust has been evident in these pages, there is hope. The power and love of each individual being makes a difference in a system. And when that individual energy is united with other beings of power and love, we have the ability to transform Life-deadening, power-over systems into Life-affirming ones.

Finally, the Dance of We is the dance of joy that arises when we truly see ourselves and each other as unique expressions of Life, and in that moment re-awaken to our mysterious, interconnected participation in the larger, ever-unfolding dance – the Dance of Life.

Would you like to dance?

INTRODUCTION TO APPENDICES

LOVE AND POWER PRACTICES

I have tried to give enough examples in this book for you to get a taste of the practical application of the principles of Interconnection, Honoring Life, Inherent Value and the Double Golden Rule. These are four of several tenets of what might be called the fundamentals of "Right Relations." Since systems are comprised of myriad reciprocal relationships, coming into right relationship with others is a way of healing dysfunctional systems.

The two areas where I believe these principles of right relations can make the most difference to you as an individual and in your family, your workplace, and in society are, 1) how you see yourself and others, and 2) how you communicate. I touched upon your view of yourself and others – what I have called mindsets – in Chapter Five about objectification and self-objectification and in Chapter Thirteen on love and the process of seeing and being seen. Examples of dysfunctional communication processes as well as mindful communication using a balance of love and power, are mentioned throughout the book.

In addition, there are several good books that explain mindsets and a few about how to work with them. There are also many excellent books on how to improve communication skills in daily life and in difficult conversations. All of these books are *implicitly* based on the fundamental laws of right relations, but I have stressed more *explicitly*, and in more detail, how the four principles inform the skills and techniques of mindsets and communication.

When you understand the principles and values behind the different skills and techniques, you realize that by holding them *explicitly*, you improve your ability to maintain successful relationships. In other words, it is even more important to be mindful of where you are coming from when using these techniques as it is to carry out the techniques themselves. If the skills or techniques do not work as you intended, the first place to look is not at the other person, but at whether you were holding yourself and the other person within the light of these fundamental tenets of right relations.

In the two appendices that follow, there are a few examples and stories of how these principles might inform your work with mindsets and how you communicate with others. If you wish to pursue these ideas in more detail, at the end of each appendix there is a list of books that I have found useful in the practical application of the four principles presented in *The Dance of We*. In addition, I encourage you to check out my website www.newcontextcoaching.org for more material about how to use the principles in this book in relation to mindful communication and working with mindsets.

Finally, Appendix C is the version of the purpose exercise that I mentioned in Chapter 11. I use this short visualization in my classes and workshops to help people begin to explore the unique note they are sounding in the great symphony of Life. I hope you enjoy it and find it useful.

APPENDIX A

LOVE AND POWER PRACTICES: WORKING WITH MINDSETS, MENTAL MODELS, AND BELIEFS*

Thinking here was a cartoon in the New Yorker of two women walking down the street with one saying to the other: "I've never forgiven him for that thing I made up in my head." Like the woman in the cartoon, most of us know we make up stories about people and situations. On some level, we also know that these mindsets, beliefs, or prejudices are not the whole truth about a person or situation. And yet, like the woman, we still believe them and act as if they are true. In my work in families, corporations and universities, I have come to see that people do not fully understand the power that our mindsets have over our lives and the effect they have on others and on our systems. We think we understand the power of mindsets, but on the fundamental level of daily practice, we don't.

You cannot successfully practice bringing a balance of love and power into your life without understanding how strongly your mindsets influence you and keep you from seeing yourself and others more clearly and with compassion.

In addition, you will not be able to exercise power with others to change dysfunctional systems into more Life-affirming ones unless you first understand the strength of systemic mindsets and how they affect the

---

This is an excerpt of a longer article of the same title (see Introduction to Appendices). Much of the material here and in the longer article was developed over the years with many colleagues including: Roger Evans, Peter Russell, Bill Joiner, Michael Sales, Jonathan Milton. Lee Farmelo, Bobbi Harvey, & Grady McGonagill.

12 LEVERAGE POINTS IN SYSTEMS

(from weakest to strongest)

12   **Numbers:** Constants and parameters such as subsidies, taxes, and standards

11   **Buffers:** The sizes of stabilizing stocks relative to their flows

10   **Stock-&-Flow Structures:** Physical systems and their nodes of intersection

9   **Delays:** The lengths of time relative to the rates of system changes

8   **Balancing Feedback Loops:** The strength of the feedbacks relative to the impacts they are trying to correct

7   **Reinforcing Feedback Loops:** the strength of the gain of driving loops

6   **Information Flows:** The structure of who does and does not have access to information

5   **Rules:** Incentives, punishments, constraints

4   **Self-Organization:** The power to add, change, or evolve system structure

3   **Goals:** The purpose or function of the system

2   **PARADIGMS:** The mindset out of which the system – its goals, structure, rules, delays, parameters – arises

1   **TRANSCENDING PARADIGMS**

---

behavior and "stuckness" of a group or organization. Systems educator, Donella Meadows, in her paper, "Leverage Points: Places to Intervene in a System,"[3] lists twelve places where systems might be influenced (see sidebar). Meadows maintains that the most effective and powerful way to change a system is to change the "mindset or paradigm out of which the system – its goals, power structure, rules, its culture – arises."

The thirteenth amendment to the constitution changed the rules of our system (#5 on Meadows' list) by abolishing slavery, but the mindsets or prejudices out of which slavery arose have yet to fully change. (#2 on Meadow's list.) The only leverage point that is stronger is the ability to transcend the paradigm, which is what I am referring to when I talk about disidentifying from the mindset.

Mindsets and The Dance of We

I am using the word 'mindset' synonymously with 'mental models,' 'worldview,' 'beliefs,' 'prejudices,' 'assumptions,' and 'paradigms.' The term mindset refers to the frame of reference through which we see and understand the world. Mindsets can be positive as well as negative and both can be problematic: the belief that "Sherry is the only woman in the world for me" can cause just as many difficulties in your relationship as the belief that "Sherry is a conniving manipulator."

The power that mindsets have over us and our systems lies in the fact that how we see the world affects both how we act and how we interpret the actions of others. Seeing Sherry as the only woman in the world for me might create a strong fear of losing her. I might smother her with love, but I might also become very paranoid and possessive. When Sherry feels my smothering and possessiveness, she might start to believe that I am trying to control her life. This might make her want to back off from the relationship a little. When she backs off, I get even more afraid and possessive. And so it goes, in an escalating circle of my trying to hold on and her trying to get away. How I see her and vice versa creates the dynamic and also keeps it going.

Mindsets also drive the behavior of larger systems. Sometimes the mindsets are conscious, but the strongest ones are usually unconscious and therefore have more powerful influence. In our cult, our belief that we were doing "God's work" was conscious (not accurate, but conscious). Some beliefs that were unconscious and therefore unable to be challenged, were a) that there was such a thing as "God's work", and b) that we knew what that was. So we judged other people and groups based on our worldview. We became righteous and withdrew from our colleagues who clearly were not doing this good work. They felt the judgment and separation and, in their anger, tried to show us how arrogant we were becoming. Of course, when they got angry and waved our arrogance in our faces, that only confirmed how evil they were.

What a system believes about itself and the world, either positively or negatively, has a powerful effect both within and outside of the system. For example, the financial community's belief in the 1990's and early 2000's that they were 'masters of the universe' ultimately had disastrous effects on many of those companies as well as the global economy.

Everything that I have been writing about in *The Dance of We* in some way ties back to our mindsets and how we see each other and the systems we inhabit. Seeing systems is itself a broadening of perspective from a simple, linear cause-and-effect mental model.

Here are some of the ways that mindsets or mental models relate to the other topics in this book:

1 When you see a person as an 'object,' for example a boss, a mother, a resource, a cashier, that is a mindset you may or may not be conscious of and that shapes your behavior toward them.

2 When you blame another, that is an assumption about their causality based on your linear, cause-and-effect mental model of how the world works.

3 Mindsets are lenses through which you look at another. Therefore they are 'between' you and separate you from others.

4 Mindsets are only partial views of another person and keep you from seeing the other as multi-dimensional, complex and 'deeper' than what you can see in their outward behavior.

5 You have mindsets about yourself that keep you from being fully who you are in the world, from exercising the power *of* your being.

6 If dysfunctional systems kill the creative expression of who you are, breaking out of systemic mindsets restores your creativity and aliveness.

7 Questioning mindsets allows you to question the values you are operating from – yours and/or the system's.

8 If information flow is the lifeblood of the system, individual and systemic mindsets can either prevent or encourage members from sharing information freely.

9 Mindsets or paradigms are powerful forces that either keep you from experiencing the principle of interconnectedness or encourage you to base your actions on our mutual interdependence.

I am aware that The Principle of Interconnection and The Principle of Respect and Inherent Value and The Double Golden Rule and The Principle of Respect for Life are themselves beliefs or mindsets that I hold. My experience is that they are models or perspectives that are useful because they help me create the kind of relationships I want with individuals and in groups. My beliefs are reinforced by the fact that these principles have been around in various forms for centuries and are referred to in most major religions. However, that doesn't make the beliefs true. You can make them 'true for you' by trying them out over time and seeing if they are useful in your life. I continue to test these beliefs and look for places where they might stop serving me and start limiting me. As I find such places, they help me to refine or expand the beliefs and principles.

The Dynamics of Mindsets

Let me share some stories that might help demonstrate how prevalent mindsets are and how subtle and yet powerful they are in shaping our lives.

We create our own realities that both serve us and limit us

Story one: I have a somewhat well-known friend who believes fairly strongly that all personal emails should be answered and that they should be answered in a timely manner, which for him means no more than a day after receiving it. This attitude serves him, because he pushes himself to answer all his emails promptly and people appreciate the thoughtfulness that his responsiveness demonstrates, especially from such a well-known person. However, it also limits him. When he is unable to keep up with the emails he gets very stressed and curses the email system and the fact that he is in such demand. In other words, in these times of stress he sees email and his fame as the problem rather than the mindset he is holding that *all* personal emails need responding to and promptly.

This mindset also limits him when other people do not respond to his emails or they do not respond within what he feels is the respectful amount of time. When this happens, he begins to make up stories about why these

people aren't answering. He begins to think that they don't care about or respect him, or that he must have done something wrong to upset them, and then begins to worry about what it was that he did. He often creates an elaborate story with the corresponding feelings to explain why he hasn't heard from someone after a day or two.

Does this sound like a familiar process to you? Do you ever make up stories about why you haven't heard from your children, or your boss, or your friend when you were expecting to? Of course you do. We all do this. It becomes a problem, however, when we believe these stories and start to blame the other person for their behavior in *our* story, like the woman in the cartoon I mentioned. As my friend has become aware that it is his own expectations or mindsets that are causing his problems, he is now able to sometimes sheepishly make fun of himself for the whole 'reality' he creates around one simple email.

So two of the dynamics to understand about mindsets are: a) *mindsets can both serve and limit us* and b) *we create our own reality.* This is not the new age belief that, for instance, you created your cancer, your rejection by the college of your choice, or your car's dead battery. Things happen in life that we have no control over. We do, however, have control over the stories we tell ourselves about the things that happen. These stories are the reality we create about the event and they determine how we relate to that event. As the Buddha said, "All that we are arises with our thoughts. With our thoughts, we make our world."[4]

When you truly comprehend that we all create our own reality, it can remind you to pay attention to your assumptions. For example, you might stop assuming that you are hearing other people and start asking if you are understanding them correctly. You also might remember that the other person's behavior is arising out of their frame of reference and you might try to understand that frame rather than attributing meaning to their behavior from your own frame of reference. You might begin to assume less and inquire more.

When we truly grasp that we make up stories about people and situations that in turn become our realities, then telling our own stories and hearing others' becomes a healthy systemic practice. You want to draw out as many of the 'realities' that people are experiencing as possible because that gives everyone valuable information about what is going on in the system as a whole.

HÄGAR The Horrible

by DIK BROWNE

We see what we expect to see and Mindsets limit what we see

Story two: When my son, Eli, was about 3 or 4 years old, he was wild about dinosaurs. He would walk around with a little plastic stegosaurus in one hand and a T Rex in the other and was always playing with his extensive collections. He also had scores of books and pictures about dinosaurs. When the Museum of Science in Boston opened up an exhibit of life-size, moving dinosaur models I thought he might be excited to see 'the real thing.' On the way to the museum, however, I began to have doubts. What if he got scared? Would I traumatize him for life? When we walked into the exhibit, my fears were magnified by how realistic these beasts appeared. I looked down to gauge Eli's reaction but he was looking around with a puzzled expression. "Where are the dinosaurs, daddy?" he asked, even though he was standing right next to one's leg. "Right there," I said, pointing up. He looked up at the brontosaurus, then at the one in his hand, and then back up and exhaled, "Wooooaah." I realized that he was looking around for three-inch plastic models or pictures in books, and did not even *see* the life-sized models because he wasn't expecting them to be so big. This is a good demonstration of another dynamic of mindsets: *mindsets can limit what we see* or *mindsets cause us to see what we expect to see.* Eli's mindset that dinosaurs were 3 inches tall kept him – literally – from seeing the huge dinosaur right next to him!

Changing our mindsets can change our reality

> *"Man alone, of all creatures of earth, can change his thought pattern and become the architect of his destiny."*
>
> SPENCER W. KIMBALL

If we create our own reality through the mindsets we form and the stories we tell ourselves, then it should follow that by changing our mindsets and telling different stories, that we can change our reality. Most of us have had experiences in our lives where we've had one idea about a situation, but when we've heard the whole story or understood the situation better, our idea about it changes. It might be as simple as the stories you create about yourself and your friends when you hear about a party that you weren't invited to. Then, the next day, when you find the invitation in your junk email folder, your reality in relation to yourself, your friends and the party totally changes.

There is a simple experiment you can do in relation to the idea that changing your mindset can change your reality. The next time you are faced with a difficult task or an obstacle in relation to a goal, see if you can shift your perspective to seeing it as an opportunity. Focus on the difficult task or obstacle and see if you can turn it into an opportunity for something, anything – to work with someone new, to learn something new, to see how creative or funny or strong you can be, for example. Then really focus on that opportunity and see if it changes your experience in relation to that task or obstacle. I once saw a cartoon of two people in a car stuck in a horrific traffic jam that stretched for miles in either direction. One of the people had a big smile on his face and the caption read, "Hey, is this great traffic or what?!" This taps into the obvious – most of us hate being stuck in traffic or in long ticket lines. Now whenever I am in one of those situations, I say to whoever I am with, "Hey, is this a great ticket line, or what?!" It definitely helps lighten our feelings about the wait.

Story three: One night my wife and I were returning to Boston and our plane landed late. We had to rush to the theater where we had tickets for the last night's performance of a popular dance troupe. We had difficulty finding a place to park, as is always the case in Boston, but were able to squeeze into a tight space in a line of cars next to a construction site. We barely made it to our seats before the opening curtain. We enjoyed the performance and took our time leaving the theater. By the time we got to our parking place all the cars were gone – including our own. We were tired from travelling and our joy from the dance performance had totally evaporated as we began worrying that our car had been stolen with our suitcases in the back. It didn't make sense, since we didn't have a very nice car, but we thought maybe they wanted the suitcases.

When we called the police and told him our location, the dispatcher said, "Oh, you're not supposed to park there. We tow cars from there every night." He gave us the phone numbers of the two towing companies the police use and told us to call them before he would file a stolen car report. Sure enough, when we looked around, high on the fence was a "No Parking Tow Zone" sign. Oddly, that perked us up and gave us hope because as troublesome and expensive as it would be, being towed was much better than having our car stolen. However, after we spent a long time on the phone and neither towing company had our car, we again became discouraged.

We were both starting to panic at the thought that our car really had been stolen and worrying about what to do without our car, clothes and computers. I called the police again to report that our car had indeed, been stolen. There was a different dispatcher and we told her the whole story. She started to pull up the stolen car report on her computer, but then she hesitated and told us that there was one other small towing company that they sometimes used on busy nights such as when there were plays and concerts. She gave us their number and I anxiously called that company. I was very excited when I turned to Abby and exclaimed, "Good news, our car has been towed!" We both laughed at the fact that we thought that it was *good* news that our car had been towed and would cost $200 to retrieve. This is a clear example of how our changed mindset completely changed our experience of the reality we were dealing with.

Personal and Systemic Mindset Clues

As we discussed in Chapter 15 on Mindfulness, in order to change something in your life, you need to first be aware of it. This also applies to mindsets. Our mental models or beliefs are very hard to see because they are so fundamental to our worldview. Our mindsets are the lenses through which we look at the world and since we are looking through them, we don't see the lens, we see what is beyond. Or at least we think we do. Since our beliefs can limit what we see or affect our interpretation of what we see, how can we know whether we are operating out of a mindset or not? The fact is that we are always acting from our beliefs about how the world works, so the safest thing is to assume that we are always seeing and understanding only a part of what is in front of us. If we carry *this* belief and assume that our understanding is only partial, we will inquire more about what other people are seeing and understanding. We will be less certain and absolute about things we believe to be true. And we will acknowledge and act from the awareness that we have opinions and not truths.

But as humans, we will continually fall back into unconsciously assuming that what we see and understand is true and that everyone else sees it the same way, or should. At those times, what cues might wake us up to the fact that we are stuck in a mindset so that we might do something about it? Remember, mindsets can be either positive or negative and each will both serve and limit us. Here are a few examples of clues that people have shared in my classes and trainings that alert them to the fact that they might be stuck in a mindset. These are just a few examples to get you thinking about what your personal cues might be:

- I get caught up in winning the argument and being right.
- I don't listen to the other person; I'm preparing my counter-argument.
- I clench my teeth as if I'm biting my tongue so I won't tell the other person how stupid she is.
- I use a lot of 'you shoulds' and 'you need to...' as I start preaching. I also use a lot of 'always' and 'never.'
- I keep making the same painful mistake over and over because there is something I am not seeing or understanding – like about boyfriends.
- I make other people wrong, bad, stupid and somehow 'less' than me.
- I can only see things one way. I refuse to hear or believe other possibilities or interpretations of events.
- I see things in very rigid terms: black or white; right or wrong; me or you. There are no shades of gray or compromises.
- People keep disappointing me. I look for the best in people, but inevitably they let me down.
- I keep feeling like a failure. I believe that I should be able to do anything I set my mind to and that everything has to be perfect.

There are also system-wide beliefs or mindsets. How can we tell when our system is stuck in a particular worldview that is limiting what is seen and understood, and therefore how the system behaves? There are many examples in the business world of missed opportunities or failed projects because companies were stuck in one way of doing things – Blockbuster Video turning down startup Netflix's offer to be Blockbuster's DVD distribution channel; or energy companies not pursuing conservation strategies because of their belief in an endless supply of oil – are two of countless examples. A family system might also have beliefs about such things as who is considered family and who is not, for example, or what should be expected from family members, or what 'suitable' employment might be for the children. These beliefs can certainly serve the family, but they can also become limiting if they are held too rigidly.

How might you or others know when your system is stuck in a limiting belief? What would the cues be for you or the system? How could our cult have woken up to the fact that our mindsets were warping everything we did? Interestingly, some of the cues for systems are similar to the cues for individuals. Here are a few examples to help you investigate what would alert your systems – your family, your organizations, your workplace, your church – to the possibility that the system is trapped in a particular, sometimes limiting, worldview:

- Polarizing with other groups or ideologies and making them bad, wrong, stupid and somehow less than your group.
- Making the same mistake over and over and experiencing painful results.
- Seeing things in absolute terms – black or white; right or wrong, etc.
- Creating and excluding 'outsiders'.
- Not letting certain information into the system. Refusing to listen to input from inside or outside the system.
- Believing there is only one way of seeing things and one way of doing things.

Think about some of the systems you are in. Can you recognize any mindsets or beliefs that those systems might be following?

Working with Mindsets

Once you become aware of mindsets, then you can begin to look at what to do about them. Much can be said about how to work with mindsets. I will give a short summary here and then list some readings that I have found helpful. For additional information, see my website at www. newcontextcoaching.org.

Put the mindset into words

The first step in working with a mindset is to put it into words. Often, when the mindset is just becoming conscious, it is experienced as a vague sense or subtle pressure that you or your organization keeps bumping into. Or you see a set of behaviors being repeated over and over, but have a hard time putting words on what the problem is. So the first step is to think about it yourself and, if it is a systemic mindset, to talk about it with others in the system. The discussion brings the mindset more into awareness and helps clarify it for everyone. This type of discussion is a love practice. Some examples of personal and systemic mindsets that people have put into words are:

- Most people are incompetent. I can do things better and faster myself.
- All men care about is power, sex and money.
- In this company, how many hours you work demonstrates how committed you are.
- We have the most innovative products in the field. No one else can touch us.

How does the mindset affect your behavior?

Once you've put the mindset into words, then it is helpful to look at how the mindset affects your (or the system's) behavior. How does this belief cause you to act? For example, the person that had the belief that "most people are incompetent and that it is better to do things myself" listed the following behaviors that came from that belief:

- I don't delegate tasks to others.
- I don't pay attention to others' ideas about how to do things.
- I end up micromanaging the work that I do delegate so that I don't have to do it over."

How does the mindset serve you and how does it limit you?

After you have seen how the mindset affects your behavior, it is important to look at how it serves you (what do you get out of it? How does it help you?) and how it limits you (what does it keep you from doing, seeing or being?). The person who believed that it was better to do things herself, saw that:

- It serves me because things get done the way I want them to; it keeps me from getting angry at people for making mistakes; and I am seen as doing excellent work.
- It limits me because it keeps me from asking for help; it means my subordinates never learn how to do things for themselves, they keep trying to guess what I want; and I am over-worked."

Disidentify from the mindset

All of the above steps help you to disidentify from the belief (see Chapter 10 on disidentification) because you are stepping out of the mindset and trying to look at it more objectively. This stepping back gives you some distance and usually lessens the control the mindset has over you. But it is helpful to take the process of disidentification one step further and ask yourself, "If this mindset or belief is not the *whole* truth, what else might be true here? What other possibilities might it open for me?"

- If it is not the whole truth that people are incompetent and I can do everything better myself, what possibilities does that open up for me?

    I can start trying to discern what others' competencies actually are and delegate things that match their competencies.

    I can train people both to think for themselves and to think like me (there are things I do better).

    I can ask for help or delegate things and, if something is important, I can be clear from the beginning what I need and how I need it so I don't have to micromanage.

I think you can see that all of these steps would also apply to systems. You can think on your own about how these steps apply to your system, but it is most useful when you can bring people together to talk about them. People in various parts of the system might have different wording for the same belief, or it might cause their part of the system to behave differently than another part. Also, the same belief might serve one part of the system quite well while severely limiting another part. One company I worked with, for example, believed that sales growth was the key component of success and this is what they measured and rewarded. This caused the sales department to over-promise on quality and deadlines, which put a huge pressure on manufacturing that they were unable to deliver on.

Deep-seated, Problematic Mindsets

Unfortunately, some individual and systemic mindsets are very deep-seated and therefore extremely difficult to see without outside help. However, as was true for our cult, sometimes the mindset actually keeps us from seeing the need for help, or pushes it away when it is offered. These deep-seated mindsets tend to cause us to see the problem as external, rather than internal, thus protecting itself from discovery. Since most mindsets were originally formed to serve or protect us, this is understandable. But even though the mindset may have served us or the system quite well for a long time, because we continue to grow and the environment changes, eventually the mindset will start to limit us or the system. In those cases, usually the individual or systemic pain has to grow large enough for the individual or system to find the will to try to uncover and confront the limiting belief and develop a more conscious and appropriate one.

I believe that humanity is currently going through this process around our beliefs about the use of the earth's resources and the earth's ability to absorb the waste created by unbridled development. System thinkers know that there is no 'away' to throw things to and most of us are left wondering how much more pain the system will have to experience before our collective mindsets will begin to change.

From Ego-Centric to Poly-Centric Perspectives

Why is it so hard to remember and act on the fact that we possess a self-created perspective on Life and that there are *billions* of other such perspectives?! I don't know why it is so hard, but I do know that part of the work of re-humanizing systems is to shift individual and system perspectives from ego-centric worldviews to poly-centric ones. This is the essence of *The Principle of Inherent Value*: "*You* are a unique human being with inherent value as an expression of Life while simultaneously and equally *I* am a unique human being with inherent value as an expression of Life." If this is true, then your perspective has as much credence and value as mine, and both of our perspectives, as well as others', must be taken into consideration to understand and resolve any issue at hand.

Resources

For more about mindsets, see my website www.newcontextcoaching.com and check out the following books that I have found particularly useful:

- Adams, James L. *Conceptual Blockbusting: A Guide to Better Ideas.* Reading, MA: Addison-Wesley, 1986.
- Durrell, Lawrence, *The Alexandria Quartet.* London: Faber, 2012.
- Evans, Roger, and Peter Russell. *The Creative Manager.* Unwin Hyman, 1989. Chapter 4, "Creating the World We See."
- Janis, Irving L. Groupthink: Psychological Studies of Policy Decisions and Fiascoes. Boston: Houghton Mifflin, 1982.
- Korn, Peter, *Why We Make Things And Why It Matters: The Education of a Craftsman,* Boston: David R. Godine, 2013. Chapter 10, "Mapping a Craftsman's Mind."
- Macy, Joanna. *Mutual Causality in Buddhism and General Systems Theory: The Dharma of Natural Systems.* Albany: State University of New York, 1991. Chapter 7, "The Co-arising of Knower and Known."
- Mayfield, Marlys. *Thinking for Yourself: Developing Critical Thinking Skills through Writing.* Belmont, CA: Wadsworth Pub., 1991. Particularly chapters 3–8.
- Ray, Michael L., and Rochelle Myers. *Creativity in Business.* New York, NY: Broadway, 2000.
- Senge, et. al, The Fifth Discipline Fieldbook: Strategies and Tools for Building a Learning Organization. New York: Currency, Doubleday, 1994. Section on "Mental Models."
- Watzlawick, Paul, John H. Weakland, and Richard Fisch. *Change: Principles of Problem Formulation and Problem Resolution.* New York: W.W. Norton &, 2011. Chapters 7–9.

APPENDIX B

LOVE AND POWER PRACTICES: MINDFUL COMMUNICATION*

Since you spend most of your waking hours in some type of communication with other people, what better place to practice trying to balance love and power? How you communicate demonstrates your respect for self and others. When you communicate, you express who you are and make yourself available to be seen. It is also how you let another person know that he or she has been seen. When you really listen to another you get the opportunity to learn something about the amazing diversity of Life. When you express yourself authentically you are sounding your unique note and contributing to Life.

The principles outlined in this book are about preserving a sense of self and staying in relationship with other human beings when system pressures separate and objectify us. Communication, one of the essential ingredients of relationship, is extremely vulnerable to these system pressures because it is so hard to do well. When you break down the process of communication and look at it carefully, you begin to see that there are so many places where it can go wrong it is a miracle that we understand each other at all, let alone stay in relationship.

The complexity of the communication process also means that some humility is appropriate. Understanding and being understood is not easy, and it is important not to take for granted your ability or another's to do so. Being mindful and taking care during the communication process helps

---

This is an excerpt of a longer article of the same title (see Introduction to Appendices)

bring you closer to understanding each other (a love practice) rather than increasing separation (a sign of a dysfunctional system).

Mindful Communication: Central Principle

The Principle of Inherent Value states that: You are a unique human being with inherent value as an expression of Life, while simultaneously and equally, I am a unique human being with inherent value as an expression of Life.

Based on this principle:

Love practices will honor the other's humanity and uniqueness. Love practices respect and value another simply because he or she is an expression of Life. Love practices treat the other as a Thou. In the communication process, love practices include such methods as mindful listening, genuinely curious inquiry, and reflecting back or mirroring so that the other person knows that he is seen, understood, and valued. Love practices move us toward the other.

Power practices will honor your own humanity and uniqueness. Power practices respect and value yourself simply because you are an expression of Life. Power practices are the expression of the power of your being – the I of the I-Thou relationship. In the communication process, power practices would include advocating for yourself, expressing your wants and needs clearly through "I" statements, saying no when appropriate, and being visible, which often means having the courage to be vulnerable. Power practices flow from your deepest sense of self in the moment and the impulse to express that self in the world.

The Principle in Practice

Have you ever had your own version of the following conversation?

> **Wife:** "Aren't you going to do the dishes?"
> **Husband:** "No, it's not my turn."
> **Wife:** "Yes it is."
> **Husband:** "No it's not!"
> **Wife:** "Yes it is. I did the dishes last night."
> **Husband:** "I wasn't even here last night. I was at a meeting, remember?"
> **Wife:** "So? I still had to do the dishes for the kids and me, and that made
> two nights in a row. It's your turn."
> **Husband:** "It's not my turn, but I'll do them."
> **Wife:** "Good."

Let's analyze this exchange in more detail:

Wife: "Aren't you going to do the dishes?"	(How would this question make you feel?) It is a statement worded as a question. Blames the husband for not doing what wife thinks he should be doing. [The blame could have been a mindfulness alert (see Chapters 6 & 15)] Blame creates separation rather than connection. Doesn't acknowledge or respect husband as a separate human being who might have a different perspective and needs.
Husband: "No, it's not my turn."	Husband does not feel seen and becomes defensive, which increases separation. [If husband had used his defensiveness as a mindfulness alert, how might he have responded to decrease rather than increase the separation?]
Wife: "Yes it is."	
Husband: "No it's not!"	

Wife: "Yes it is. I did the dishes last night."	Wife does not feel heard and provides facts to bolster her position. Win-lose dynamic, creates more separation
Husband: "I wasn't even here last night. I was at a meeting, remember?"	Husband provides counter-facts. Does not acknowledge wife's perspective as a valid but different perspective than his. Pushes wife further away.
Wife: "So? I still had to do the dishes for the kids and me, and that made two nights in a row. It's your turn."	Wife does not feel seen as a human being who might have a valid perspective.
Husband: "It's not my turn, but I'll do them."	Husband capitulates, but neither feels particularly good about the interchange. What will he do to regain his power?
Wife: "Good."	"I win!" Re-inforces a win-lose dynamic in the relationship

With the mindful use of love and power practices, consider how the conversation about the dishes *might* have gone:

> **Wife:** "Technically I'm not sure whose turn it is to do the dishes since you weren't here last night, but I've done the dishes two nights in a row and am feeling really tired right now. Would you be willing to do them tonight? I'll do them tomorrow night."
>
> **Husband:** "Hmm. I'm torn. Here's the deal: I understand that you've done the dishes several nights now and are really tired, but I was hoping to watch the game on TV."
>
> **Wife:** "If you are willing to do the dishes, how about taping the beginning of the game while you do them?"
>
> **Husband:** "Definitely, I'll do the dishes. How about if I leave the mess until after the game?"

Wife: "Sure, as long as they get done before we go to bed. I've got the girls coming for book club in the morning."

Husband: "OK by me. Want to relax and watch the game with me?"

What is different about these two scenarios? Clearly they are being nicer to each other in the second one, but they are not just being nice. They each are coming from a place of respect for oneself and the other, and skillfully practicing techniques that communicate that respect. Let's analyze this conversation in more detail:

Wife: "Technically I'm not sure whose turn it is to do the dishes since you weren't here last night, but I've done the dishes two nights in a row and am feeling really tired right now. Would you be willing to do them tonight? I'll do them tomorrow night."	Wife respects: The relationship by acknowledging their previous agreement; Herself by using a power practice to state clearly what she needs; Her husband, by recognizing that he might have other plans and by asking if he is willing to do the dishes
Husband: "Hmm. I'm torn. Here's the deal: I understand that you've done the dishes several nights now and are really tired but I was hoping to watch the game on TV."	Husband feels seen and respected. Husband demonstrates respect for wife by mirroring back what he's heard her say – a love practice. Husband uses a power practice to state clearly his plans and to acknowledge their dilemma. He has not, however, stated his willingness to do the dishes.
Wife: "If you are willing to do the dishes, how about taping the beginning of the game while you do them?"	Wife is implicitly inquiring whether he is willing to do the dishes. (How could she have done this better?) She respects his needs by proposing a win-win solution – a love practice, while simultaneously holding on to her need to have the dishes done – a power practice.
Husband: "Definitely, I'll do the dishes. How about if I leave the mess until after the game?"	Husband respects wife by staying in relationship and answering her question directly – a love practice. He also proposes an alternative solution that better meets his desires – a power practice. He also uses love practices by proposing a win-win solution and by respecting her enough to inquire if it is, in fact, a win for her.

Wife: "Sure, as long as they get done before we go to bed. I've got the girls coming for book club in the morning."	Wife feels seen and acknowledged and accepts solution. She does not assume that he understands the importance of the dishes being done that night and provides her whole context – a power practice.
Husband: "Okay by me. Want to relax and watch the game with me?"	By using a combination of love and power practices, they have maintained mutual respect in the relationship while coming up with a creative solution that works for both.

Mindful Listening – A love practice

The CEO of a very large real estate development company hired my partners and me to do a communication skills training for his executive team because, as he put it, "*They* need to learn how to work together better." During the section of the training on mindful listening and inquiry, we broke into groups of three to practice simply listening to someone. The CEO would listen for a few sentences and then would interrupt and give his solution to the issue that the person was describing. The others would remind him just to listen and inquire without judgment, interpretation, or having to respond. He would nod and listen for a few more sentences and then inquire by asking, "Don't you think you should . . .?" The others gently pointed out that this was a judgmental inquiry and not an open one, such as, "Could you say more about that?"

To his credit, he was open to the feedback and was really trying hard to put it into practice. At the end of the exercise we usually ask the listener to reflect back to the speaker what he has heard. Then we ask the speaker to estimate the percentage of what was said that the listener actually heard. The CEO was shocked to realize that he could repeat back very little of what was said and that the speaker said he had only heard about 15% of her meaning. He was sober and quiet for the rest of the day.

To my surprise, the next day the CEO was very excited and wanted to go first in the morning's sharing. He told this story:

"Yesterday I thought the listening exercise was pretty silly when we started. I already knew I was a good listener – ha, ha! Boy was I surprised and humbled. I want to thank everyone in my small group for giving me feedback. I thought you guys needed the communication skills. I promise I will try to do better.

"I also really want to share with you the most amazing thing! My 15-year-old daughter and I have been having trouble for a year or so now. We seem to always be arguing. She never listens to anything I say and is acting out a lot. Last night, after the seminar, I got home and at dinner my wife told me that my daughter had been required to stay after school because she had gotten into a loud argument with someone in her class.

"When I went into her room I was furious with her for misbehaving yet again. I was going to yell at her but, because of our seminar yesterday, I thought I'd try to see her like you said – a person deserving of respect as an expression of Life – and just try to listen to what she had to say.

"I asked her to tell me what happened. Almost immediately she sat up and looked at me with surprise.

"What?" I asked.

"You never ask me what happened. You always just yell at me," she said.

"I still might," I said, "but tell me what happened."

"I tried to really listen without criticizing her or telling her how she should have acted. It was very hard for me and my tongue was sore from biting it. The more I listened the more she spoke. She hadn't said that many words to me in months! At one point I had a memory of what it was like for me when I was her age. I was awkward socially and tried to be tough to cover up my fears. It was a hard time for me. I don't know where it came from, but I found myself saying, 'It's really hard being 15 years old isn't it?' She burst into tears and fell into my arms. I just melted. I hadn't felt that close to her since she was 9 years old! I'm still not sure exactly what happened, but I know it had something to do with listening to her."

By the end of the story he had tears in his eyes, as did several of his team. There was a lot of appreciation and respect for him for the vulnerability of his sharing. Listening to his story allowed his team to see a side of him they had not seen and brought all of them closer to him and to each other. This is part of the value of storytelling as a system-wide communication process, a) it gives people an opportunity to express who they are (a power practice), and b) it deepens understanding of others and usually brings people closer together (a love practice).

The Systemic Practices of Love and Power in Communication Processes

We have looked at the practices of love and power in individual and small group relationships. What would these practices look like if used by the system as a whole?

Information is the lifeblood of the system. It is the way the system knows itself. If the teenage son closes himself in his room playing video games and does not share the notes the school sends home with him, the family is missing vital information about what is going on with him and therefore, with the family system that he is a part of. If the sales department doesn't receive timely information about product returns and quality control problems, they keep selling more of the defective product, which makes even bigger problems for the company as a whole.

If the whole is greater than, and different than, the sum of its parts, then the way for that whole to know itself is for as many of the parts as possible to have access to high-quality information about what is going on in the system as a whole. In addition, systemic problems are often best solved when as many relevant parts of the system as possible can be brought together (a love practice) in the problem-solving process.

My partners and I were asked to facilitate the process of a Fortune 100 paper company trying to develop toilet paper made from recycled paper. The U.S. government had mandated that any paper products sold to them needed to be 50% recycled material, and all paper companies were trying to figure out how to meet this requirement. The resistance throughout the many divisions of the paper company was great, with each division pointing to another to explain why making a 50% recycled toilet paper was impossible for them: manufacturing pointed to procurement saying that they could not get enough high-quality used paper to run through their machines; procurement pointed to the financial department saying that their numbers didn't allow them to purchase high-quality used paper; and the budgeting department pointed to marketing saying that their price points weren't realistic.

When we called the first meeting of representatives from all of the divisions, the chaos and resistance in the room was so great that everyone in the room questioned whether the goal was even possible. We all felt that even if it were possible, it would certainly take a long time. Everyone was worried about this because the government was one of their biggest customers and they were afraid of losing such a big part of their business.

We set up regular meetings with leaders of all the divisions in the same room, with research and homework in between. We designed and facilitated a process whereby each division took turns telling their story. We asked them to share the obstacles they were facing in producing and selling a 50% recycled toilet paper and what they would need from other divisions and from within their own division to make it happen. As the meetings went on over several months, people began to get frustrated that nothing concrete was happening, but we insisted that every division be heard.

Eventually, several things developed in the process. First, as we established the safe space for each division to present their obstacles and needs in a non-blaming way (a love practice), the other divisions were more able to hear that division's dilemmas (also a love practice). Second, when the division felt that the environment was safe, they were more able to share their internal obstacles and vulnerabilities and that made it acceptable for other divisions to do the same (authentic expression of what is true is a power practice). This added to the feeling of safety. Third, as they listened to each other, they began to get a more complete picture of what the system as a whole was dealing with in trying to produce this product. The system was beginning to know itself in a deeper way.

As the process went on, each division came more and more prepared with its problems and needs, and the divisions that had already told their story took time to present their research about the issues that had been raised during their presentations. There were no longer any complaints about how long it was taking.

It took a total of nine months (meeting once or twice a month) to finish all of the stories and the research that arose out of the stories. At the end of the nine months, when all of the information was in the room, we posed the simple question: "You all now know the obstacles and the needs of the system in order to produce a 50% recycled toilet paper. As a group, if your back was to the wall, how would you do it?" In the next several meetings they worked cross-functionally, solving all the issues that had been raised and coming up with some rather innovative and cost-cutting solutions not just for this product but also for others. At the end of three months, they had a sample of the product rolling off of their papermaking machines. As a group they were amazed that the whole process had taken only 12 months when product development usually took 18!

During the final meeting we did an evaluation of the project and asked people why it had worked so well. A few of their answers were:

- We took the time to listen and build relationships.
- We learned about the problems everyone else was facing.
- You created a safe space to share our problems and we felt like we were in this together.
- It became clear that if a solution was going to work it had to work for all the divisions.
- We were open to other divisions' different perspectives on the task, and to their ideas about the problems our division was facing.

As you can see, they were describing love practices and power practices as instituted on a system-wide basis.

The Effectiveness of Mindful Communication

The stories that I have shared above are just a few examples of the practical application of the Principle of Inherent Value in individual and system-wide communication processes. I share them not only because they demonstrate how to use the principle, but also to show how *effective* it can be when you use a balance of love and power in your communications. Mindful communication is about getting results while at the same time practicing right relations and nurturing Life-affirming systems.

I have only shared a few examples here. If this appendix whets your appetitie, you can download my longer article, *Love and Power Practices: Mindful Communication*, from my website www.newcontextcoaching.com. The article includes sections on:

- The Anatomy of the Communication Process
- Love Practices in the Communication Process
    - *Mindful Listening*
    - *Inquiry and Mirroring*

- Fear of True Dialogue
- Power Practices in the Communication Process
  - *Advocacy and I-statements*
  - *I-statements as Requests*
- Collaboration: Balancing Love Practices and Power Practices in the Communication Process
- When the Other(s) Don't Know How, Can't, or Won't Play Win-win
- The Systemic Practices of Love and Power in Communication Processes
- Storytelling

In addition, if you wish to pursue this topic more deeply, some of the most useful books I have found on the individual and systemic use of love and power practices in communication are:

- Joiner, Bill, and Stephen Josephs. *Leadership Agility: Five Levels of Mastery for Anticipating and Initiating Change.* San Francisco: Jossey-Bass, 2007. "Pivotal Conversations" chapter and throughout.
- Kegan, Robert, and Lisa Laskow Lahey. *How the Way We Talk Can Change the Way We Work: Seven Languages for Transformation.* San Francisco: Jossey-Bass, 2001.
- Smith, Diana McLain. *Divide or Conquer: How Great Teams Turn Conflict into Strength.* New York: Portfolio, 2008.
- Stone, Douglas, Bruce Patton, and Sheila Heen. *Difficult Conversations: How to Discuss What Matters Most.* New York, NY: Viking, 1999.
- Ury, William. *The Power of a Positive No: How to Say No and Still Get to Yes.* New York: Bantam, 2007.
- Yeomans, Thomas, "The Corona Process: Group Work within a Spiritual Context" in *Soul on Earth: A Spirituality for the 21st Century.* Concord: Concord Institute.

APPENDIX C

YOUR NOTE IN THE SYMPHONY
An Exercise for Identifying Purpose

There is a vitality, a life force, an energy, a quickening that is translated through you into action, and because there is only one of you in all of time, this expression is unique. And if you block it, it will never exist through any other medium and it will be lost. The world will not have it. It is not your business to determine how good it is nor how valuable nor how it compares with other expressions. It is your business to keep it yours clearly and directly, to keep the channel open. You do not even have to believe in yourself or your work. You have to keep yourself open and aware to the urges that motivate you.

MARTHA GRAHAM, dancer and choreographer

The Timeline of Your Life Exercise

This is an exercise that I often do in my classes, trainings and coaching. It is based on the assumption that Life is always flowing through us and that we give it a unique articulation, like a particular note in a symphony or a particular color in a palette (see Chapter 11). I am calling this unique expression your purpose in Life. You are always expressing your unique purpose whether you are aware of it or not. There may not be just one purpose, or it may evolve as you grow. This exercise is to help you identify and put words to that purpose in order to be able to live it more consciously and intentionally.

The exercise helps you review your life and look for threads that weave through it. In trying to identify these threads, you are looking for qualities or values or core beliefs that you have held and acted from whether you were aware of them or not. It is not specifically about the jobs you have done or the career you have chosen, but rather about the qualities and values that you have expressed or are expressing in your work and other aspects of your life. By qualities or values, I mean such things as caring, steadfastness, beauty, healing, humor, justice, peacemaking, strength, clarity, love, or joy. This is a very short list of the myriad qualities that we express as human beings. You may be expressing many qualities and values in your life, but I think you will notice as you do the exercise that there are a handful that standout as threads or recurring themes. Have fun identifying them!

1   Take a sheet of paper and turn it horizontally so that it is in 'landscape' position. Draw a horizontal line across a page and mark off seven-year intervals, e.g. 0 – 7, 7 – 14, 14 – 21, etc. up to your present age.

2   This is a visualization exercise through the timeline of your life so far. You will be looking for qualities you expressed at different stages or what values you held. You will be looking for what was important to you, and what thread or threads emerge as you have travelled along this journey we call life. At any point you can make notes below that period on your timeline. (or, if it you choose, you can draw a picture that represents that quality or value).

3   As you look at each seven year period of your life, here are some of the questions to consider:

- What do you love doing? What makes you excited? Why? What is important to you? Why?

- What do others say about you at this age? What do they see in you? Why do the people who want to be with you want to be with you? What kinds of friends do you have? What type of things do you all care about?

- If you are in a relationship, what are the qualities you most admire in your partner? Why?

- If you have children, what is important to you in how you raise or raised them? What qualities of yours would you like to pass on?

- You might want to look at the jobs you have held or are holding. What attracts you to this kind of work? What particular skills or qualities do you have that makes you suited for these jobs? Is there a thread that runs through your work like creativity, teaching, serving others, or curiosity?

4   When you reach current age and the last seven year block, look at your life now and ask these same type of questions.

5   Now go back and look for threads that seem to be there through your whole life:

   -   You are looking for qualities, purpose, and values. What are you trying to express in the world? What do others see you expressing? What is the essence of what you are putting out into the world?

   -   Spend some time thinking and writing about what you see and understand.

6   If you want to take this exercise a little further, you can explore the following questions as well:

   -   What inner obstacles get in the way of you expressing what you are being moved or called to express?"

   -   Investigate more deeply, for example if it is fear, fear of what, e.g if fear of failure, what does this mean, specifically?

   -   What would you need to develop in yourself to overcome these internal obstacles?"

   -   What outer obstacles get in the way of you expressing what you are being moved or called to express?"

   -   Sometimes it's difficult to tell inside blocks from outside blocks. Some examples might include:

   -   This quality is not valued by the culture and I can't support myself economically if I express it.

   -   Women are discouraged in this area of expression.

   -   My family is expecting me to . . .

   -   I'm too young (or too old) to . . .

   -   What would you need to do or to develop in yourself to overcome these external obstacles?

Be yourself. Everyone else is already taken.

OSCAR WILDE

RECOMMENDED READING
AND RESOURCES

Ackoff, Russell Lincoln, and F. E. Emery. *On Purposeful Systems*. Chicago: Aldine-Atherton, 1972.

Ackoff, Russell Lincoln, and Sheldon Rovin. *Redesigning Society*. Stanford, CA: Stanford UP, 2003.

Adams, James L. *Conceptual Blockbusting: A Guide to Better Ideas*. Reading, MA: Addison-Wesley, 1986.

Almaas, A. H., *Being and the Meaning of Life*. Berkeley, CA: Diamond, 1990.

Argyris, Chris, and Donald A. Schön. *Organizational Learning II: Theory, Method and Practice*. Reading, Mass: Addison-Wesley, 1996.

Assagioli, Roberto. *Psychosynthesis: A Collection of Basic Writings*. Amherst: Synthesis Center Publishing. 2000.

Assagioli, Roberto. *The Act of Will*. Amherst: Synthesis Center Publishing, 2010.

Atlee, Tom, and Rosa Zubizarreta. *The Tao of Democracy: Using Co-intelligence to Create a World That Works for All*. Cranston, RI: Writers' Collective, 2003. And Tom Atlee's website at: www.co-intelligence.org

Bohm, David Joseph. *On Dialogue: David Bohm*. London: Routledge, 1996.

Bohm, David. *Wholeness and the Implicate Order*. London: Routledge & Kegan Paul, 1981.

Brown, Molly Young. *Growing Whole: Self-realization on an Endangered Planet*. New York: HarperCollins, 1993.

Brown, Molly Young. *The Unfolding Self: The Practice of Psychosynthesis*. New York: Helios, 2004.

Buber, Martin. *I and Thou*. New York: Scribner, 1958.

Chödrön, Pema. *Start Where You Are: A Guide to Compassionate Living*. Boston: Shambhala, 1994.

Chödrön, Pema. *The Places That Scare You: A Guide to Fearlessness in Difficult times.* Boston: Shambhala, 2001.

Covey, Stephen R. *Principle-centered Leadership.* New York: Free, 1992.

de Vries, Marco, *Chosing Life: A new perspective on illness and healing,* Lisse: Swets & Zeitlinger, 1993.

Donella Meadows Institute: uses systems thinking and collaborative learning to solve economic, social and environmental problems. www.donellameadows.org

Evans, Roger, and Peter Russell. *The Creative Manager: Finding Inner Vision and Wisdom in Uncertain times.* San Francisco, CA: Jossey-Bass, 1992.

Evans, Roger. *5DL: Five Dimensions of Leadership,* in publication.

Ferrucci, Piero. *The Power of Kindness: The Unexpected Benefits of Leading a Compassionate Life.* New York, NY, USA: Jeremy P. Tarcher, 2007.

Firman, John, and Ann Gila. *A Psychotherapy of Love: Psychosynthesis in Practice.* Albany, NY: State University of New York, 2010.

Firman, John, and Ann Gila. *Psychosynthesis: A Psychology of the Spirit.* Albany: State U of New York, 2002.

Firman, John, and Ann Gila. *The Primal Wound: A Transpersonal View of Trauma, Addiction, and Growth.* Albany, NY: State University of New York, 1997.

Frankl, Viktor E. *Man's Search for Meaning: An Introduction to Logotherapy.* Boston: Beacon, 1992.

Gall, John, *The Systems Bible: The Beginner's Guide to Systems Large and Small: Being the Third Edition of Systemantics.* Walker, MN: General Systemantics, 2002.

Glassman, Bernie. *Bearing Witness.* New York: Random House International, 2000, and The Zen Peacemakers newsletter: http://zenpeacemakers.org

Hassan, Zaid. *The Social Labs Revolution: a new approach to solving our most complex challenges.* San Francisco: Berrett-Koehler, 2014.

Hirasuna, Delphine, and Kit Hinrichs. *The Art of Gaman: Arts and Crafts from the Japanese American Internment Camps, 1942-1946.* Berkeley, CA: Ten Speed, 2005.

Joiner, Bill, and Stephen Josephs. *Leadership Agility: Five Levels of Mastery for Anticipating and Initiating Change.* San Francisco: Jossey-Bass, 2007.

Kabat-Zinn, Jon. *Coming to Our Senses: Healing Ourselves and the World through Mindfulness.* New York: Hyperion, 2005.

Kahane, Adam. *Power and Love: A Theory and Practice of Social Change.* San Francisco, CA: Berrett-Koehler, 2010.

Kahane, Adam. *Solving Tough Problems: An Open Way of Talking, Listening, and Creating New Realities.* San Francisco: Berrett-Koehler, 2004.

Kegan, Robert, and Lisa Laskow Lahey. *How the Way We Talk Can Change the Way We Work: Seven Languages for Transformation.* San Francisco: Jossey-Bass, 2001.

Kegan, Robert. *In Over Our Heads: The Mental Demands of Modern Life.* Cambridge, MA: Harvard UP, 1994.

Korn, Peter, *Why We Make Things And Why It Matters: The Education of a Craftsman,* Boston: David R. Godine, 2013.

Kramer, Gregory. *Insight Dialogue: The Interpersonal Path to Freedom.* Boston: Shambhala, 2007.

Leverage Networks: Organizational Learning, Systems Thinking, and System Dynamics tools, resources and information. www.leveragenetworks.com

Macy, Joanna. *Mutual Causality in Buddhism and General Systems Theory: The Dharma of Natural Systems.* Albany: State University of New York, 1991.

Macy, Joanna and Molly Brown, *Coming Back to Life: The Updated Guide to the Work That Reconnects.* Canada: New Society Publishers, 2014..

Maslow, Abraham H. *Toward a Psychology of Being.* New York: J. Wiley & Sons, 1999.

Meadows, Donella H., *Thinking in Systems: A Primer.* White River Junction, VT: Chelsea Green Publishing, 2008.

Mingyur, Yongey, and Eric Swanson. *Joyful Wisdom: Embracing Change and Finding Freedom.* New York: Harmony, 2009.

Oshry, Barry. *Leading Systems: Lessons from the Power Lab.* San Francisco, CA: Berrett-Koehler, 1999.

Oshry, Barry. *Seeing Systems: Unlocking the Mysteries of Organizational Life.* San Francisco: Berrett-Koehler, 2007. And at www.powerandsystems.com

Public Conversations Project: Designs and facilitates conversations on divisive issues and provides training in their methodology. www.publicconversations.org

Quiñones Rosado, Raúl. *Consciousness-in-Action: Toward an Integral Psychology of Liberation & Transformation.* Caguas, Puerto Rico: Ilé publication, 2007.

Ray, Michael L., and Rochelle Myers. *Creativity in Business.* New York, NY: Broadway, 2000.

Rogers, Carl R. *A Way of Being.* Boston, MA: Houghton Mifflin, 1980.

Russell, Peter. *From Science to God: A Physicist's Journey into the Mystery of Consciousness.* Novato, CA.: New World Library, 2005.

Sales, Michael, and Anika Ellison Savage. *Life Sustaining Organizations: A Design Guide.* 2011. www.artofthefuture.com

Schumacher, E. F. *A Guide for the Perplexed.* New York: Harper & Row, 1977.

Seixas, Abby. *Finding the Deep River Within: A Woman's Guide to Recovering Balance and Meaning in Everyday Life*. San Francisco, CA: Jossey-Bass, 2006.

Senge, Peter M. *Senge, et. al, The Fifth Discipline Fieldbook: Strategies and Tools for Building a Learning Organization*. New York: Currency, Doubleday, 1994.

Senge, Peter M. *The Fifth Discipline: The Art and Practice of the Learning Organization; with a New Introduction and Tips for First-time Readers*. New York: Doubleday/Currency, 1994.

Siff, Jason. *Unlearning Meditation: What to Do When the Instructions Get in the Way*. Boston: Shambhala, 2010.

Simpson, Steve and Roger Evans. *Essays on the Theory and Practice of a Psychospiritual Psychology*. Institute of Psychosynthesis, London, 2014

Smith, Diana McLain. *Divide or Conquer: How Great Teams Turn Conflict into Strength*. New York: Portfolio, 2008.

Society for Organizational Learning: founded by Peter Senge, "The purpose of sol is to discover, integrate and implement theories and practices for the interdependent development of people and their institutions." www.solonline.org

Starhawk, *Truth or Dare: Encounters with Power, Authority, and Mystery*. San Francisco: HarperSanFrancisco, 1988.

Stone, Douglas, Bruce Patton, and Sheila Heen. *Difficult Conversations: How to Discuss What Matters Most*. New York, NY: Viking, 1999.

Thich Nhat Hahn and Arnold Kotler. *Peace Is Every Step: The Path of Mindfulness in Everyday Life*. New York, NY: Bantam, 1991.

Tillich, Paul, and Peter J. Gomes. *The Courage to Be*. New Haven: Yale UP, 2000.

Ury, William. *The Power of a Positive No: How to Say No and Still Get to Yes*. New York: Bantam, 2007.

Wachtel, Paul, *The Poverty of Affluence,* Philadelphia: New Society Publishers, 1989.

Waters Foundation: the application of systems thinking concepts, habits and tools in classroom instruction and school improvement. www.watersfoundation.org

Watzlawick, Paul, John H. Weakland, and Richard Fisch. *Change: Principles of Problem Formulation and Problem Resolution*. New York: W.W. Norton & Co., 2011.

Wilber, K. *Integral Spirituality: A Startling New Role for Religion in the Modern and Postmodern World*. Boston, Integral Books imprint of Shambala Publications; 2006.

Wilber, Ken. *A Theory of Everything*. Boston, MA: Shambhala, 2000.

Yeomans, Thomas, *Readings in Spiritual Psychology.* (Concord: Concord Institute, 1998)

Yeomans, Thomas. *Soul on Earth: A Spirituality for the 21st Century*. Concord: Concord Institute.

ENDNOTES

Author's note

1 There are many different types and schools of systems theory that try to understand the behaviors of systems as a whole. I am using 'human systems theory' to point particularly to the human aspect of systems, the behaviors of the systems as a whole, and the behaviors of individual people within those systems. I believe that there is a fertile area for research in understanding the reciprocal relationships between individual psychology and the dynamics of human systems.

Introduction

1 Some of the individuals who are working (or have worked) on creating Life-affirming systems are Donella Meadows, Peter Senge, Adam Kahane, Zaid Hassan, Otto Sharmer, Ken Wilber, William Joiner, Michael Sales, Grady McGonnagil, Roger Evans, Thomas Yeomans, and David Stroh among others. I have included a bibliography of inspiring work on Life-affirming systems at the end of the book.

Chapter one

1 Wachtel, Paul. *The Poverty of Affluence,* (Philadelphia, PA: New Society Publishers, 1989) p. 145.

2 Oshry, Barry. *Seeing Systems: Unlocking the Mysteries of Organizational Life.* San Francisco: Berrett-Koehler, 2007.

3 Ackoff, Russell & Sheldon Rovin, *Redesigning Society* (Stanford, CA: Stanford University Press, 2003), p. 3.

4 de Vries, Marco, *Choosing Life: A new perspective on illness and healing,* (Lisse: Swets & Zeitlinger, 1993), p. 31.

5 Kauffman, J R., Draper L., *Systems One: An Introduction to Systems Thinking. https:// engineering.purdue.edu/~engr116/ENGR19500H_spr/General_Course_Information/ Common/ReadingMaterial/Kauffman_Systems_One_1980.pdf*

6 Associated Press in Boston Globe, January 21, 2007.

7 The reader can look up the system principle of 'Indeterminacy/equifinality' for more of a discussion of causality.

8 Meadows, Dana, *Whole Earth Review*

9 Sufi teaching story, quoted in Donella H. Meadows, *Thinking in Systems: A Primer,* (White River Junction, VT: Chelsea Green Publishing, 2008), p. 31.

Chapter two

1 Meadows, Donella, "Whole Earth Models and Systems," *CoEvolution Quarterly*, (Summer, 1982), pp. 98–108

2 Michael Goodman, Principal at Innovation Associates Organizational Learning, and at Applied Systems Thinking

3 Haley, Jay, *Leaving Home: The Therapy of Disturbed Young People*, (New York: McGraw-Hill, 1980).

4 As an example of another system principle – delays, it took 30 years for me to admit that the conservatives were right that if Vietnam fell to the communists so would most of Indochina, and for my father to admit that even though that had happened, the war was not worth the cost in lives, money and the affect on America as a whole.

5 Seixas, Abby. *Finding the Deep River Within: A Woman's Guide to Recovering Balance and Meaning in Everyday Life.* San Francisco, CA: Jossey-Bass, 2006.

6 Some would point to the still powerful forces of systemic racism in the U.S. as being responsible for this behavior. I think that this certainly played a significant role in trying to keep our first black president from succeeding. But I'd like to make two additional points: 1) it is not just "those racists" (*parts* of the system) that were responsible for this behavior, but *all of us* who allow the perpetuation of the *system* of racism; and 2) this same paralyzing gridlock happened when Bill Clinton took over as president and, not just coincidentally, focused on the issue of gays in the military and health care. So what is it about the 'life of America' as an entity that needs people to scapegoat and which needs to have a healthcare industry that is beyond government control? (And, of course, these are probably not disconnected issues!)

Chapter three

1 Oshry, Barry. *Leading Systems: Lessons from the Power Lab.* San Francisco, CA: Berrett-Koehler, 1999.

2 Hans Christian Andersen, *The Emperor's New Clothes*, adapted by Stephen Corrin in *Stories for Seven-Year-Olds*. (London:Faber & Faber, 1989).

3 *Buying The War: How Big Media Failed Us*, Bill Moyers' Journal, April 25, 2007. http://billmoyers.com/content/buying-the-war/

4 All the following quotes are from the transcript of the documentary found at http://billmoyers.com/content/buying-the-war/

5 http://www.powerandsystems.com

6 Oshry (2007)

7 Oshry (1999) p. 1–2

8 Oshry also demonstrates the system forces affecting the 'customers' of these organizations, whether in the true business sense or in the sense of 'those receiving services' e.g. students, homeless, patients, etc. But for the sake of brevity, I'll let you read about this in his books.

9 Because many dysfunctional systems are based on rules that allow some people to have power over others, there are real victims of oppressive systems. But as you will read in later chapters where I talk about Viktor Frankl's experience in Nazi concentration camps and Japanese experiences in U.S. internment camps, there are ways to counteract victimhood even in the most oppressive of situations.

10 Corn, David, *SECRET VIDEO: Romney Tells Millionaire Donors What He REALLY Thinks of Obama Voters*, Mother Jones Online, Mon Sep. 17, 2012. http://www.motherjones.com/politics/2012/09/secret-video-romney-private-fundraiser

Chapter four

1 Starhawk, *Truth or Dare: Encounters with Power, Authority, and Mystery*. San Francisco: HarperSanFrancisco, 1988, p 256.
2 Green, Hardy, "In good company: Welfare capitalism", Boston Globe, 9/3/10 p. A13.
3 ibid
4 Hardin, Garrett, "The Tragedy of the Commons," *Science* 13 December 1968: Vol. 162 no. 3859 pp. 1243–1248.
5 "The federal VA has been widely criticized for the backlog. As of Sept. 28, the VA said there were 725,469 cases pending, 58% of them for more than 125 days." http://www.usatoday.com/story/news/nation/2013/10/03/veterans-va-government-shutdown/2914485/
6 "The average annual earnings of the top 1 percent of wage earners grew 156 percent from 1979 to 2007; for the top 0.1 percent they grew 362 percent (Mishel, Bivens, Gould, and Shierholz 2012). In contrast, earners in the 90th to 95th percentiles had wage growth of 34 percent, less than a tenth as much as those in the top 0.1 percent tier. Workers in the bottom 90 percent had the weakest wage growth, at 17 percent from 1979 to 2007." Economic Policy Institute website: http://www.epi.org
7 Quiñones Rosado, Raúl. *Consciousness-in-Action: Toward an Integral Psychology of Liberation & Transformation*. Caguas, Puerto Rico: Ilé publication, 2007, p. 81
8 Ibid, p. 81–82
9 Six African-American CEO's of Fortune 500 companys = 1.2%. 21 women CEO's = 4.2%; https://www.diversityinc.com/diversity-facts/wheres-the-diversity-in-fortune-500-ceos/
10 Based on median annual earnings for full-time, year-round workers, women earned 76.5% of men's earnings in 2012. Based on the median weekly earnings for full-time workers, (which excludes self-employed and full-time workers who work only part of the year), in 2012 women earned 80.9% as much as men. US Census Bureau, "Income, Poverty, and Health Insurance Coverage in the United States: 2012" (2013), p. 7.
11 See Quiñones Rosado (above) for an explanation of internalized inferiority and superiority.
12 Global Issues, *Poverty Facts and Stats,* by Anup Shah. http://www.globalissues.org/article/26/poverty-facts-and-stats
13 "Nearly 15 million children in the United States – 21% of all children – live in families with incomes below the federal poverty level – $22,350 a year for a family of four. Research shows that, on average, families need an income of about twice that level to cover basic expenses. Using this standard, 44% of children live in low-income families." National Center for Children in Poverty, Mailman Center of Public Health, Columbia University – website.
14 *Preventable diseases killing children*, 29 JUNE 2010 by Rita Mu. http://www.reportageonline.com/2010/06/preventable-diseases-killing-children/

Chapter five

1 Bookchin Murray, *Post Scarcity Anarchism,* Berkeley: Ramparts Press, p. 63
2 See: Evans, Roger, and Peter Russell. *The Creative Manager.* Unwin Hyman, 1989. Chapter 4, "Creating the World We See"
3 See: Senge, Peter M. *The Fifth Discipline: The Art And Practice Of The Learning Organization.* New York: Doubleday/Currency, 1990. Chapter 9, "Mental Models"

Chapter six

1 For longer explanation, see Oshry, Barry, *Leading Systems* and *Seeing Systems*
2 Gamm, Gerald, *Urban Exodus: Why the Jews Left Boston and the Catholics Stayed,* Cambridge, Harvard University Press, 1999. And, Levine, Hillel, and Lawrence Harmon. *The Death Of An American Jewish Community: A Tragedy Of Good Intentions.* New York: Free Press, 1992.

Chapter seven

1 *Question time with Hannah Pool: Jerry Greenfield, co-founder of Ben & Jerry's, on starting out 30 years ago, selling out to Unilever – and his favourite flavour --* The *Guardian,* Wednesday 30 July 2008
2 Argyris, Chris, and Donald A. Schön. *Organizational Learning II: Theory, Method and Practice.* Reading, Mass: Addison-Wesley, 1996.
3 Lager, Fred. *Ben & Jerry's: The inside Scoop : How Two Real Guys Built a Business with Social Conscience and a Sense of Humor.* New York: Crown, 1994, p. 112
4 ibid, p. 119
5 ibid, p. 120
6 ibid, p. 94
7 Page, Anthony, and Katz, Robert A., *The Truth About Ben and Jerry's: Contrary to myth, the sale of Ben & Jerry's to corporate giant Unilever wasn't legally required.* SSIReview.org Fall 2012
8 Steiker, Jim, and Golden, Michael, *Hot Fudge Partners: Insiders tell how social investors tried to (but couldn't) buy Ben & Jerry's.* Business Ethics: The Magazine of Corporate Responsibility, Volume 14, Issue 3, May/June 2000, p. 7
9 Page and Katz, ibid.
10 Hays, Constance, *Ben & Jerry's To Unilever, With Attitude,* New York Times: April 13, 2000, http://www.nytimes.com/2000/04/13/business/ben-jerry-s-to-unilever-with-attitude.html
11 Ibid
12 Page and Katz, ibid.
13 http://www.benjerry.com/company/b-corp
14 Reuters report: By Maggie Fox, Health and Science Editor WASHINGTON | Wed Jun 23, 2010 4:48pm EDT http://www.reuters.com/article/2010/06/23/us-usa-healthcare-last-idUSTRE65M0SU20100623
15 http://www.photius.com/rankings/healthranks.html
16 http://www.photius.com/rankings/healthy_life_table2.html
17 http://www.reuters.com/article/2010/06/23/us-usa-healthcare-last-idUSTRE65M0SU20100623
18 http://www.politico.com/news/stories/0809/26078.html
19 Kunen, James S., *Enron's Vision (and Values) Thing,* NY Times Opinion Section, January 19, 2002.

20 Harris, Gardiner, and Wilson, Duff, *Glaxo Pays $750 Million for Sale of Bad Products,* New York Times: October 26, 2010 (all quotes about Glaxo are from this article) http://www.nytimes.com/2010/10/27/business/27drug.html?pagewanted=2&_r=3&ref=glaxosmithkline_plc

21 Harris and Duff, Ibid

22 Urbana, Ian, *Oil Rig's Owner Had Safety Issue at Three Other Wells.* NY Times (online): August 4, 2010: All quotes and facts from this article. http://www.nytimes.com/2010/08/05/us/05transocean.html?pagewanted=all&_r=0

23 Ibid

24 Tapper, Jake, *President Obama Says AIG Bonuses An 'Outrage,' Violation of 'Our Fundamental Values.'* Political Punch (ABC.com): March 16, 2009.

25 Wolfe, Tom. *The Bonfire of the Vanities.* New York: Farrar, Straus Giroux, 1987.

Chapter eight

1 Wachtel (1989)

2 Senge (1990)

3 Joiner, Bill, and Stephen Josephs. *Leadership Agility: Five Levels of Mastery for Anticipating and Initiating Change.* San Francisco: Jossey-Bass, 2007.

4 Kegan, Robert. *In over Our Heads: The Mental Demands of Modern Life.* Cambridge, MA: Harvard UP, 1994.

5 Wachtel (1989)

6 Maslow, Abraham H. *Toward a Psychology of Being.* New York: J. Wiley & Sons, 1999.

7 Assagioli, Roberto. *Psychosynthesis: A Collection of Basic Writings.* Amherst: Synthesis Center Publishing. 2000.

8 Yeomans, Thomas, *Readings in Spiritual Psychology.* (Concord: Concord Institute, 1998)

9 Cameron, James, director, *Avatar,* A Twentieth Century Fox Presentation, 2009.

10 http://www.chopra.com/community/online-library/terms/namaste

11 I am using the phrases "seeing" someone and holding them with "empathic love" somewhat interchangeably in this section. They are not totally synonymous but are close enough for my purpose here.

12 Rogers, Carl R. *A Way of Being.* Boston, MA: Houghton Mifflin, 1980, pp. 154–5.

13 Firman, John, and Ann Gila. *A Psychotherapy of Love: Psychosynthesis in Practice.* Albany, NY: State University of New York, 2010, p. 33

14 Ibid, p. 32

15 Firman, John, and Ann Gila. *The Primal Wound: A Transpersonal View of Trauma, Addiction, and Growth.* Albany, NY: State University of New York, 1997, p. 71.

16 Buber, Martin. *I and Thou.* New York: Scribner, 1958, pp. 112–13.

17 Firman and Gila, (1997), pp. 172–3.

18 Firman and Gila, (2010), pp. 40–1.

19 Deikman, Arthur, and Doris May Lessing. *Them and Us: Cult Thinking and the Terrorist Threat.* Berkeley, CA: Bay Tree Pub., 2003, p. 65–6

Chapter nine

1 Seixas, Peter, *Historical Agency as a Problem for Researchers in History Education,* American Educational Research Association, Seattle, April 11, 2001, p. 4

2 Almaas, A. H., *Being and the Meaning of Life.* Berkeley, CA: Diamond, 1990, p. 172

3 Assagioli (2000) p. 22

4 Ibid, p. 119

5 Firman and Gila. (2010) p. 24.

6 Gibney, Alex, Director, *Enron: The Smartest Guys in the Room.* (2005)

7 For a more detailed account of systemic liberation, see Quiñones, Rosado Raúl (2007)

8 Frankl, Viktor E. *Man's Search for Meaning: An Introduction to Logotherapy.* Boston: Beacon, 1992. pp. 103–4

9 Frankl, Viktor E. *Viktor Frankl - Recollections: An Autobiography.* New York: Insight, 1997, p. 97

10 Hanus, Julie K., *Beauty in a Bleak World*, American Craft Magazine, December/January 2011, p. 48 – See more at: http://craftcouncil.org/magazine/article/beauty-bleak-world#sthash.ni7iw8Ms.dpuf

11 Hirasuna, Delphine, and Kit Hinrichs. *The Art of Gaman: Arts and Crafts from the Japanese American Internment Camps, 1942–1946.* Berkeley, CA: Ten Speed, 2005.

12 Ibid, p. 48

13 Ibid, p. 50

14 Ibid, pp. 51–3

15 Ibid, pp. 52–3

Conclusion Part one

1 Die Wahlverwandtschaften, Hamburger Ausgabe, Bd 6 (Romane und Novellen I), dtv Verlag, München, 1982, S. 397 (II,5)

2 For more on nested hierarchies, see the works of Ken Wilber.

Chapter ten

1 Roberts, Charlotte, quoting George Sheehan, physician/author in, Senge, et. al, *The Fifth Discipline Fieldbook: Strategies and Tools for Building a Learning Organization.* New York: Currency, Doubleday, 1994, p. 230.

2 Scharmer, Claus Otto, *Grabbing the Tiger by the Tail*, Conversation with Robert Kegan,
Harvard Graduate School of Education, March 23, 2000, p. 18.

3 Assagioli, Roberto. *The Act of Will.* Amherst: Synthesis Center Publishing, 2010. p. 7.

4 Radhakrishnan, quoted by Assagioli in *The Act of Will*, p. 128.

5 Nietzsche, Friedrich, *Thus Spake Zarathustra: A Book for All and None,* Thomas Common, trans., in *The Complete Works of Friedrich Nietzsch*, Oscar Levy ed., vol. 11 (NY: Russell & Russell, 1964), II.23.

6 Maslow (1968).

7 Kahane, Adam. *Power and Love: A Theory and Practice of Social Change.* San Francisco, CA: Berrett-Koehler, 2010, p. 2

8 Yeomans, Thomas, spiritual psychologist, personal communication

9 de Mille, Agnes. *Martha: The Life and Work of Martha Graham.* NYC: Random House, 1991.

10 Lao-tzu, and Witter Bynner. *The Way of Life According to Laotzu ; Translated by Witter Bynner Illustrated by Frank Wren*. New York: Putnam, 1986, No. 47.

11 For more on presence see Chapter 8, "Practice Presence" in Abby Seixas (2006).

12 Fuller, R. Buckminster. *I Seem to Be a Verb*. New York: Bantam, 1970.

13 Heschel, Abraham Joshua, and Susannah Heschel. *Moral Grandeur and Spiritual Audacity: Essays*. New York: Farrar, Straus & Giroux, 1997. "No Religion is an Island", p. 264.

14 Macy, Joanna. *Mutual Causality in Buddhism and General Systems Theory: The Dharma of Natural Systems*. Albany: State University of New York, 1991, p. 86.

15 Gandhi, M.K. *Non-violent Resistance*. New York: Schocken, 1961, p. 6.

16 King, Martin Luther. *Letter from Birmingham City Jail*. Valley Forge, PA: Division of Social Concern, American Baptist Convention, 1963, pp. 30–1.

17 Oshry, Barry, Organization Workshop simulation. See www.powerandsystems.com

Chapter eleven

1 Overton, Patrick. *The Leaning Tree*. Saint Louis: Bethany, 1975.

2 Starhawk (1988)

3 Schwartz, Richard C. *Introduction to the Internal Family Systems Model*. Oak Park, IL: Trailheads, 2001.

4 Lorde, Audre. *Sister Outsider: Essays and Speeches*. Trumansburg, NY: Crossing, 1984.

5 Castaneda, Carlos. *Journey to Ixtlan: The Lessons of Don Juan*. New York: Simon and Schuster, 1972.

6 Tillich, Paul, and Peter J. Gomes. *The Courage to Be*. New Haven: Yale UP, 2000, p. 39

7 Sarton, May. *Journal of a Solitude*. New York: Norton, 1973.

8 Yeomans, Thomas, "The Corona Process: Group Work within a Spiritual Context" from, *Readings in Spiritual Psychology*. Concord: Concord Institute, 1998.

9 Kahane (2010) pp. 17–18.

Chapter twelve

1 Senge (1990) p. 171

2 King, Jr., Martin Luther, "Speech at Riverside Church in New York City," 1967. http://en.wikiquote.org/wiki/1967"1967-HYPERLINK

3 Assagioli (2010) p. 96

4 Bill O'Brien, former president, Hanover Insurance – in Kahane, *Power and Love*.

5 Assagioli, ibid

6 Rilke, Rainer Maria. *Rilke on Love and Other Difficulties: Translation and Considerations by John J.L.Mood*. New York: Norton Paperback, 1994.

7 Stanley, Elizabeth PhD, Captain. "Bringing Mindfulness to the Military to Enhance Performance and Build Resilience." Mindful Society Conference 2012, http://live.soundstrue.com/mindfulsociety/

8 Used with permission of the authors

9 Merton, Thomas. *No Man Is an Island*. New York: Harcourt, Brace, 1955.

10 Firman and Gila (2010)

11 Buber (1958)

12 Frankl (1992) pp. 176–7

13 Fuller, R. Buckminster. *Critical Path*. New York: St. Martin's, 1981.

14 Thich Nhat Hahn and Arnold Kotler. *Peace Is Every Step: The Path of Mindfulness in Everyday Life*. New York, NY: Bantam, 1991.

15 Ellison, Ralph. *Invisible Man*. New York: Vintage International, 1995.

16 Schweickart, Rusty, from White, The Overview Effect, p. 13 (Originally in Earth's Answer: Explorations of Planetary Culture at the Lindisfarne Conferences West Stockbridge, MA, Lindisfarne/Harper & Row, 1977. http://www.overviewinstitute. org/featured-articles/54-the-overview-effect-astronauts-unique-view-of-the-earth-and-what-we-all-can-learn-from-it

17 Whitmont, Edward C. *The Symbolic Quest; Basic Concepts of Analytical Psychology*. New York: Published by Putnam for the C.G. Jung Foundation for Analytical Psychology, 1969, p. 169

18 Assagioli (2010) p. 91

19 Firman and Gila (2010) p. 21

20 King, Jr., Martin Luther, "Address to the Southern Christian Leadership Conference," 1967. http://www.indiana.edu/~ivieweb/mlkwhere.html

21 *Super 8*. Paramount, 2011.

22 Macy (1991)

23 Mitchell, Stephen. *The Enlightened Mind: An Anthology of Sacred Prose*. New York, NY: HarperCollinsPublishers, 1991.

24 Alexander, Eben. *Proof of Heaven: A Neurosurgeon's Journey into the Afterlife*. New York, NY: Simon & Schuster Paperbacks, 2012, p. 78.

Chapter thirteen

1 Assagioli (2010) p. 91

2 King, M.L. "Where Do We Go From Here?" Speech delivered at the 11th Annual SCLC Convention, Atlanta, Georgia, 16 August 1967.

3 Assagioli ibid. p. 95

4 Gottlieb, Lori, , "How to Land Your Kid in Therapy," *Atlantic Magazine*, July/ Augus, 2011.

5 Faber, Adele, and Elaine Mazlish. *How to Talk so Kids Will Listen & Listen so Kids Will Talk*. New York: Scribner, 2012.

6 Kahane (2010) p. 7

7 Ibid., p.50

8 Ibid, p. 7

9 Introduction to Martin Buber: article by Harry James Cargas. http://essays-articles-texts.blogspot.com/2010/05/this-article-is-by-harry-james-cargas.html

10 Buber, M., translation: Smith, R.G. *I and Thou*. 2nd ed., New York, Charles Scribner's Sons; 1958, p. 11.

11 Buber, M., translation: Kaufmann, W. *I and Thou*. New York, Charles Scribner's Sons; 1970, p. 62

12 Ibid, p. 53

13 Ibid, p. 54

14 Ibid.

15 Ibid, p. 62

16 Ibid, p. 85

17 Ibid, p. 111
18 Ibid, p. 67
19 *Talking with the Enemy*, This story ran on page F1 of the Boston Globe on 1/28/2001 or see, http://www.publicconversations.org/dialogue/policy/abortion
20 Wilber, K. *Integral Spirituality: A Startling New Role for Religion in the Modern and Postmodern World.* Boston, Integral Books imprint of Shambala Publications; 2006.

Chapter fourteen

1 Society for Organizational Learning – http://www.solonline.org/ amd Co-Intelligence Institute – http://www.co-intelligence.org
2 Janice Marturano, http://www.mindful.org/mindful-voices/on-leadership
3 Barry Oshry is pointing to the reflexive responses in the various worlds so that people can use them as cues that they have other choices in that world in that moment. He calls these alternative choices "empowered stands" and they are all concrete expressions within systems of love or power or a combination of both.

Conclusion

1 Glassman, Bernie, The Zen Peacemakers newsletter: http://zenpeacemakers.org
2 One of the places that has provided us with an opportunity to share what we have learned, is the Harmony Institute and its International School of Psychotherapy, Counseling, and Group Leadership in St. Petersburg, Russia. One of our former group members contributed to the founding of the International School and several of us have supported and taught there over the last twenty-five years. It has been a blessing to be able to contribute to an organization that is fulfilling the vision that we had hoped to achieve at our graduate school.

Appendix A

1 Meadows (2008)
2 Buddha, *Dhammapada*, as translated by T. Byrom, Shambhala Publications (1993)
3 Kimball, Spencer W. , twelfth president of The Church of Jesus Christ of Latter-day Saints, in his *Miracle of Forgiveness* (1969), p. 114.

Acknowledgements

1 Buber (1958) p. 67
2 Ibid p. 112-113

INDEX

in, 85; objectification of, 101; power and teams in, 209–210; power over and, 205; primacy of values and, 128–129; self-objectification and, 103; system pressures on Tops in, 114–115; as system within systems, 45–46, 124–128; values and, 124–128

Buying the War (television documentary), 70–72

Casteneda, Carlos, 201
Catholic Church, 25, 136
Cause and effect: mutually influential relationships and, 33–34, 36; separation and, 107–108
Change, system resistance to, 29–30, 55–56
Changing perspective, disidentification via, 166–168
Children, culture's power over, 90–91
Chodron, Pema, 201
Choice, power and, 79–80
Civil rights movement, 118, 199, 206
Clinton, Bill, 93
Cohen, Ben, 124, 126, 127
Cointelligence, 254
Collective action, power with and, 206–207
Communication, mindful. *See* Mindful communication
Communication skills, 274
Compassion: self and Largest Whole and, 220; system forces and lack of, 80–81
Conformity, 205
Conscious values, 121–124
Consequences, unintended, 34–35
Control, of system, 24–25
Corona process, 254
Courage, 199–202; to be mindful, 258–260; effects of not expressing power of being and, 202–203; internal obstacles to expressing one's power and, 191–193; Life force and, 195–196; to love, 216–218; mindfulness and learning, 197–199; mutual influence relationships between inner and outer systems and, 196–197; overcoming external obstacles and, 203–207; struggle with fear and, 200–202; subpersonalities and, 192–194, 197–199
The Courage to Be (Tillich), 201
Creativity: dysfunctional systems and, 153; system pressures and, 79, 80
Critic subpersonality, 193–194, 195

Cults, 7–11, 17–18; blame and, 108–109; emergence of, 43–44
Culture of imposition, 88
Cultures, system pressures in different, 68
Curiosity, seer and, 221, 222

Dance of We, 233–248; balancing love and power and, 234–239; creating conditions for true meeting, 242–243; Double Golden Rule and, 245–246; I-Thou relationships and, 239–245, 248; learning opportunities and, 246–248; mindful, 272–273; Principle of Respect and Inherent Value and, 241–242; re-humanizing systems through I-Thou relationships and, 243–245
Death, fear of, 199
Deep ecology, 27n
Deepwater Horizon oil spill, 137
Deikman, Arthur, 147, 148
Delays, systems and, 34–35
Democratic Party, objectification and, 92–93
Design of system, 38–41
DeVries, Marco, 27
Dialogue Process, 254
Discernment, seer and, 221–223
Disidentification, 62–64, 156–174; changing perspectives as way of, 166–168; in extreme situations, 171–174; from human system or ideology, 162–164; identification, 159–161; individual, 157–158, 162–164; from larger system, e.g. country, 164–166; leaving system as form of, 168–170; from mindset, 289; multiple effects of, 166; process of, 161–162; remaining in system and, 170–171; stages of, 176
Double Golden Rule, 22, 245–246, 263, 269, 274, 279
Dysfunctional separation, 112
Dysfunctional systems, 7–11, 17, 152–153; blame and, 108; clash of values and change in, 134–135; disidentification from, 169–170; experiences of love and, 212; Larger Whole and, 135–138; mindfulness and, 266; mutual influence and caring breaking down in, 85–86; objectification and, 94, 96–97, 175, 184; power of and, 204; re-humanization of, 184–185, 227–228; relationship between whole and its parts in, 48; seeing and being seen and re-humanization of,

Learning: balancing love and power and opportunities for, 246–248; desire of seer and, 221; mindfulness and, 197–199

Leaving Home (Haley), 57

Legacy of power over, 88–89

Lehman Brothers, 136

"Leverage Points: Places to Intervene in a System" (Meadows), 277

Levinson, Barry, 107

Life: force of, 179, 195–196; guided imagery exercise, 177–180; individual and, 185–186; meaning of term, 21; persistence of, 177; Principle of Honoring, 22, 274; qualities of, 177; self and, 142–143

Life-affirming principles, 21–22

Life-affirming systems, 17; from dysfunctional systems, 153–154; power of being in, 186–190; practice of seeing and creation of, 150; relationship between people and, 47–48; subpersonalities and, 196–197

Life-deadening systems. *See* Dysfunctional systems

Like, as precondition for love, 213–215

Linear, causal seeing, 151–152

Listening, mindful, 297–298

Logotherapy, 172

Lorde, Audre, 200

Love, 208–232; balanced use of, 19–20; balancing with power, 233–248; defined, 210–212; degenerative side of, 235; having courage to, 216–218; intention to, 214; I-Thou relationship and balance with power, 248; limitations of, 236–237; as mindfulness component, 251; mindful practice of, 260–263; of other, of self, of Life, 229–232; 230; positive aspects of, 236; power and love feeding each other's growth, 218; power and loving fully, 223–228; power with, 208–210; Principle of Interconnectedness and, 212–213; relation between like and, 213–215; seeing and being seen and, 219–223; seeing is loving, 215–216; systemic practices of, in communication processes, 299–301

Love and power practices, 274–275; mindful communication, 292–302; mindsets, 276–291

Love of Life/loved by Life, 231–232

Love practices, 293. *See also* Love and power practices

Macy, Joanna, 185, 231

Mao Zedong, 136

Margolis, Diane, 147

Marturano, Janice, 258–259

Maslow, Abraham, 142, 180

Massing, Michael, 72

Matsumoto, Kazuko, 174

May, Rollo, 205

Meadows, Donella, 35, 50, 59, 60, 277

Media, system pressures and, 70–72

Mental models. *See* Mindsets

Merton, Thomas, 218

Middles of system, 74, 75–76, 77–78; forces of separation and, 115–116

Military, breakdown of mutual influence relationships in, 85–86

Mindful communication, 292–302; central principle of, 293; effectiveness of, 301–302; mindful listening, 297–298; principle in practice, 294–297; resources, 302; systemic practices of love and power in communication, 299–301

Mindfulness: in action, 263–266; courage to be mindful, 258–260; individual, 249–254; learning and, 197–199; mindful practice of love and power, 260–263; practice of, 221, 249, 260–263; systemic, 254–258

Mindfulness alerts, 261–263

Mindfulness meditation, 249–250

Mindsets, 94–96, 274, 278–280; benefits and limitations of, 288; changing, 277; deep-seated, problematic, 290; defined, 278; disidentifying from, 289; dynamics of, 280–285; effect on behavior, 288; limitations created by, 283; personal and systemic clues to, 285–289; putting into words, 287–288; resources on, 291; separation and, 113; values and systems within systems and, 127

Mollner, Terry, 127

Mother Teresa, 144

Moyers, Bill, 70–72

Mutual influence relationships, 30–38, 84–86; between inner and outer systems, 196–197

Mutuality, recognition of, 221

My Lai massacre, 105, 159

Nazi concentration camps, disidentification and, 171–172

Needs, fear about getting own met, 146–149

Sheehan, George, 175
Sister Outsider (Lorde), 200
Social Labs, 254
Soviet Union, cause of fall of, 213
Stalin, Josef, 136
Stanley, Elizabeth, 216
Starhawk, 82, 191
Stonyfield Farm Dairy, 128
Strobel, Warren, 71, 72
Subject, becoming, to one's life, 175–177
Subpersonalities, 192; critic, 193–194, 195; inadequate one, 194, 195; in Life-affirming system, 196–197; mindfulness and learning, and, 197–199; Mr. Nice Guy, 194, 195
Suicide: disidentification and, 168–169; internment camps and, 174
Super 8 (film), 230
Survival personality, 146–147, 148
Synergy of system, 41. *See also* Emergence
System dynamics, 27n
System forces, 64, 66–81; agency and, 156–157; balancing love and power and, 247; choice and power, 79–80; effect on individual, 80–81; Emperor's New Clothes, 68–70; life of bottoms, 76; life of middles, 75–76; life of tops, 74–75; overcoming external obstacles, 203–207; power and systems, 73–79; power with and overcoming, 206–207; reality of, 66–68; real-life example, 70–72; results of, 77–79; of separation, 113–118
Systemic cues to mindsets, 285–289
Systemic dysfunction, interaction with personal dysfunction, 105–106
Systemic "ego," 56
Systemic mindfulness, 254–258. *See also* Mindfulness
System(s), 4, 24–49; behavior and rules of, 13–14; benign, 48; blame and, 107–119; change and, 55–56, 134–135; clash of values and, 134–135; control of, 24–25, 49, 59–62; courage and (*See* Courage); definitions, 27–28; design, order, and rules of, 38–41; disidentification from (*See* Disidentification); examples of, 28; expressing power of being and, 183–185; fear and loathing in, 146–149; healing within, 271–272; homeostasis of, 55–58, 72, 135; identity of, 52–55, 64; individual part (*See* Individual part of system); information for, 29–30, 56

(*See also* Feedback); leaving, 168–170; leverage points in, 277; Life and power of, 187; Life-deadening, 17; as "living" whole, 28–29; loss of humanity, 80; mindsets and, 278–280; mutual influence relationships and, 30–38; objectification (*See* Objectification); overview of, 16–17; personality of, 41, 42, 55; power and, 73–79 (*See also* Power); power of member's being and growth of, 184; power of people within, 21–22; power over people and, 20, 22, 82–91, 154; purpose of, 21; re-humanizing, 243–245; relation of individuals to, 13–14; relationship between inner and outer, 196–197; relationship between people and, 47–49; relationships within, 16; seeing and being seen and, 144–146, 227–228; seeing systemically, 14–16; within systems, 41–47, 124–128; values and (*See* Values); visualizing, 25–27; wholeness of, 28–30. *See also* Dysfunctional systems; Life-affirming systems
System sight, 25
Systems modeling, 27n
Systems theory, 11–12

The Teachings of Don Juan (Casteneda), 201
Teams, power with and, 209–210
Terrorism, blame and, 110–111
Them and Us (Deikman), 147
Thich Nhat Hahn, 222–223
Thrall of organization, 147
Thus Spake Zarathustra (Nietzsche), 180
Tillich, Paul, 201
Timeline of Your Life exercise, 303–305
Tops, of systems, 73–75, 77–78, 89; forces of separation and, 114–115; objectification of, 101; self-objectification of, 103–104
Tragedy of the commons, 85
Transocean Inc., 137
The Truman Show (film), 168
Truth or Dare (Starhawk), 82
Tsunami, Indian Ocean, 259–260
2008 financial crisis, 44

Unconscious values, 121–124; colliding with system's, 130–131
Unilever, 126–127
United States, healthcare system overhaul in, 131–133

ACKNOWLEDGEMENTS

My friend, John Firman, was the first to recognize the relevance of my thoughts on human systems and to encourage, gently push, chide, and demand that I write them down. His work in Psychosynthesis with Ann Gila was influential in my later thinking and is widely referenced here. John died in June of 2008, well before he had finished sharing his wisdom, love, and humor with the world. This book would have been better for his reading and consulting around key ideas. I am sure there are parts of *The Dance of We* he would have taken issue with, but even if ultimately we hadn't agreed, my thinking would have been clearer because of our discussions. I think this book would have made him proud and I am sorry I never got to feel his loving, knowing smile at seeing it completed.

There were other readers, however, who picked up John's mantle and gave me early feedback and strong encouragement. In particular, Didi Firman, Molly Brown and Toni Brooks were the earliest readers who insisted that I had a useful book here and that it needed to be completed and published. In my head (but never to their faces, heaven forbid!) I referred to them as my three cheerleaders, and their affirmations kept me going during my times of doubt while writing in a vacuum.

Many others read pieces or all of early drafts and gave me useful advice which has been gratefully incorporated: Tom Yeomans, Bill Joiner, Grady McGonagill, Alexander Badkhen, Mark Pevzner, Richard Burg, Steve Dunn, Roger Evans, Ron Krouk, and Michael Sales.

Donella (Dana) Meadows and Barry Oshry are two friends of mine and the first teachers to shape my thinking about systems. Dana was a systems thinker, a global citizen and a farmer who lived what she taught. She, too, died much too soon with many gifts unshared. Barry Oshry made me aware of the tangible existence of system forces and how formidable and resistant to change they are. He is generous in the sharing of his knowledge and experience and practices the partnership he teaches.

Marilyn, Bob and Otis Kriegel, in addition to supplying a great deal of coaching and publishing advice, also introduced me to my editor, Susan Suffes. Susan managed to prune a mammoth manuscript into merely a large one. I, and readers who read the entire book, owe her a debt of gratitude for her heroic effort.

Many others contributed pieces large and small to this endeavor: Sara Hunter offered support and publishing advice all along the way. Isobel Gillan designed the book as well as the cover and Emma Levitt produced most of the graphics. Rich and Antra Borofsky generously contributed their poem on pages 217–218, which I feel beautifully summarizes the chapter on love. The Institute of Psychosynthesis London lent considerable credence to my thinking on balancing love and power by publishing an early version of Chapter 13 in their 40th anniversary book of readings, *Essays on the Theory and Practice of a Psychospiritual Psychology*. Ted Slawski of the Synthesis Center Press shepherded the manuscript through the many tedious steps of turning it into an actual printed volume. And the impatience of our chavura – a Jewish eating, drinking, laughing and celebrating group – kept me going with their constant inquiries, "So nu, when's it due?"

I want to extend a special appreciation to Sasha and Marina Badkhen, Mark Pevzner, and the staff and faculty of the Harmony Institute for Psychotherapy and Counseling and the International School for Psychotherapy, Counseling and Group Leadership in St. Petersburg, Russia. Harmony has created a true, Life-affirming learning environment that offers its students experiential education in how to liberate themselves and their clients even in the midst of the post-Soviet chaos and continuing government control. Over the last 18 years, the students at the International School have been eager and welcoming recipients of all that I have had to offer, and over the last five years, have helped me clarify the thinking that led to this book. Martin Buber captured my relationship with those at the International School when he wrote in *I and Thou*, "Relation is reciprocity. My Thou acts on me as I act on it. Our students teach us, our works form us . . . Inscrutably involved, we live in the currents of universal reciprocity."[1]

And finally, who would I be without Abby Seixas, my wife of 41 years? We have swum together in those same currents of universal reciprocity and she has helped shape me into the man I am today. So if you have any complaints, please speak with her. Abby and I have often marveled at the miracle of finding each other at such a young age when at least one of us was immature and totally out of touch with his feelings. Somehow I trusted the one feeling I was in touch with and asked her to marry me before anyone else could. It is rare that a couple can grow in the same directions over time – emotionally, mentally and spiritually – and become best friends, respected colleagues, trusted partners and lifetime lovers. Abby understood the importance of this book to me and in addition to supporting us financially while I worked on it, she spent many hours editing it for clarity and meaning. There is no one else I would have trusted enough to hand my baby over to in such an unguarded way. Buber also wrote, "The purpose of relation is the relation itself – touching the You. For as soon as we touch a You, we are touched by a breath of eternal life."[2] Abby, You have touched me.

THE AUTHOR

MARK HOROWITZ is a leadership and organizational development consultant, an experienced educator, and board certified coach. He trained in Humanistic Psychology with Abraham Maslow, Ph.D. and in Psychosynthesis with Roberto Assagioli, M.D. He has studied the field of human systems for over thirty-five years as a licensed individual and family therapist and as a management consultant and coach for businesses in the United States, Europe, Scandinavia, and Russia. He has facilitated numerous leadership training programs and large-scale corporate change projects, and has served as coach to senior business leaders undertaking team and organizational development initiatives. He is a faculty member of the International School of Psychotherapy and Group Counseling in St. Petersburg, Russia, and has been an adjunct faculty member at John F. Kennedy University and Antioch San Francisco in California, and at Suffolk and Lesley Universities in Boston. Mark has taught Psychosynthesis at many centers around the world, including the Psychosynthesis Institute in San Francisco, and the Institute of Psychosynthesis, London. He is an amateur woodworker and a founding board member of The Center for Furniture Craftsmanship in Rockport, Maine. He is also the founder and president of The Uniterra Foundation, an international non-profit committed to the practical application of spiritual values to social change. He lives outside of Boston with his wife, Abby Seixas. He can be reached at www.newcontextcoaching.com.